Collected
Prose

Poets on Poetry   Donald Hall, General Editor

Collected
Prose

JAMES WRIGHT

Edited by Anne Wright

Ann Arbor   The University of Michigan Press

Copyright © by The University of Michigan 1983
All rights reserved
Published in the United States of America by
The University of Michigan Press and simultaneously
in Rexdale, Canada, by John Wiley & Sons Canada, Limited
Manufactured in the United States of America

1986   1985   1984   1983   6   5   4   3   2   1

Library of Congress Cataloging in Publication Data

Wright, James Arlington, 1927-
   Collected prose.

   (Poets on poetry)
   I. Wright, Anne.   II. Title.   III. Series.
PS3573.R5358A6   1982   809   82-23692
ISBN 0-472-06344-8 (pbk.)

To Irving Silver

Acknowledgments

To the Ingram Merrill Foundation for such generous help in making this book possible.

To Roland Flint, Roger Hecht, Galway Kinnell, Gibbons Ruark, and Peter Stitt for the care, thought, and help in advising on the manuscript.

To Betsy Fogleman, Belle McMaster, Jane Robinett, and *Ironwood* for their checklists of James Wright's work.

To my editor Donald Hall for patience and encouragement.

To Beth Tornes who worked with me on the manuscript and was of invaluable help.

Grateful acknowledgment is made to the following publishers, journals, and individuals for permission to reprint copyrighted material written by James Wright:

American Poetry Review for "Secrets of the Inner Landscape," *American Poetry Review* 2, no. 3 (May/June 1973).

Michael André for "An Interview with Michael André" which first appeared in the *Unmuzzled Ox* 1, no. 2 (February 1972).

Robert Bly for "A Note on Trakl" from *Twenty Poems of Georg Trakl;* for "A Note on Cesar Vallejo" from *Twenty Poems of Cesar Vallejo;* and for "The Work of Gary Snyder" from *The Sixties* 6 (Spring 1962).

Bobbs-Merrill Educational Publishing and William Heyen for "On the Occasion of a Poem: Richard Hugo"; for "On the Occasion of a Poem: Bill Knott"; and for "The Infidel"; all originally published in *American Poets in 1976*.

Deluca [Rome] for "Meditations on René Char" from *René Char's Poetry*. Copyright 1959.

The English Institute, Indiana University, for "The Delicacy of Walt Whitman."

E.N.V.O.Y., a publication of the Academy of American Poets, for "Some Notes on Chinese Poetry," *E.N.V.O.Y.* 40 (1981).

Farrar, Straus and Giroux for "Translator's Note on Herman Hesse" by James Wright, from *Poems* by Herman Hesse, selected and translated by James Wright. Copyright © 1970 by James Wright.

Kenyon Review for "The Stiff Smile of Mr. Warren," *Kenyon Review* 20, no. 4 (Autumn 1958). Copyright 1958 by Kenyon College. Reprinted by permission of the *Kenyon Review*.

Minnesota Review for "The Few Poets of England and America," *Minnesota Review* 1 (1961); and for "Gravity and Incantation," *Minnesota Review* 2, no. 3 (1962).

New American Library for an afterword to *Far from the Madding Crowd*, 1960; for an afterword to *The Mystery of Edwin Drood*, 1961; and for "Theodor Storm," an introduction to *The Rider on the White Horse*, 1964. Reprinted by permission of New American Library.

New Orleans Review for "Poetry Must Think," *New Orleans Review* 6, no. 3 (1978).

Poetry for "A Shelf of New Poets," *Poetry* 99 (December 1961); and for "I Come to Speak for Your Dead Mouths," *Poetry* 112 (June 1968).

William S. Saunders for "Childhood Sketch" as it appeared in *James Wright: An Introduction* (Ohio Authors Series, 1978); and *Antaeus* for "Ohio: Childhood Sketch" as it appeared in *Antaeus* 45/46 (Spring/Summer 1982). Reprinted by permission of author and publisher.

Sewanee Review for "The Terrible Threshold," first published in the *Sewanee Review* 67, no. 2 (Spring 1959). Copyright © by the University of the South. Reprinted with the permission of the editor.

Southern Humanities Review, Jerome Mazzaro, and Joseph McElrath for "Something to Be Said for the Light," first published in the Spring 1972 issue of the *Southern Humanities Review.*

University of Illinois Press and Dave Smith for "The Pure Clear Word."

Voyages for "James Wright on Roger Hecht," *Voyages* 1, no. 1 (1976).

Washington Square Press for "Frost: 'Stopping by Woods on a Snowy Evening'" from *Master Poems,* edited by Oscar Williams, 1967.

Every effort has been made to trace the ownership of all copyrighted material in this book and to obtain permission for its use.

Contents

Introduction

For several years before his death, James Wright planned to collect his essays, reviews, and other prose writings. In 1978, when he received a grant from the Guggenheim Foundation, he was able to take leave from Hunter College and reserve a block of time for writing. He spent most of this leave traveling and working in Europe. Here, he completed much of *This Journey*, and planned this prose book in journal notes and in letters to his friends.

In his journal he noted a table of contents for the book. James intended to divide it into four sections: Essays, Memoirs, Reviews, and Notes and Travel Letters. He listed his selection of essays, memoirs, and reviews—together with a sketch of childhood written for the Ohio Public Library Series. Another journal entry reminded him to include the sermon given at the Methodist Church in Old Chatham, New York, an event arranged by Orrin and Katherine Bly. In a letter to Robert Mezey, James mentioned including a dozen travel letters and perhaps one interview.

I started working on the book of prose in the summer of 1981. There was little editing to be done, as James had planned the formation of the book so carefully. With the invaluable help of Beth Tornes, I assembled the material. We made only one addition to the original format at this time—"The Work of Gary Snyder," an essay called to my attention by Robert Bly who had published it, under the pseudonym Crunk, in *The Sixties*.

After the University of Michigan Press accepted *Collected Prose* for "Poets on Poetry," we made several further changes. Galway Kinnell and Donald Hall suggested that we omit the travel letters, because they were inappropriate to the theme of the series. Donald Hall advised that we include three more interviews.

James wrote the majority of essays and reviews in *Collected Prose* during the fifties and the early sixties, when he taught at the University of Minnesota. He describes the circumstances of the review, "The Stiff Smile of Mr. Warren," in his interview with Dave Smith. In a letter to his old teacher, John Crowe Ransom, James mentioned that he and his friend Morgan Blum had been reading and discussing the work of Robert Penn Warren. When Ransom suggested that they write about Warren, James wrote this review and Blum wrote one of his own.

Both in conversation with me, and in early letters, James said that he wrote and published prose for money. Doubtless financial reasons formed part of his motive, for trying to raise and support a family on a teacher's salary was certainly difficult. However, it is obvious that James wrote only about writers whom he greatly admired and respected. He reviewed only books he cared about. In some cases he knew the writers. In others, as with René Char, he enjoyed exploring the work and establishing a correspondence. There are letters between James and Char, and a watercolor signed by Char hangs in our hallway.

The essays on Trakl, Vallejo, and Chinese poetry come from the days when James visited the Bly farm to talk with Robert. They discussed the work of poets in Spanish and Chinese, the German poets Trakl and Rilke, and the Japanese haiku of Issa and Bosho. James' interest in Spanish and German writers continued through the years, as he translated Theodor Storm, Herman Hesse, and wrote a review of Neruda in 1968. Then he took part in two conferences about Chinese poetry sponsored by the Academy of American Poets.

In 1970, after our first trip to Europe together, James began to experiment with a form he referred to as his "prose pieces."

He wrote about places we had seen on that trip as well as events from his childhood in the Ohio valley. Two chapbooks of prose pieces about Europe were published: *Moments of the Italian Summer* and *The Summers of Annie and James Wright*, the latter a combination of pieces by both of us. He included many other prose pieces in his last books of poetry.

James' article on Richard Hugo for the *American Poetry Review* was more an essay than a review. He took great delight in this article, for Hugo was a friend of long standing from University of Washington days. They had much in common: poverty in childhood, a couple named Ed and Zetta Bedford, a love of Italy, fishing, and late evenings (on the rare occasions when they could get together) spent in long and involved discussion.

In 1975 William Heyen asked James to contribute to the anthology *Poets in 1976*. James decided to include travel letters to his son Franz and his nieces Karin East and Laura Lee, some prose pieces about Italy which later appeared in *Moments of the Italian Summer,* and several reminiscences written especially for Heyen's book. In two of these pieces he interwove early memories about the poets Bill Knott and Richard Hugo with critical notions about their poetry—pieces touched with the earthy, somewhat cynical wit that was characteristic of James Wright.

James continued to be deeply committed to the prose piece. His journals from 1978 to 1980 are filled with drafts and completed selections. During the last months of his life he worked on a series of ten poems and prose pieces for the *American Poetry Review*. He broke off his work three days before entering the hospital. Left as a legacy is a small brown notebook whose pages are filled with the beauty of words set down as only James Wright could do.

Anne Wright

I
Essays

The Delicacy of Walt Whitman

The public mask, the coarse Whitman, is false. Then what is true? Is there a private Whitman who is delicate, and if there *is* a delicate Whitman, what is his poetry like? Where can we find it? And what does it have to do with those of us who want to read it? Is Whitman's delicacy a power that is alive in American poetry at the present moment? If so, who is displaying it? And is it capable of growth?

The *delicacy* of Walt Whitman. I do not mean to imply that Whitman was delicate as Nietzsche, for example, was in delicate health. Whitman really does seem to have been a strong man, in spite of the public mask's strident insistence on his own vigor. His actions were often modest and yet they demonstrate a physical condition astonishingly robust. When the war began, Whitman was forty-two years old. He went into the war. He did not have to go. I am not concerned with arguing the ethical significance of his relation to the war. I point only to the fact. In an essay recently published in the *Sewanee Review,* Mr. James M. Cox eloquently describes Whitman's exploit in terms which reveal the abundant physical strength of the man:

> Whitman's role in the Civil War stands as one of the triumphs of our culture. That this figure should have emerged from an almost illiterate background to become a national poet, that he

From *The Presence of Walt Whitman,* ed. R. W. B. Lewis (New York: Columbia University Press, 1962).

should have at the age of forty-two gone down into the wilderness of Virginia to walk across the bloody battlefields ministering to the sick and wounded, that he should have paced through the hospitals and kept a vigil over the mutilated victims on both sides, that he should have created the war in prose and poetry of an extraordinarily high order—that he should have done these deeds shows how truly he had cast himself in the heroic mould.

So the delicacy I have in mind is not an empty gentility, nor the physical frailty that sometimes slithers behind arrogance. It is the delicacy of his *poetry* that concerns me. It has its source in the character of Whitman himself, and it is, I believe, available to American poetry at the present time.

Whitman's poetry has delicacy of music, of diction, and of form. The word "delicacy" can do without a rhetorically formal definition; but I mean it to suggest powers of restraint, clarity, and wholeness, all of which taken together embody that deep spiritual inwardness, that fertile strength, which I take to be the most beautiful power of Whitman's poetry, and the most readily available to the poetry, and indeed the civilization, of our own moment in American history.

If what I say is true, then we are almost miraculously fortunate to have Whitman available to us. For some time the features of American poetry most in evidence have been very different from Whitman's: in short, recent American poetry has often been flaccid, obtuse and muddied, and fragmentary, crippled almost. Yet there is great talent alive in our country today, and if the spirit of Whitman can help to rescue that talent from the fate of so many things in America that begin nobly and end meanly, then we ought to study him as carefully as we can. What is his poetry like?

Let us consider first the delicacy of his music. And since I want to listen to the music closely, a few notes on traditional prosody are in order. At this point Whitman himself is ready to help us. As a stylist, he did not begin as a solitary barbarian (in Ortega's sense of that word). He is many things that are perhaps discomforting and even awkward, but he is not a smug fool—he is not an imitation Dead End Kid pretending that no poet or man of any kind ever existed before he was born upon the earth. Whitman realizes that the past has existed.

He also understands how the past continues to exist: it exists in the present, and comes into living form only when some individual man is willing to challenge it. Whitman dares, like Nietzsche, to challenge not only what he dislikes but also what he *values*. "The power to destroy or remould," writes Whitman in the 1855 Preface to *Leaves of Grass,* "is freely used by him (the greatest poet) but never the power of attack. What is past is past. If he does not expose superior models and prove himself by every step he takes he is not what is wanted."

It seems to me of the gravest importance that Whitman's relation to established traditional forms of poetry and of society itself be clarified, so that we may free him from the tone of pretentious ignorance that has been associated with his mere name, from time to time, by fools. He knows that the past exists, and he knows that, as a poet and as a man, he has a right to live. His duty to the past is precisely this: to have the courage to live and to create his own poetry.

This is the great way of learning from the noble spirits of the past. And the most difficultly courageous way of asserting the shape and meaning of one's own poetry and one's own life is to challenge and surpass those very traditions and masters whom one can honestly respect. This deep spiritual kinship between a truly original man and the nobility of the past is formulated thus by Goethe: "People always talk of the study of the ancients; but what does that mean, except that it says, turn your attention to the real world, and try to express it, for that is what the ancients did when they were alive" (*Conversations with Eckermann*). And so in Whitman's music we find him turning away from one masterfully delicate verbal musician, Longfellow, toward the real world. Whitman respected Longfellow for his true gifts, as we ought to do. Our own scorn of Longfellow is cant. It is like the scorn of the great Victorian Englishmen that prevailed until recently under the influence of Lytton Strachey; we scurry forth like insects to deface them as soon as a serious, honorable man like Strachey assures us that Dickens, Tennyson, and Florence Nightingale are safely dead. So let us turn, for just a moment, to Longfellow, whose lovely poetry, even in his own time, was in the strict sense a musical embodiment of the European past. In *Specimen Days* ("My Tribute to Four Poets"), Whitman records a visit to Longfellow which unmistakably reveals his true respect for the poet who was almost universally celebrated as the great poet whom Whitman himself would like to be: "I shall not soon forget his lit-up face," says Whitman, "and glowing warmth and courtesy in the modes of what is called the old school." And then Whitman suddenly, and rather startlingly, remarks on his own poetic relation to Longfellow and others (Emerson, Whittier, and Bryant):

> In a late magazine one of my reviewers, who ought to know better, speaks of my "attitude of contempt and scorn and intolerance" toward the leading poets—of my "deriding" them, and preaching their "uselessness." If anybody cares to know what I think—and have long thought and avow'd—about them, I am entirely willing to propound. I can't imagine any better luck befalling these States for a poetical beginning and initiation than has come from Emerson, Longfellow, Bryant, and Whittier. . . . Longfellow for rich color, graceful forms and incidents—all that makes life beautiful and love refined—competing with the singers of Europe on their own ground, and with one exception, better and finer work than that of any of them.

Furthermore, Whitman's deep humility (an intellectual as well as a moral virtue) appears in his note on the "Death of Longfellow" (*Specimen Days*). There, in the very act of praising Longfellow for his best gift ("verbal melody") he speaks of his radical inadequacy; and thus Whitman inadvertently, almost as an afterthought, identifies his own great strength:

> Longfellow in his voluminous works seems to me to be eminent in the style and forms of poetical expression that mark the present age, (an idiosyncrasy, almost a sickness, of verbal melody,). . . . He is certainly the sort of bard and counter-actant most needed for our materialistic, self-assertive, money-worshipping, Anglo-Saxon races, and especially for the present age in America—an age tyrannically regulated with reference to the

manufacturer, the merchant, the financier, the politician and the day workman—for whom and among whom he comes as the poet of melody, courtesy, deference—*poet of the mellow twilight of the past* in Italy, Germany, Spain, and Northern Europe. . . . He strikes a splendid average, and does not sing exceptional passions, or humanity's jagged escapades. He is not revolutionary, brings nothing offensive or new, does not deal hard blows. . . . His very anger is gentle, is at second hand, (as in the "Quadroon Girl" and the "Witnesses"). . . . To the ungracious complaint-charge of his want of racy nativity and special originality, I shall only say that America and the world may well be reverently thankful—can never be thankful enough—for any such singing-bird vouchsafed out of the centuries, without asking that the notes be different from those of other songsters; adding what I have heard Longfellow himself say, that ere the New World can be worthily original, and announce herself and her own heroes, she must be well saturated with the originality of others, and respectfully consider the heroes that lived before Agamemnon.

The whole passage is moved by an impulse to pass beyond. Not merely to pass beyond what one hates—the phoniness, the counterfeit poetry which is always among us in its thousand blind, mean, sly forms. But to pass beyond what one loves, to open one's ears, to know what one is doing and why. It is a noble statement by a delicate and reverent man.

Let us apply the statement to Whitman's own music. In effect, he tunes his verses toward those very crass and difficult subjects which Longfellow (for whatever reason) avoided. And yet, even so, Whitman's music is not "jagged" like the escapades of that American humanity he often sings of. It is a *delicate* music, a deeper sound than that of Longfellow; it is alive, and it hurts, as men are hurt on the jagged edges of their own lives.

So Whitman respected Longfellow, a traditional prosodist. In spite of his poems like "Evangeline," which we are told to read as though they were written in the classical dactylic hexameter, Longfellow is predominantly an iambic writer. Moreover, he writes the iambic meter with a masterful grasp of its permissive variations: the elisions, the trochaic substitutions, the spondaic effects and their euphonious combination within regular iambic patterns. But Longfellow does not write about American life. He does not write about its externals. And, shunning its externals, he does not penetrate to its spirit. Whitman notices these radical limits in the very act of praising Longfellow for his mastery—mastery of a kind which forces him to turn away from the living world and to sing either of Europe or of the American past.

Whitman also brings a rare technical understanding of prosody to bear on the living American present. But in his concern to surpass tradition, he deliberately shuns the iambic measure and all its variations, except in a very few instances (like the notorious "O Captain! My Captain!" and the less frequently quoted "Ethiopia Saluting the Colors") which offer a helpful contrast to the inventive delicacy of music in Whitman's greater poems.

He shuns the iambic measure. He says, in the 1855 Preface, "The rhythm and uniformity of perfect poems show the free growth of metrical laws, and bud from them as unerringly and loosely as lilacs and roses on a bush, and take shapes as compact as the shapes of chestnuts and oranges." Does Whitman mean that "free growth" is aimless? No, he speaks of "metrical laws." Listen to his poem "Reconciliation":

Word over all, beautiful as the sky,
Beautiful that war and all its deeds of carnage must in time
     be utterly lost,
That the hands of the sisters Death and Night incessantly
     softly wash again, and ever again, this soil'd world;
For my enemy is dead, a man divine as myself is dead,
I look where he lies white-faced and still in the coffin—I draw
     near,
Bend down and touch lightly with my lips the white face in
     the coffin.

We cannot understand this poem's music in traditional prosodic terms. Still, it's fun to note that Whitman did not write noniambic verse out of pique at his inability to control its rules.

Listen again to Whitman's opening line: "Word over all, beautiful as the sky." The line is a flawless iambic pentameter; he uses a trochaic substitution in the first foot, a hovering spondaic echo between the second and third feet, a daring and yet perfectly traditional inversion; and he successfully runs two light stresses before the final strong stress.

It seems to me wonderful that Whitman should have written that line, which is not only iambic, but as bold in its exploitation of the iambic possibilities as the masters themselves: Campion, Herrick, Wyatt, even Milton. And that is not so strange. In a note on "British Literature" (*Collect: Notes Left Over*), Whitman writes the following: "To avoid mistake, I would say that I not only commend the study of this literature, but wish our sources of supply and comparison vastly enlarged." The trouble is that "the British element these states hold, and have always held, enormously beyond its fit proportions . . . its products are no models for us." So he does not hate traditional British prosody, which is of course predominantly iambic. He loves its great craft, and he shows his ability to emulate it. But he is an adventurer; he wants to listen beyond the admittedly rich music of iambic, and to report what he hears.

In prosody, then, Whitman is sometimes a destroyer, but we must see that he knows exactly what he is destroying. He is both theoretically and practically ready to replace it with a new prosody of his own. He begins with a supremely sensitive ear for the music of language; he moves beyond the permissive variations of iambic; and he is not afraid of the new musical possibilities out there, so he brings some of them back with him. Perhaps they were there all the time; perhaps they are the quantitative possibilities of the classical languages that have drifted around in English. In any case, the iambic conventions do not seem to make much provision for them; and yet they can be incredibly beautiful in Whitman. We need only listen:

> Come lovely and soothing death,
> Undulate round the world, serenely arriving, arriving,
> In the day, in the night, to all, to each,
> Sooner or later delicate death.

Whitman really does have something to teach current American poets, in spite of his entering American poetry once again, in Mr. Randall Jarrell's wicked phrase, as "the hero of a De Mille movie about Whitman"—a movie, one might add, which costars the Dead End Kids.

To summarize, Whitman can teach us about some possibilities of musical delicacy in our language. He sympathetically understood iambic forms (exemplified by Longfellow) which in his own poems he is trying to break and surpass. He can also teach courage, for he has great rhythmical daring; he seeks constantly for a music which really echoes and fulfills his imaginative vision.

He becomes a great artist by the ways of growth which Nietzsche magnificently describes in the first speech of *Thus Spake Zarathustra:* the Three Metamorphoses of the Spirit. The spirit that truly grows, says Nietzsche, will first be a camel, a beast of burden, who labors to bear the forms of the past, whether in morality or art or anything else; then he will change into a lion, and destroy not merely what he hates but even what he loves and understands; and the result of this concerned and accurate destruction will be the spirit's emergence as a child, who is at last able to create clearly and powerfully from within his own imagination.

Whitman says of the great poet, "He swears to his art, I will not be meddlesome, I will not have in my writings any elegance, or effect, or originality, to hang in the way between me and the rest like curtains. I will have nothing hang in the way, not the richest curtains" (Preface, 1855). And Whitman is well aware of the many curtains that can hang in the way. There is not only the old-world elegance of Longfellow—which may stand for the prosodic traditions of England, beautiful in themselves—but there is also the curtain of aimless destructiveness, which is eventually not even destructive but just trivial. In "After Trying a Certain Book" (*Specimen Days*), Whitman says that the difficulty of explaining what a poem means is not to be taken as evidence that the poem means nothing: "Common teachers or critics are always asking 'What does it mean?' Symphony of fine musician, or sunset, or sea-waves rolling up the beach—what do they mean? Undoubtedly in the most subtle-elusive sense they mean something—but who shall fathom and define those meanings? (*I do not intend this as a warrant for wildness and frantic escapades. . . .*)" (my italics). Every scholar and every Beat who mentions Whitman ought to read that salutary note beforehand.

Now I want to speculate on the delicacy of Whitman's diction, his choice of words. What is remarkable is not merely his attempt to include new things—objects, persons, places, and events—in his poems. Something more interesting and complex goes on: in the face of this sometimes difficult and prosaic material ("humanity's jagged escapades"), he is able to retain his delicacy, which is a power of mind as well as a quality of kindness. In a crisis, he keeps his head and his feelings alert. He can be as precise as Henry James, as Mr. Jarrell rightly says; but he is sensitively precise about things that are often in themselves harsh, even brutal.

Mr. Jarrell has written one of the liveliest accounts of Whitman's delicacy of diction, and I refer the reader to that essay. Perhaps Mr. Jarrell does not sufficiently emphasize the enormous strength and courage it required even to face some of the horrible things Whitman faced, much less to claim them for the imagination by means of a diction that is as delicate as that of Keats.

One of my favorite poems in Whitman is "A March in the Ranks Hard-Prest, and the Road Unknown" from *Drum-Taps.* It reveals perfectly what I mean about Whitman's delicate diction: his power of retaining his sensitivity right in the face of realities that would certainly excuse coarseness, for the sake of self-defense if for no other reason. But Whitman does not defend himself. As he had told us in a Virgilian line, one of the noblest lines of poetry ever written, "I was the man, I suffered, I was there." The line is great because it is not a boast but a modest bit of information, almost as unobtrusive as a stage-direction or perhaps a whispered aside to the reader. (Whitman is always whispering to us—that is another of his musical delicacies.) There he certainly is, gathering the horror into his delicate words, soothing it if possible, always looking at it and in the deepest sense imagining it:

A march in the ranks hard-prest, and the road unknown,
A route through a heavy wood with muffled steps in the
    darkness,
Our army foil'd with loss severe, and the sullen remnant
    retreating,
Till after midnight glimmer upon us the lights of a dim-
    lighted building,
We come to an open space in the woods, and halt by the
    dim-lighted building,
'Tis a large old church at the crossing roads, now an
    impromptu hospital,
Entering but for a minute I see a sight beyond all the
    pictures and poems ever made,
Shadows of deepest, deepest black, just lit by moving candles
    and lamps,
And by one great pitchy torch stationary with wild red
    flames and clouds of smoke,
By these, crowds, groups of forms vaguely I see on the
    floor, some in the pews laid down,
At my feet more distinctly a soldier, a mere lad, in
    danger of bleeding to death, (he is shot in the abdomen,)
I stanch the blood temporarily, (the youngster's face
    is white as a lily,)
Then before I depart I sweep my eyes o'er the scene fain to
    absorb it all,
Faces, varieties, postures beyond description, most in
    obscurity, some of them dead,
Surgeons operating, attendants holding lights, the smell of
    ether, the odor of blood,
The crowd, O the crowd of the bloody forms, the yard
    outside also fill'd,
Some on the bare ground, some on planks or stretchers,
    some in the death-spasm sweating,
An occasional scream or cry, the doctor's shouted orders or
    calls,
The glisten of the little steel instruments catching the glint of
    the torches,

These I resume as I chant, I see again the forms, I smell the
    odor,
Then hear outside the orders given, *Fall in, my men, fall in;*
But first I bend to the dying lad, his eyes open, a half-smile
    gives he me,
Then the eyes close, calmly close, and I speed forth to the
    darkness,
Resuming, marching, ever in darkness marching, on in the
    ranks,
The unknown road still marching.

I want to draw attention to a single small detail of diction, which becomes huge because of its delicacy. I mean the phrase about the wounded young man's face. He suddenly looms up out of the confusion and darkness; he has been shot in the abdomen; and his face, buffaloed by shock, is "white as a lily."

There have been many poets in America who would compare a white face with a lily. There are also many poets who attempt to deal with a subject matter that is, like Whitman's, very far from the traditional materials of poesy as Longfellow understood them. Moreover, I know that there are many brave American men who write about painful experiences. But what is special about Whitman, what makes his diction remarkable in itself and fertile for us today, is that he does all three of these things at once, and in him they become a single act of creation. Unless we can see the nobility of his courage, then we have neither the right nor the intelligence to talk about the delicacy of his style.

Whitman's diction contains a lesson that can actually be learned, and it does not require the vain imitation of his personal appearance and stylistic mannerisms. It is more spiritually inward than any external accident can suggest. It is this: he deliberately seeks in American life the occasions and persons who are central to that life; he sometimes finds them harsh and violent, as in the war; and he responds to the harshness with a huge effort of imagination: to be delicate, precise, sensitive.

I realize that it is difficult to distinguish between the delicacy of Whitman's diction and his sensitivity as a man. But that is just the point. When a certain kind of diction, like a certain kind of meter, is employed by a coarse man, it automatically becomes a mannerism, or perhaps a stock device, detachable from the body of the poem, like a false eyelash, or a shapely artificial breast. Any concentration upon Whitman's stylistic mannerisms alone betrays an obsession with external, accidental things. Perhaps that is why so many bad poets have claimed Whitman as an ancestor.

I want also to say something about the delicacy of form in Whitman's poems. I think at once of the sentence in the 1855 Preface about rhythm and what he calls "uniformity." Here is the sentence again: "The rhythm and uniformity of perfect poems shows the free growth of metrical laws, and bud from them as unerringly and loosely as lilacs and roses on a bush, and take shapes as compact as the shapes of chestnuts and oranges."

This sentence can help us to understand what "form" meant to Whitman and also what it might mean to contemporary poets in America and elsewhere, if they have truly learned from Whitman and still wish to learn from him. The word "form" itself, however, may be ambiguous. So I will shun rhetorical definitions, which often threaten to mislead or oversimplify; and I will discuss a single short poem that, I believe, is a great poem because of the almost perfect delicacy of its form:

I heard you solemn-sweet pipes of the organ as last Sunday
    mourn I pass'd the church,
Winds of autumn, as I walk'd the woods at dusk I heard your
    long-stretch'd sighs up above so mournful,
I heard the perfect Italian tenor singing at the opera, I heard
    the soprano in the midst of the quartet singing;
Heart of my love! you too I heard murmuring low through
    one of the wrists around my head,
Heard the pulse of you when all was still ringing little
    bells last night under my ear.

Does this poem have a form? If so, how can I describe it without losing in a general classification the very details that give the poem its life? I can think of at least two possibly helpful ways of answering these questions. First, Mr. Gay Wilson Allen (in his definitive biography of Whitman) supplies us with a crucial bit of textual information. The version of "I heard you solemn-sweet pipes" which I just quoted is not the only one. An earlier version, one of three poems which Whitman published in 1861, is quoted and discussed by Mr. Allen. The revisions are almost all deletions. The earlier version (printed in the New York *Leader*, October 12, 1861) contained apostrophes to "war-suggesting trumpets," to "you round-lipp'd cannons." In the version which Whitman apparently considered final (printed in the "Deathbed" edition of 1892), the references to war are deleted. Whitman also deleted a whole single line, in which he addresses a lady who played "delicious music on the harp."

What is left? A simple poem of five lines. Whitman addresses four different sounds. In these apostrophes and in his arrangement of them we can find the form of his poem.

The form is that of parallelism. But immediately we have to distinguish between the grammatical signification of "parallelism" and Whitman's actual use of it. A grammatical parallelism is primarily concerned with sentence structure: noun balances noun, verb balances verb, either as repetition or as antithesis. But in Whitman's poem, the appearance of grammatical parallelism is so rare as to be almost accidental. In fact, he almost seems to avoid it. For he uses parallelism not as a device of repetition but as an occasion for development. For this reason, we take a certain risk when we read "I heard you solemn-sweet pipes." After the first two lines, we can know only two things: first, we cannot hope to rest on mere parallel sentence structure; second, the poet is probably going to sing about another sound, but it might be the sound of anything. (The possibility is a little scary in a country where, for example, President Coolidge's taciturnity is automatically considered a joke, instead of a great civic virtue. Behind the uneasy joke lies the dreadful suspicion that we talk too much.) There is no way to read Whitman's poem at all unless we yield ourselves to its principle of growth, a principle that reveals itself only in this particular poem, stage by stage.

Whitman first tries to make sure that we will not confuse his poetic forms with the rules of grammar; and then he lets his images grow, one out of another; and finally, we discover the form of the poem as we read it, and we know what it is only after we have finished.

It is this kind of formal growth that, I believe, gives special appropriateness to Whitman's mention of "shapes as compact as the shapes of chestnuts and oranges." These fruits do indeed have "shapes"—delicate shapes indeed. And they are compact, not diffuse. Their life depends on their form, which grows out of the forms of blossoms, which in turn grew out of the forms of trees, which in turn grew out of the forms of seeds. If I followed the changes that overwhelm an orange seed, I should be startled at the unexpected form of each stage of growth; but the form would be there nevertheless, however unexpected: at once undreamed-of and inevitable.

I have avoided the term "organic unity" because I wanted to read Whitman's poem afresh; and I am afraid that we might confuse the philosophical definition of a term in aesthetics with our empirical attempt to pay attention to the form of a poem. Just as bad poets tend to substitute the external accidents of Whitman's personal mannerisms and habits of dress for his poetry, so we readers might tend to substitute a general term for our reading of poetry—any poetry. If you mention the name of Laforgue, for example, it is a rare graduate student who will not immediately say, or think, the phrase "romantic irony," just as certain famous dogs helplessly salivated when a bell was rung. That's a good simile, as W. C. Fields once observed in another connection. Moreover, the simile is horrible; I wish I could make it even more so.

What is "form"? It is not simply the rules of grammar. And it cannot simply be equated with certain conventions of iambic verse. When reviewers of current American verse say that a certain poem is written "in form," they usually mean it is predominantly iambic, either skillful or clumsy. But the form in Whitman's poems is not iambic. Form, in Whitman, is a principle of growth: one image or scene or sound *grows* out of another. The general device is parallelism, not of grammar but of action or some other meaning. Here is a further example of the parallel form, which is delicate and precise and therefore very powerful but which is not based on the repetition of the sentence structure:

The little one sleeps in its cradle,
I lift the gauze and look a long time, and silently
    brush away flies with my hand.

The youngster and the red-faced girl turn aside up
    the bushy hill,
I peeringly view them from the top.

The suicide sprawls on the bloody floor of the bedroom,
I witness the corpse with its dabbled hair, I note where the
    pistol has fallen.

                        ("Song of Myself," section 8)

Form in Whitman is a principle of imagination: the proliferating of images out of one unifying vision. Every real poem has its own form, which cannot be discovered through rhetoric, but only through imagination. Whitman can teach current American poets to destroy their own rhetoric and trust their own imagination. I shudder to think what would happen if every current versifier in America were to do that. (Is it a shudder of joy? A risky question.)

I began by asking what Whitman has to do with us, and where he is to be found. Some great writers of the past continue to exist as objects of veneration and study. They are no less great for all that. But Whitman is different, at least for us in America today, scholars and poets alike. Of course he deserves veneration, and he receives it. But he is also an immediate presence. He demands attention whether he is venerated or not. His work is capable of exerting direct power upon some conventional divisions in American life; and the power can heal the division. For example, in America today we still suffer from the conventional division between scholarly study of poetry on one hand and the attempt to practice the living art of poetry on the other. But consider Mr. Malcolm Cowley's 1959 reprinting of the first edition of *Leaves of Grass.* The reprinting is a work of the most careful scholarship: textual, historical, and biographical. It fully deserves the attention of scholars in the most dignified learned journals. It is respected by scholars who modestly accept their role as "academics"—men who labor faithfully by day at the scholarly profession, and are not especially interested in reading current American verse during their evenings at home with their families. And yet . . . Mr. Cowley's reprinting of the 1855 *Leaves of Grass* is not only an act of sound scholarship; it is also an act of living poetry. I am sure that Mr. Cowley felt the relevance of Whitman's first edition to any lively interest in current American verse; but I doubt if he could have anticipated the effect of its living presence. The book itself is the newest poetry we have. It is as though the true spirit of Whitman had returned among us in order to rescue himself from the misinterpretations and abuses of his coarse imitators. He is, quite literally, living among us at this very moment; he has just published a new book; his poetry doesn't sound at all like the vast (too vast) clutter of work in two fairly representative anthologies of recent American verse: *The New Poets of England and America* (Meridian Books, 1957) and *The New American Poetry* (Grove Press, 1960). He is newer than both; he is precise, courageous, delicate and seminal—an abundant poet. I think it would be entirely appropriate to award a prize to Whitman for a beautiful first book; and to Mr. Cowley for a revelation in which scholarship and thrilling poetic vitality are one and the same.

I think Whitman can also be found in other places, and I will mention two of them.

The delicate strength of Whitman was recognized and loved long ago by poets in the Spanish language. It is remarkable how often they speak of him. Often they speak of him in poems. I have in mind Federico García Lorca's magnificent

"Ode to Walt Whitman," written in New York City at the end of the twenties. But the spirit of Whitman is everywhere present among Spanish and South American poets: in the form which rejects external rhetoric in order to discover and reveal a principle of growth; in the modesty and simplicity of diction; in the enormously courageous willingness to leap from one image into the unknown, in sheer faith that the next image will appear in the imagination; in the sensitive wholeness of the single poems which result from such imaginative courage; and, above all, in the belief in the imagination as the highest flowering of human life (the phrase belongs to Jorge Guillen), not just a rhetorical ornament. These are all powers of Whitman's spirit. They have been enlivening Spanish poetry for at least fifty years.

Moreover, we are in the midst of a wave of translation in the United States. The September, 1961, issue of *Poetry* (Chicago) is entirely devoted to translation. The poems of Pablo Neruda of Chile, Cesar Vallejo of Peru, and of several great writers from Spain—Juan Ramon Jimenez, Antonio Machado, Jorge Guillen, Miguel Hernandez, and Blas de Otero, to name only a few—are being not only read but also translated by several American writers, and this effort cannot help but lead to Whitman. It is sometimes said that the true spirit of Poe was absorbed into contemporary American literature only after Poe had been truly understood by the French. Perhaps the true Whitman may return to the United States from Spain and South America "through the sky that is below the ground" (Jimenez).

We have spirits capable of welcoming him. Louis Simpson's imagination is obsessed with the most painful details of current American life, which he reveals under a very powerfully developed sense of American history. Several of his latest poems directly address Whitman as a figure who discovers that the Open Road has led to the barren Pacific, to the used-car graveyard, to the earthly paradise of the real-estate agents. Mr. Simpson describes America and Americans in a vision totally free from advertising and propaganda, just as Whitman described the Civil War soldiers, not as "Our Boys" or suchlike, but rather as startled white faces of youths shot in the abdomen.

Robert Bly's Whitmanesque powers include the ability to write about what he calls "the dark figures of politics." A remarkable sequence describing such "figures" is *Poems for the Ascension of J. P. Morgan*, published in *New World Writing #15*. I want to quote a new poem of Bly's. It is called "After the Industrial Revolution, All Things Happen at Once."

> Now we enter a strange world, where the Hessian Christmas
> Still goes on, and Washington has not reached the other
>   shore;
> The Whiskey Boys
> Are gathering again on the meadows of Pennsylvania
> And the Republic is still sailing on the open sea.
>
> In 1956 I saw a black angel in Washington, dancing
> On a barge, saying, Let us now divide kennel dogs
> And hunting dogs; Henry Cabot Lodge, in New York,
> Talking of sugar cane in Cuba; Ford,
> In Detroit, drinking mothers' milk;
> Ford, saying, "History is bunk!"
> And Wilson saying, "What is good for General Motors—"
>
> Who is it, singing? Don't you hear singing?
> It is the dead of Cripple Creek;
> Coxey's army
> Like turkeys are singing from the tops of trees!
> And the Whiskey Boys are drunk outside Philadelphia.

Denise Levertov, an extremely gifted poet, suggests Whitman in several ways: her reverence for the civilization of the past, so deep as to be utterly modest; her willingness to discover the new forms of her imagination; and her nobility of spirit, which knows what is worthy of celebration and is capable of great moral understanding. Two of her recent poems (included in her superb book from New Directions, *The Jacob's Ladder*), "In Memory of Boris Pasternak" and "During the Eichmann Trial," embody this nobility perfectly. The latter sequence includes a cry of pity for Adolf Eichmann; and Miss

Levertov sees everyone in the twentieth century caught and exposed in Eichmann's glass cage. The subject is almost unendurably horrible; and it is treated with a tenderness which is in itself an imaginative strength of great purity.

So Whitman is alive; in person, with his own poems; in spirit, among the Spanish writers who long ago understood him; and among certain American writers, in their translations and in their own spiritual courage. Whitman has delicacy; moreover, he dared to subject his delicacy to the tests of the real world, both the external world of nineteenth-century America, with its wars and loud cities and buffaloes vanishing into herds of clouds, and the inner world of his spirit. He loved the human body, he knew that when you kill a man he dies, and he exposed his feelings to the coarsest of wars in order to record its truth. He had nothing against British literature; but he felt that Americans have even greater stores of imagination to draw upon. Here are some of his words, from *Collect: Notes Left Over:*

> I strongly recommend all the young men and young women of the United States to whom it may be eligible, to overhaul the well-freighted fleets, the literature of Italy, Spain, France, Germany, so full of those elements of freedom, self-possession, gay-heartedness, subtlety, dilation, needed in preparations for the future of the States. I only wish we could have really good translations. I rejoice at the feeling for Oriental researches and poetry, and hope it will continue.

The man who wrote those words was not only a very great poet. He was also a generous human being, and he rejoiced in the hopes of his fellows. I believe that American poetry at this moment is able to show itself worthy of Whitman's intelligence, his courage, his supremely delicate imagination. At any rate, many living American poets cherish Whitman's best powers; and one cannot love such things without being inwardly changed. We honor Whitman; and we share the happy thought that he would have been delighted and would have wanted to honor us in return. Surely he would have loved another new American poem which occurs to me, for it speaks with his own best voice—uncluttered, courageous, and kind. The poem is Mr. David Ignatow's "Walt Whitman in the Civil War Hospitals," which I quote in its entirety:

Prescient, my hands soothing
their foreheads, by my love
I earn them. In their presence
I am wretched as death. They smile
to me of love. They cheer me
and I smile. These are stones
in the catapulting world;
they fly, bury themselves in flesh,
in a wall, in earth; in midair
break against each other
and are without sound.
I sent them catapulting.
They outflew my voice
towards vacant spaces,
but I have called them farther,
to the stillness beyond,
to death which I have praised.

Far from the Madding Crowd
An Afterword

To read the work of any famous author is in itself something of an art. A reader must develop the poise of courage, in order to stay the judgments of his elders until he can read the work for himself.

Such a warning is especially pertinent to a reading of Hardy's novels. He is a "classic," and to turn an author into a classic, according to Shaw, is one way of making sure that no one will read him. Thus, *The Return of the Native* is often required reading for high school or college classes because it is supposed to illustrate Hardy's "fatalism," or because it has a symmetrical plot; and I sympathize with the students who have the good taste to prefer the version in Classics Comics to the plot-outlines and prejudgments given them by their teachers.

There is other temptation to irrelevancy. A new reader may have heard that Hardy had some difficulty in publishing certain novels (such as *Tess of the d'Urbervilles* in 1891) serially in magazines, because he wrote of sexual matters. So the reader may be tempted to read *Tess,* not for its own sake, but for the opportunity it provides him to congratulate himself on his moral superiority to the smug Victorians. Similarly, professional students of literature sometimes seem more interested in attacking or defending T. S. Eliot's judgment of Hardy ("scarcely edifying") than in reading Hardy's books.

From Thomas Hardy, *Far from the Madding Crowd* (New York: New American Library, Signet Classics, 1960).

When one undertakes to read a Hardy novel, it is probably best to remember only the simple, general things: that Hardy lived for a long time; that his career developed in such a way and in such a period of time as to make him a major author of both the nineteenth and twentieth centuries; that he wrote many books that were controversial for one reason or another. Some of his books have survived both excessive praise and intelligent devaluation. For example, Henry James found *Far from the Madding Crowd* a clever but uninspired imitation of George Eliot's manner. James makes a serious case; and yet the novel continues to be read, even now that James's own writings are granted the attention they were not receiving in 1874. Often the great literary damnations have themselves survived only as curiosities of pigheadedness, or they have succeeded in obliterating their victims from the public consciousness. I remember how strange I felt when I discovered that Thomas Shadwell's poetry was not half bad. The power of critics and authors to react upon each other is difficult to assess. It is a subject which ought to be carefully studied, for it is important as well as strange. Henry James's review of Hardy's *Far from the Madding Crowd* is one of the most thorough and clear critical devastations I have ever read. And yet, at this very moment, both James's review *and* Hardy's novel are still in print. There is obviously some quality in *Far from the Madding Crowd* which eluded James, a quality which has kept the attention of professional scholars and the general public alike. There is something in the book that inspires people to love it; and love, like other passions, does not yield to argument, even judicious argument. For this reason, it is especially appropriate that a brief discussion of this novel should be an "afterword." Let the reader discover first whether or not he can love the book. If he cannot, then he will not read the commentary. If he can, then he will welcome it.

Hardy published fourteen novels in all, from *Desperate Remedies* (1871) to *Jude the Obscure* (1895). It is futile to divide his literary career into sections. Though he did not publish his first book of verse (*Wessex Poems*) till 1898, he had wanted to be a poet in his youth, and he wrote some poems even while he was working on his novels. From scattered comments in his wife's edition of his memoirs, I think we may safely assume that Hardy thought of himself primarily as a poet.

And yet, it is not adequate to say that he was essentially a poet, that he gave up the attempt to publish his poems when he discovered that the popular reading-public was more likely to be interested in fiction, and that he returned to the writing—and the publishing—of poetry only after his literary reputation had been established by his novels and after he had become disgusted with the arguments that his past novels provoked. For the poet is always there. Some of the characteristics of his best poems often crop up in his novels.

I do not mean that there are detachable sections of merely florid prose. Of course, Hardy could write startlingly bad prose sometimes. There is scarcely a novel which contains no signs of his awkwardness, his heavy-handed comparison of delicate women's faces with the sketches of some forgotten artist, his guidebook-descriptions of architecture, and other bad mannerisms. But the quality of his best poetry appears just where the prose itself is most supple, concrete, and precise.

We should try to avoid yet another discussion about the difference between poetry and prose. That discussion is physically depressing, like a stupid joke which everyone present has known and loathed for years. I should like to record my gratitude to Mr. Yvor Winters for his beautifully impatient statement that poetry is written in verse whereas prose is written in prose. The statement may not have solved any problems of aesthetics, but it made the actual reading of books a little easier; and, as such, Mr. Winters's words clear my mind and lighten my heart, as though an ancient burden had been lifted from my back. One can escape such dreadful toils by simply noting, to begin with, that the language of Hardy's novels is often most beautiful when it is most like the language of his poems. This remark is particularly relevant to three of the novels: *Under the Greenwood Tree, The Woodlanders,* and *Far from the Madding Crowd.*

Under the Greenwood Tree (1872) had impressed Leslie Stephen, editor of the *Cornhill Magazine,* who wrote Hardy and requested a story. Though Hardy had not yet begun the tale that was to become *Far from the Madding Crowd,* he had been thinking about it; and, in his answering letter, he told Stephen of "a pastoral tale . . . in which the chief characters would be a woman-farmer, a shepherd, and a sergeant of the Dragoon Guards." The first exchange of letters between editor and author took place late in 1872; and early in the next year Hardy submitted a few completed chapters and the remainder in outline. *Far from the Madding Crowd* was published serially in the *Cornhill* from January to December, 1874.

However it may be with other novelists, the mention of an outline by Hardy is sure to raise one of those attractive irrelevancies which have kept thousands of Teutonically conditioned contributors to literary journals off the already crowded streets by providing occasions for the relief of anxiety through the writing of "articles." They have also contributed little to the intelligent reading of literature. One such irrelevancy is the equation of rhetorical manners with literary worth. For example, Hardy's way of writing a novel sometimes involved the sketching of an outline. Sometimes, as in *Far from the Madding Crowd,* the central actions of the novel can be summarized so as to suggest an almost perfect symmetry. At the beginning, we see the shepherd Oak wooing Bathsheba. Shortly after his failure, he begins to blend with the landscape in his silent devotion to the heroine. Then Bathsheba more or less promises herself to Boldwood. Just as she is to accept Boldwood's offer of engagement, she becomes infatuated with Sergeant Troy. Boldwood joins Oak in a hopeless patience. Shortly after Bathsheba's marriage to Troy, she begins her descent. She learns that he is a cad, and marriage seems hell to her. After the incident of Fanny Robin's death, Troy vanishes. Boldwood emerges from the background to woo Bathsheba again. Troy returns, and is killed. Boldwood is imprisoned. At last, Bathsheba and Oak are together, as they were at the beginning. We might schematize the action according to the number of wooers surrounding Bathsheba as the novel progresses: 2–3–4–3–2.

The scheme is charmingly neat; it is also satanically false to Hardy.

At one time Hardy would have been praised as a great novelist merely because he could write a symmetrical story. More recently, we have humorlessly misread Flaubert, and memorized the "idea" that evidence of the mechanics of the action is in itself enough to damn the novel.

But a reader is not very likely to worry about the symmetry of the plot as he reads *Far from the Madding Crowd.* It is obvious enough, and it is not especially obtrusive. In fact, it is rather entertaining. But what really matters is that the outline provides Hardy with a series of occasions wherein he can realize the figure of Gabriel Oak, and, by the blending of Oak with the rustics and of the rustics with nature, give body to a vision profoundly close to his best poems.

It is a vision in the strictest sense *embodied.* Nothing could be more striking than the contrast, almost the contradiction, between the character of Oak as it seems promised by a mere outline of the action and the actual character of Oak as Hardy presents it to us page by page. In a summary, Oak seems sure to be one of those prigs who are easily reconciled to a loveless life because they have no emotion to lose. But in the book itself we find Oak a man of deep and serene feeling. He is always surrounded by things which fill him with inexorable affection, and with which, at last, he becomes miraculously identified: sheep, dogs, plants, trees, items of clothing, his pocket watch. Take a passage in Chapter Thirty-six: Oak leaves the revelers asleep in the barn, walks to his hut, and discovers signs of the coming thunder and rain:

> Gabriel proceeded towards his home. In approaching the door, his toe kicked something which felt and sounded soft, leathery, and distended, like a boxing-glove. It was a large toad humbly travelling across the path. Oak took it up, thinking it might be better to kill the creature to save it from pain; but finding it uninjured, he placed it again among the grass. He knew what this direct message from the Great Mother meant. And soon came another.
>
> When he struck a light indoors there appeared upon the table a thin glistening streak, as if a brush of varnish had been lightly dragged across it. Oak's eyes followed the serpentine sheen to the other side, where it led up to a huge brown

garden-slug, which had come indoors to-night for reasons of its own. . . . Oak sat down meditating for nearly an hour.

There are many such descriptions in Hardy's novels. He is not "padding." He is not merely sketching in the details that are supposed to conceal the plot outline. It is not only the details themselves that so sharply strike the reader's attention, but also Hardy's feeling about those details. The physical description is clear enough, and does not require comment. But look at the word "humbly," in the passage on the toad. And the phrase "for reasons of its own," about the garden-slug. The qualities that these phrases have in common are their unobtrusiveness and their originality. An unobtrusive phrase is one which draws the reader's attention to something more dramatically important than itself and then slips out the back-door without saying goodbye. An original phrase is one whose meaning is perfectly adequate to the details which it introduces. The unobtrusiveness and the originality come together in a "moment of vision" (to use a phrase which Hardy used as title for one collection of his poems) that is distinguished, though not wholly explained, by its being simultaneously natural and unpredictable. Perhaps the most quietly astonishing instance of such mastery of language—by the author who knows in his bones just what stock-response the reader's most secret heart expects and who thereupon produces a word or phrase which mildly devastates the stock-response—is to be found in *A Midsummer Night's Dream*, where King Oberon reminds Puck of the mermaid on the promontory, who sang so sweetly "That the rude sea grew civil at her song." Nobody else would have thought of the word "civil" beforehand; and yet, when you think about it afterwards, it is hard to imagine how any other word would possibly do. In Hardy's little phrase of comment on his description above, the unobtrusive naturalness is plain; but something helpful might be said about the unexpected originality.

We are brutalized by the crude, hollow, extravagant language hurled at us by commerce. Words remain weapons, not for any noble cause, but against the human imagination. We may turn for nourishment to authors who, humbly and for reasons of their own that the Reason knows not of, take walks in the evening over fields and under trees, hold out their words, and stand patiently until the night fills them. But our usual impatience is our blindness; our abstraction is our coarseness; and our sloth is our starvation. We fail in the struggle to stand still. We want devoutness: the grace to see that a toad walks humbly and to understand that a garden-slug comes into a house for reasons of its own. Whatever these reasons may be, Hardy's poems show his respect for them and for the creatures themselves:

> A shaded lamp and a waving blind,
> And the beat of a clock from a distant floor:
> On this scene enter—winged, horned, and spined—
> A longlegs, a moth, and a dumbledore;
> While 'mid my page there idly stands
> A sleepy fly that rubs it hands . . .
>
> Thus meet we five, in this still place,
> At this point of time, at this point in space.
> —My guests besmear my new-penned line,
> Or bang at the lamp and fall supine.
> "God's humblest, they!" I muse. Yet why?
> They know Earth-secrets that know not I.

In plain terms, this poem states Hardy's warning that the most commonplace creatures are not to be approached with condescension. He is often affectionate with nature, it is true; but what gives his affection for living creatures its power is his awe in the presence of his own ignorance of them. Lovers of Hardy rightly cherish the honesty of the man and the plainness of his language at its best; but it is not often remarked that the plainness—the reserve, almost the shyness—is an artistic response to the serious strangeness of nature which Hardy's honesty compels him to look upon with such close attention. He is aware of the seriousness of life to those who live it, and of the strangeness in which they have a share whether they know it or not. I think he is one of the most truly devout authors in

English. He is indeed scarcely edifying; but he is often edified. Though he occasionally speaks with the tongues of men, he does not speak with the tongues of angels. His gifts lie elsewhere.

D. H. Lawrence writes of a "quality which Hardy shares with the great writers, Shakespeare or Sophocles or Tolstoi, this setting behind the small action of his protagonists the terrific action of unfathomed nature; setting a small system of morality, the one grasped and formulated by the human consciousness within the vast, uncomprehended and incomprehensible morality of nature or of life itself. . . ."

Gabriel Oak the shepherd is not only a part of the "small action"; he is also a part of the "terrific action of unfathomed nature." He seems always to be listening for something; moreover, he sometimes hears it. His very identity comes into existence according to his relation to the foreground and the background of the novel. He is necessary to the main action, and yet it is through his eyes that we often see, and join, the background. Through his wise passiveness, the sorrows of Bathsheba are given their shape. By the end of the novel she has indeed returned to her beginning. But she has not merely returned to Oak for lack of a better man. Hardy says otherwise; he presents Bathsheba before her marriage with the shepherd: "though so plainly dressed, there was a certain rejuvenated appearance about her. . . . Repose had again incarnadined her cheeks; . . . at Gabriel's request, [she had] arranged her hair this morning as she had worn it years ago on Norcombe Hill. . . ." And so Bathsheba's return to Oak is also her return to the occasion of life where he had first seen her: a girl alone in a wagon, waiting for her driver to find her hat which had fallen, touching her hair and smiling into herself, surrounded by household goods and window plants—"the myrtles, geraniums, and cactuses packed around her were fresh and green." Returning to Oak, she comes home to herself. The other wooers have simply fallen away like dead leaves.

Gabriel is the genius of the places that are fresh and green. He has waited for Bathsheba, not because of any priggish assurance that she would come to a most satisfactory grief. In fact, he had given her up for lost several times. He has waited simply because he is not in any particular hurry.

The shepherd owned a pocket watch that, "being several years older than Oak's grandfather, had the peculiarity of going either too fast or not at all . . . though the minutes were told with precision, nobody could be quite certain of the hour they belonged to." When the false hours strike for Bathsheba's engagement to Boldwood or her infatuation and marriage with Troy, Oak neither retreats nor attempts to outrace time itself. He checks the minutes on his watch; and, the hour for perfect human glory and happiness being a bit off schedule as usual, he walks outside and examines the sky, "to ascertain the time of night from the altitudes of the stars."

The Absorbing Eye of Dickens

*". . . that curious, all-absorbing eye—the child's eye
of David Copperfield, which he never lost."*
—Kathleen Tillotson

*"Poetry is childhood willfully recovered; genius is
childhood lucidly formulated."*
—Baudelaire

Whatever the range of one's interests in writing about Dickens,
it is hardly possible to ignore his concern with children and
madmen. The concern has both biographical and artistic im-
plications. Edmund Wilson, whose masterful essay on Dickens
("The Two Scrooges") has figured so often in modern criti-
cism, is the most vivid example of the modern critic who dis-
covers a living relation between Dickens' own childhood and
his work. But examples of an interest in the artistic implica-
tions of Dickens' concern with children and madmen are to be
found everywhere. The concern itself is obvious.

To make this observation is to say nothing about critical
evaluation; and critics of Dickens have used his references to
childhood as bases of either praise or condemnation, accord-
ing to their preferences. Mrs. Tillotson's remark, quoted as

From "The Comic Imagination of the Young Dickens," Ph.D. disser-
tation, University of Washington, 1959.

one epigraph to this essay, appears in her discussion of *Sketches by Boz* in the recently published *Dickens at Work;* and the remark is an offhanded way of praising Dickens for the freshness of his vision. But the reader must be wary of inferring that such an assumption of praise is a matter of universal agreement. For other critics of Dickens have pointed to his absorption in children as plain evidence of his "immaturity," his failure to understand and explain the worldly relations of truly adult men and women—adult people, in other worlds, like the characters of Jane Austen, Dostoevsky, Cervantes, Sophocles, Dante, the critic's friend and colleague Prof. Peachie Budnutt, and finally (though most important) the critic himself. I am speaking of fools, of course. But what complicates the problem of the student who wishes to grasp the artistic meaning of Dickens' interest in children and madmen is the fact that Dickens has so often been damned for this interest, not merely by the universal fool (the "fool that fills the sky," in Chesterton's phrase), but actually by critics of great intelligence. For example, every student of Dickens is by this time familiar with Oscar Wilde's remark about Little Nell: that a man must have a heart of stone if he can read of Nell's death without laughing. For another example of the intelligent reader who finds Dickens' interest in children an evidence of mere emotional immaturity, we may note Ford Madox Ford, who remarked in passing that Dickens is a novelist (his word is "hack") for children.[1]

Both of these evaluations of Dickens' children have their deep importance. I myself desire not so much to argue about Dickens' "maturity" or "childishness" as to consider briefly the way in which his obvious interest in children and madmen is to be reconciled with his imagination.

I think that the artistic value of Dickens' writings about children resides, not in the amount of weeping which those children can inspire in readers, but rather in the amount of illumination which the eye of childhood can cast upon the themes which Dickens' imagination is sometimes able to discover and develop. Though it is mere evasion to deny the importance of the sniffling multitudes who greeted Nell's lingering death with such licking of lips, I would remark that such importance is historical and sociological, and thus to be distinguished, though not excluded, from a study of Dickens' children.

Dickens' imagination is marked by its power of fusing his characters with places, with things, and with institutions. I seek here to focus attention on Dickens' development in a few brief but centrally significant details in *Oliver Twist*. In this novel we see Dickens for the first time in his career displaying his startling gift for seeing the physical world, in all its concrete particularity, as a small child sees it.

First, however, I believe it will be helpful to set aside a consideration that has traditionally caused some confusion to readers of the novel—a confusion which, I sometimes think, is welcome to some readers. The problem might be stated thus: if, as is often taken for granted, Dickens is a "reformer" who wrote powerful and immediate novels of "social protest," then what is the point of reading, say, *Oliver Twist* in the twentieth century? For the social abuses which Dickens is supposed to have attacked are now removed, are they not? There are no more parish workhouses. There are no more schools for pickpockets in the underworld of London. And so forth. So (the argument might go) we read Dickens only to be "entertained." Since Dickens is a "reformer," and since reformers are concerned with the removal of specific abuses, and since the specific abuses attacked by Dickens are indeed removed, we may regard the more painful aspects of *Oliver Twist* as mere historical data on our benighted Victorian ancestors' sins against children—unfortunate sins, no doubt, but now at any rate removed from the human scene; and thus we of the morally superior twentieth century may congratulate ourselves, drop a salt tear or two over the strange and anachronistic descriptions of social and personal tyranny in *Oliver Twist,* pull down the usual veil over those chambers of our minds which are set aside for "historical data," and settle ourselves for a long winter's nap of "entertainment."

This argument of evasion, or something like it, is perhaps what goes on in the mind of some twentieth-century Sowerberry when he encounters the fictional Mr. Sowerberry in *Oliver*

Twist. He cannot admit that he himself is being described; and so he calls Dickens a reformer whose problems have long since been solved, and who therefore is relevant to us only as an entertainer. As George Orwell remarks, "before I was ten years old I was having Dickens ladled down my throat by schoolmasters in whom even at that age I could see a strong resemblance to Mr. Creakle. . . . Dickens seems to have succeeded in attacking everybody and antagonizing nobody." Orwell immediately faces the inevitable question: if Dickens seems to antagonize nobody, is his attack on society somehow "unreal"? No, the attack is real enough. But it can be made to seem unreal if the objects of the attack are resourceful enough to limit Dickens' social abuses to Dickens' own time. "Any history," writes Humphrey House, "is a splendid field for benevolence and love of justice and indignation; for there they require no action. . . ."

Now, I believe that Dickens' attacks on antihuman social institutions derive their power from the very fact that they are not limited to specific arguments that can be met and either refuted or else acknowledged and acted upon. On the contrary, his attacks are powerful just because they take the shape of illuminating vision rather than of itemized grievances. At their greatest artistic intensity, they do not present blueprints for revolt against tyranny; they *expose* tyranny, and force the reader to look at it and laugh; and suddenly the reader is aware that he alone is laughing, while Dickens himself has long since become silent and is simply staring; and, finally, the reader starts to stare at himself. It is distressing.

Thus, to disregard the tradition which assumes Dickens to be a "reformer" is not to limit his range as a novelist. On the contrary, it is to give one's own imagination the chance to see things that cannot easily be subordinated to some reformist program or other.

Setting aside, then, the historical problem of Victorian reform, let us see how Dickens' imagination in *Oliver Twist* employs a child's view of the world. Concrete details become isolated and stange in a child's mind. One such detail is the word "board," and the very confusion of meaning which is invariably attached to this world in the mind of the young Oliver is Dickens' occasion for conveying one of his most important imaginative visions in the novel. And it is the vision—certainly not the plot, which is one of Dickens' celebrated worst—which remains in the reader's memory.

Exactly how does this imaginative vision take shape, and what is it supposed to illuminate? My immediate concern is with the first of these questions; but an answer to the first question would be trivial nit-picking if it were not seen in the context of the answer to the second. And I think the second question is answered truly by Mr. Arnold Kettle: "The methods of oppression are simple: violence and starvation. The workhouse is a symbol of the oppression but by no means its limit. Outside, the world is a vast workhouse with the 'parish' run by the same gentleman in a white waistcoat, assisted by magistrates fatuous or inhuman, by clergymen who can scarcely be bothered to bury the dead, by Mr. Bumble. London is no different from the parish, only bigger."[2] Now, in *Oliver Twist* this theme is not fully illuminated. The melodramatic "plot" (with its daydream of Mr. Brownlow and the Maylies) seems to be a sort of uneasy ruse by which Dickens tricks himself into thinking that the world which his imagination has so terribly evoked is not the real world after all, and that the daydream world of Mr. Brownlow is actually real for the simple reason that it is nicer. At this early stage in his career, Dickens lacks either the skill or the stamina to drive his vision to its conclusion—namely, that modern society (as he finally sees it in such works as *Bleak House, Our Mutual Friend,* and *Great Expectations*) is so hopelessly self-deluded that its villains and its so-called "good" people are alike tricked and swallowed and devoured by it.

However, to deny artistic completeness to *Oliver Twist* is not to deny the imaginative power of some of its individual scenes. Mr. Kettle observes that "millions of people all over the world (including many who have never read a page of Dickens) can tell you what happened in Oliver Twist's workhouse." How does Dickens' imagination work in order to produce such an effect?

That is where the "absorbing eye" comes in. When we look

closely at the early chapters of *Oliver Twist,* we discover that the "all-absorbing eye" of childhood belongs, not to Dickens alone, nor to his character Oliver alone, but to both; and that, as the one imaginative vision is superimposed on the other, the force of the child's blundering and concrete vision suddenly turns into the force of Dickens' own piercingly accurate and equally concrete (though much broader) vision; and that what begins, through innocent misunderstanding of the meaning of a simple word in the mind of the child Oliver, as a mere accidental detail, becomes an image of Dickens' own vision—in short, an image of his illuminated theme.

The word which Oliver misunderstands is "board." And the word appears many times throughout the first four chapters of the novel. And we find that, even when the "board" itself is mentioned, the actions and images which surround the child suddenly expand with references to weapons of aggression. Furthermore, the "gentleman in the white waistcoat," one of Dickens' most memorable figures of pious brutality against children, often appears either personally or through a reference, when the word "board" is mentioned. In order to show how Dickens' imagination works in this instance, and to show how it illuminates his theme of the continuity between all the tyrannies and brutalities in society, whether they be official (like the parish board) or unofficial (like Fagin), I shall proceed now to consider the two visions in these early chapters.

First, there is Oliver's vision. It is that of a child whose confusion and misunderstanding are compounded by fear of the people officially assigned to take care of him. The first reference to the "board," with Oliver's misunderstanding of the word comes in Chapter Two, significantly titled "Treats of Oliver Twist's Growth, Education, and Board." Having been "farmed out" (like any wild beast) to the hideous Mrs. Mann until he is old enough to work in the workhouse itself, Oliver is at length taken by Mr. Bumble. Oliver's first duty is to report to . . . but it is best to quote the passage itself:

> Oliver had not been within the walls of the workhouse a quarter of an hour, and had scarcely completed the demolition of a second slice of bread, when Mr. Bumble, who had handed

him over to the care of an old woman, returned; and, telling him it was a board night, informed him that the board had said he was to appear before it forthwith.

Not having a very clearly defined notion of what a live board was, Oliver was rather astounded by this intelligence, and was not quite certain whether he ought to laugh or cry.

And immediately, in order to explain what a board is, Mr. Bumble clouts Oliver sharply with his cane. Oliver understands immediately; but he doesn't understand what Mr. Bumble wishes him to understand—namely, that he has to visit a group of gentlemen who are graciously and kindly devoted to the well-being of children. No, Oliver merely understands the truth—namely, that a "board" is a weapon, illustrated in the most concrete way by Mr. Bumble's cane.

Then the boy is led into a "large white-washed room" where several ominous and pompous gentlemen are gathered to stare down upon him, and he receives his orders from Bumble: " 'Bow to the board' said Bumble. Oliver brushed away two or three tears that were lingering in his eyes; and seeing no board but the table, fortunately bowed to that." So far, the detail might seem like just one of those many small items of illustration and even humor that Dickens always has at his beck and call. But the detail returns, and its meaning becomes clearer. In the same chapter, we have the famous scene in which Oliver "asks for more." Of course everyone recalls that Oliver's superiors are mortified at his audacity, and that eventually they sell him to Mr. Sowerberry the undertaker, from whose oppressions he escapes to London and the care of Fagin. But what helps to make the scene so memorable is, once again, Dickens' imaginative power of fusing persons with things; and the central "thing" is the "board." The scene is one of Dickens' funniest, but it is also frightening, and worth quoting briefly:

"Please, sir," replied Oliver, "I want some more."

The master aimed a blow at Oliver's head with the ladle; pinioned him in his arms; and shrieked aloud for the beadle.

The board were sitting in solemn conclave, when Mr. Bumble rushed into the room in great excitement, and addressing the gentleman in the high chair, said,

> "Mr. Limbkins, I beg your pardon, sir! Oliver Twist has
> asked for more!"
>   There was a general start. Horror was depicted on every
> countenance. . . . "That boy will be hung," said the gentleman
> in the white waistcoat."

By this time it is clear to Oliver (who is, after all, only a con-
fused child) that there are several phenomena in the sensible
world that are so identified with one another, that the mention
of any one of them immediately calls the others into existence:
boards, weapons of aggression against children, groups of
pompous gentlemen sitting around tables, requests for ade-
quate nourishment, and hanging.

So we find that, in the child's mind, the word "board" serves
to describe any person or thing which threatens his life. Thus,
when Bumble takes Oliver to see the magistrates without
whose permission he cannot be turned over to the chimney
sweep Mr. Gamfield, Oliver sees the magistrates thus: "Oliver
roused himself, and made his best obeisance. He had been
wondering, with his eyes fixed on the magistrates' powder,
whether all boards were born with that white stuff on their
heads, and were boards from thenceforth on that account."

There are other examples of Oliver's confusion—natural
enough in a small, ill-treated, and uneducated child; but those
which I have noted will show the sort of thing that Dickens
presents as going on in the child's mind.

Now, this kind of imaginative detail, slight as it may seem,
is nevertheless a major consideration in the understanding
of *Oliver Twist,* I believe. There are two reasons for its
importance.

First, what begins as little Oliver's confusion becomes, from
the artistic viewpoint of Dickens himself, one of the novel's
major visions: namely, that the official institutions which osten-
sibly are founded for the purpose of caring for the children of
the poor are, in actuality, weapons of aggression against those
very children. The imaginative—one might say the poetic—
power of this vision resides in the fact that Oliver's misunder-
standing of the word "board" turns out, when viewed in the
larger context of society shown in the child's movement from

the parish workhouse to the underworld of London, to be the deepest and clearest truth. This is the first reason for my calling the detail of the "board" a more *imaginatively* significant detail in this novel—at least in the earlier chapters—than its brevity would ordinarily suggest. Now, it is true that Dickens' imagination does indeed sometimes work through the rapid and wild accumulation of hundreds of concrete details, as many critics (Taine, for example) have noted. Such critics justly imply, in this wild kind of accumulation, the presence of great imaginative energy.

But the presence of energy does not preclude precision; and, just as Dickens is able to make the entire English judicial system and bar appear idiotic by the simple hilarious expedient of describing them (in *Pickwick*) according to their noses and whiskers and leaving out all other details, so he is able to illuminate, with dreadful and unforgettable force, the real meaning of the pious and self-congratulating social aggressors against children by the equally simple and far less comic expedient of allowing a child (Oliver) to confuse boards with weapons and weapons with boards until the two become identified—fused, in a word.

The second reason for my finding a continuous relation between the confused vision of Oliver and the clear vision of Dickens himself in this meaning of the "board" is that Dickens is carefully explicit about that meaning. I have quoted the small scene in which Oliver is presented to the "board" as soon as he arrives at the workhouse, and in which, being rapped with Bumble's cane and told to bow to the board, he bows to the table. And on the very next page, after Oliver's dismissal to the mercies of Bumble, Mrs. Thingummy, and the rest, Dickens seizes his dramatic opportunity to elucidate, and thus artistically as well as morally to sanction, Oliver's own vision:

Poor Oliver! He little thought, as he lay sleeping in happy unconsciousness of all around him, that the board had that very day arrived at a decision which would exercise the most material influence over all his future fortunes. And this was it:

The members of this board were very sage, deep, philosophical men; and when they came to turn their attention to the workhouse, they found out at once, what ordinary folks would never have discovered—the poor people liked it! It was a regular place of public entertainment for the poorer classes; a tavern where there was nothing to pay; a public breakfast, dinner, tea, and supper all the year round; a brick and mortar elysium, where it was all play and no work. "Oho!" said the board, looking very knowing; "we are the fellows to set this to rights; we'll stop it all, in no time." So, they established the rule, that all poor people should have the alternative (for they would compel nobody, not they), of being starved by a gradual process in the house, or by a quick one out of it.

And so out of the child's eye, which Mrs. Tillotson has called not only "all-absorbing" but also "implacable," Dickens' imagination—with its ready and vital power of changing people and things into each other—plucks a mote of social reality, and expands it, sometimes explicitly as in the above passage and sometimes dramatically as in the great scene of Jack Dawkins' trial, into an artistic vision too great even for himself to bear, at this early stage of his life and career. What this vision reveals is that, even more seriously and painfully than in *Pickwick*, the world of human values in *Oliver Twist* is inverted as in a nightmare, and the murderers are in the robes, not only of the magistrates, but of the very nursemaids themselves. The child Oliver muddled into the truth, and the artist Dickens seized it and went a good distance toward clarifying it, before it became too terribly glaring for him, and he gazed off into the daydream—comforting and kind—of Mr. Brownlow, the good rich man, and the daydream is Dickens' escape from the vision of the child Oliver. But the absorbing eye of the child is open and clear, even though the novel in which it stares is artistically incomplete.

NOTES

1.   Ford's observation appears in his book *The English Novel* (Philadelphia, 1929), pp. 110–115. I think it is important to remark that Ford's attitude is at least partly to be explained by the fact that he himself was an artist, and that his primary concern might conceivably

have been to knock Dickens—whether mature or immature—out of his own imagination's way. This is merely a suspicion of mine, and I have no evidence. However, if it is true, it is certainly justified. There is a similarly strong possibility in T. S. Eliot's early rejection of Milton. Milton's artistic success or failure was not what primarily interested Eliot. The real point was that Milton's way was not Eliot's, that the earlier poet had nothing to teach the later, and that—temporarily, at least—he had to be put out of mind and out of influence. It is sometimes forgotten that Keats—who worshipped Milton—nevertheless rejected him for the same reason. The critical evaluations of earlier writers by later writers should, I believe, always be taken with this reservation: that every new writer claims the right to use or to reject earlier writers according to the needs of the new.

2. Arnold Kettle, *An Introduction to the English Novel*, vol. 1 (London: Hutchinson University Library, 1957), pp. 123–38.

The Madmen in *Barnaby Rudge*

Dickens is celebrated for his interest in madmen—all the way from charming persons who happen to be mentally retarded (like Mr. Dick in *David Copperfield*) to wildly improbable foamers-at-the-mouth (like the alleged author of "The Madman's Manuscript," one of the interpolated tales in *Pickwick.*) It would be easy to turn a discussion of Dickens' madmen into a mere listing of names and types. It so happens, however, that in some of his early novels Dickens is able not only to use his imagination in order to explore the emotional states of madmen and criminals (as in his dramatization of Jonas Chuzzlewit's fear after his murder of Tigg Montague in *Martin Chuzzlewit*) but also to use the madmen themselves in order to explore and illuminate other themes.

In *Barnaby Rudge,* Dickens' employment of the mad and harmless Barnaby's viewpoint is quite similar to his use of the child Oliver's viewpoint in *Oliver Twist.* That is, what seems to the reader (and, indeed, to the other characters of the respective novels) at first glance to be a mere confusion caused by youth or idiocy in the brain of a child or a madman turns out, in the larger context of Dickens' own artistic vision, to be the very truth itself. And again, as in the case of Oliver's confusing the parish "board" with weapons of aggression against chil-

From "The Comic Imagination of the Young Dickens," Ph.D. dissertation, University of Washington, 1959.

dren, Dickens proceeds, first, to show Barnaby's visionary interpretation in action; and, second, to corroborate Barnaby's visions by explicit comment and by further dramatic development of these visions in the actions of the other important characters of the novel.

A number of these characters are indeed mad. They are all intimately bound up in the Gordon anti-Catholic riots. Barnaby Rudge, who taken by himself is a mere stock figure of the village idiot, is perhaps the sanest of them all.

Before I proceed to the madmen, it is necessary to see what I mean by the larger context of Dickens' artistic vision in this novel; for that vision is the object which his madmen help to illuminate in the same kind of complex, twofold viewpoint that existed in *Oliver Twist*. Edmund Wilson is probably the best of those recent critics who have recognized the power of the neglected novel *Barnaby Rudge,* and the following is Wilson's statement of Dickens' two "themes," one of them rather superficial and the other a fulfillment of what Wilson calls the "deeper artistic intention":

> The ostensible subject of the novel is the anti-Catholic insurrection known as the "Gordon riots," which took place in 1780. . . . On the surface he reprobates Lord George Gordon and the rioters for their fanatical or brutal intolerance; but implicitly he is exploiting to the limit certain legitimate grievances of the people. . . . The really important theme of the book—as Dickens shows in his preface, when he is discussing one of the actual occurrences on which the story is based—is the hanging under the Shop-lifting Act of a woman who has been dropped by her aristocratic lover and who has forged notes to protect her child. This theme lies concealed, but it makes itself felt from beginning to end of the book. And as *Pickwick*, from the moment it gets really under way, heads by instinct and, as it were, unconsciously straight for the Fleet prison, so *Barnaby Rudge* is deliberately directed toward Newgate, where, as in *Pickwick* again, a group of characters will be brought together; and the principal climax of the story will be the orgiastic burning of the prison.

I think that Wilson's statement of the two "themes" is perfectly clear and just. However, to speak of the "ostensible" and the "really important" subjects of this novel is to imply that the plot is in conflict with the "deeper artistic intention" and that Dickens never succeeds in unifying the two. I believe that he does so unify them. The ostensible subject is Dickens' horror at the violence of the Gordon rioters; but the burning of Newgate prison, which those rioters perpetrate and which Dickens so clearly condones, is not irrelevant to his original horror at their violence. For it is the horror of all violence, whether official or unofficial, which Dickens' imagination illuminates here. The violence of the rioters and the violence of the so-called civil authorities are the same; and Dickens' artistic vision unifies these two kinds of violence through the use of his madmen.

The vision of the novel has to do with social suppression, with irrational and sadistic punishments (illustrated by the hanging of Hugh's young mother for petty theft, and magnificently symbolized by the official hangman Dennis, who not only leads the rioters but also stands ready to execute them when they are caught), and with the actual nature of both mob violence and of officially sanctioned corporal and capital punishments. That is, Dickens' imagination here is not only stating but demonstrating (through created actions and images) the fact that mob violence and official violence can be, and often are, distinguished from each other only in the sense that the agents of official violence are a little better organized and a bit more adequately armed. The two aspects of the single artistic vision come together in Hugh and in Dennis the public hangman.

It is true that Dickens conveys a profound imaginative sympathy with the rioters. They themselves lose all human control, and do not quite understand what they are doing. But Dickens himself makes their motive perfectly clear. This motive, finally grasped by Hugh as he stands on the scaffold of the gallows, is that their only response to a blind, irrational, amoral, and physically powerful civil authority must be a repetition of the official amoralities—and the riots are Dickens' vision of those amoralities in all their horror.

The meaning of this vision, as I have said, is symbolically embodied with triumphant effectiveness in the person of Dennis the public hangman. His meaning, which Hugh announces in his speech on the scaffold, is morally clear but socially ambiguous: namely, that men who brutally tyrannize over other men, for either criminal or officially sanctioned reasons, are inhuman and ugly. Wilson's acute analysis of Dennis is worth quoting in this connection: "This hangman has a complex value: he is primarily a sadist who likes to kill. Yet he figures as a violator as well as a protector of prisons. In his role of insurgent, he attacks authority; in his role of hangman, makes it odious. Either way he represents on Dickens' part a blow at those institutions which the writer is pretending to endorse."

In the last phrase of his analysis, Wilson seems to imply that Dickens is himself unconscious of the ambiguous nature of the artistic vision which he conveys. I have my doubts about Dickens' unconsciousness in this matter. That is a biographical problem in the continuing study of Dickens as a man, and of course he was something more than uncomplicated. But the problem of his artistic intention, I believe, involves the critic's observing in the recorded vision of the novel a number of impulses and meanings which, though they seem mutually contradictory in a superficial sense, are nevertheless imaginatively unified.

In other words, I think that Wilson is wrong in supposing that Dickens' attitude toward his theme is ambiguous. On the contrary, the novel is imaginatively successful just because he is able to convey artistically his feeling that both the unofficial and the official violence are the same—both are antihuman. The young man Hugh—whose speeches and actions seem so often capricious and irresponsible—turns out to have a perfectly clear and comprehensible motive of hatred against the civil authorities who hanged his mother for petty theft and forgery. Yet Hugh is a plain criminal. Dennis, on the other hand, seems throughout the novel to have clear motives for his violence—that is, the upholding of the "law," and the maintenance of "order." But at last he is revealed as a madman who has no motive other than the revolting pleasure he takes in murder. And Dennis is one of the law's official representatives. When the rioters, whom he himself has let into Newgate Prison with his own official key, threaten to release the condemned prisoners, Dennis suddenly realizes that these prisoners are, after all, his own personal pets. He wants to kill them in the proper style, in his own good time, in order to derive the maximum pleasure from the execution.

The more one lingers over this man Dennis, the better one can understand why *Barnaby Rudge* is not often read and acclaimed. It is really not a very nice book. But its artistic vision of the fundamental identity between criminal and official violence, it seems to me, is securely established.

How does Dickens establish the identity? He does so by manipulating the viewpoints of his madmen. Thus, in the scene during which Newgate is burned, Dickens presents the mob in action from two points of view: one from the objective, or omniscient, point of view of the novelist himself, and the other from the point of view of a character—Barnaby—who is literally psychotic. The very casting aside of pious motives— the rioters commit violence in order to "preserve Protestantism against the Catholics," and the police and soldiers commit violence in order to "preserve order"—is far from coming as a result of Dickens' confusion about an ambiguous theme. On the contrary, the elimination of pious motives is one imaginative gesture toward the illumination of the theme itself: all men who kill and maim one another are morally the same; and, whatever their stated and rationalized motives, all are mad— mad in the midst of a man-created nightmare, whose distinction from the fantasies of a psychotic man like Barnaby is utterly lost.

Dickens develops this theme by manipulating the viewpoint of the mad Barnaby and the viewpoint of the objective beholder until both viewpoints are seen to reveal the same thing. First, he shows how Barnaby himself ordinarily sees the world, and he contrasts Barnaby's fantasies with commonplace things as they exist in a time and place undisturbed by either criminal or official violence. Then, having established the contrast, Dickens imaginatively creates the scene of the Newgate riot from Barnaby's point of view and then from the objective point of view. But in the second stage, there is no contrast. The way Barnaby sees the riot is a weird fantasy, a nightmare—but so is the reality.

The first crucial passage in this twofold development occurs in the tenth chapter. Barnaby, mad but harmless, loafs around the Maypole Inn, owned and operated by the really idiotic John Willet. Barnaby is called in by Willet to run an errand for a visiting stranger. The latter, a Mr. Chester, gives Barnaby a letter to deliver, and bids him "make all speed away."

"Speed!" said Barnaby, folding the little packet in his breast, "Speed! If you want to see hurry and mystery, come here. Here!"

With that, he put his hand, very much to John Willet's horror, on the guest's fine broadcloth sleeve, and led him stealthily to the back-window.

"Look down there," he said softly; "do you mark how they whisper in each other's ears; then dance and leap, to make believe they are in sport? Do you see how they stop for a moment, when they think there is no one looking, and mutter among themselves again; and then how they roll and gambol, delighted with the mischief they've been plotting? Look at 'em now. See how they whirl and plunge. And now they stop again, and whisper, cautiously together—little thinking, mind, how often I have lain upon the grass and watched them. I say—what is it that they plot and hatch? Do you know?"

"They are only clothes," returned the guest, "such as we wear; hanging on those lines to dry, and fluttering in the wind."

"Clothes!" echoed Barnaby, looking close into his face, and falling quickly back, "Ha ha! Why, how much better to be silly, than as wise as you! You don't see shadowy people there, like those that live in sleep—not you. Nor eyes in the knotted panes of glass, nor swift ghosts when it blows hard, nor do you hear voices in the air, nor see men stalking in the sky—not you! I lead a merrier life than you, with all your cleverness. You're the dull men. We're the bright ones. Ha! Ha! I'll not change with you, clever as you are,—not I!"

With that, he waved his hat above his head, and darted off.

"A strange creature, upon my word!" said the guest, pulling out a handsome box, and taking a pinch of snuff.

"He wants imagination," said Mr. Willet, very slowly, and after a long silence. . . .

Now, to suggest the imaginative unity of this novel, I wish to turn from this little scene—so unobtrusively placed in Chapter Ten of a book which contains no less than eighty-two chapters—to a scene in Chapter Sixty-five. The latter is the chapter in which the public hangman Dennis tries, and fails, to hide his private game-preserve of condemned prisoners from the very mob of rioters whom he has himself let into Newgate Prison. I ask the reader to compare the following sets of details. First, in Chapter Ten, Barnaby (looking at the clothes that flutter in the wind) says: "Do you mark how they whisper in each other's ears? . . . and then how they roll and gambol, delighted with the mischief they've been plotting. . . . See how they whirl and plunge. . . . Clothes! . . . Ha! Ha!"

And this is what the same Barnaby sees during the Newgate riot in Chapter Sixty-five: "these two lads had the weakest party, and the worst armed, and did not begin until after the others, having stopped to whisper to him through the grate. . . . At the bidding of the mob, the houses were all illuminated that night—lighted up from top to bottom as at a time of public gaiety and joy. . . . The way they heaved and gasped for breath, as though in water, when they were first plunged into the crowd . . . as though they had risen in their shrouds; and many were seen to shudder, as though they had been actually dead men, when they chanced to touch or brush against their garments."

The similarity—one would almost be justified in speaking of the identity—of the actual physical details in these passages, set so far apart in the novel, is truly striking. Having shown us the mad visions of the sick-minded Barnaby, Dickens then shows us the mad *actions* of the "sane" instigators of violence. Both are mad. And there is no escape for the reader in the comforting notion that, after all, the horrors of the riot are merely the work of the "criminal element" of the population. This criminal element is led by its own essential genius; that is, the violent mob is led by a man who is an expert in violence and murder. And he is the official representative of civil authority. He is Dennis, the public hangman.

This sudden illumination penetrates to the meaning of the Gordon Riots, and, beyond them, to the meaning of official violence.

Barnaby Rudge is often compared with *A Tale of Two Cities* because both contain extravagant descriptions of mobs. What distinguishes the one from the other, I believe, is that the latter novel is formless. That is, the mob scenes in Paris have possessed Dickens' emotions, and yet his imagination—with its powers of illumination through the fusing of people and things around them, so that the one may stand for the other—has not possessed the mob scenes in turn. M. D. Zabel and others have claimed distinction for *A Tale of Two Cities* because it is constructed around the idea of self-sacrifice and resurrection. Perhaps this idea accounts for the unformed and unpenetrated melodrama of Sidney Carton; it surely does not account for the sensationalistic extremes to which Dickens carries his description of the revolutionary mobs in Paris. Moreover, Sidney Carton figures so centrally in the plot, that the reader can quite easily employ him for purposes of evading whatever meaning Dickens' imagination might have discovered in the violent mob scenes. If you're a drunk, you can always get your head cut off, and then everyone can feel nice again. The reader has been titillated and then left to sob comfortably over the scaffold speech of Sidney Carton, a piece of bad dramatics so universally famous in its asininity that I will excuse myself from quoting it.

Dickens' imagination in *Barnaby Rudge* does not work with his characteristically lavish inventiveness. On the other hand, the book is not sterile or repressed. The imagination has precisions of its own. In order to see this precision—this ability to control many details so that they illuminate one another—we have only to compare the scaffold speech in *A Tale of Two Cities* with the scaffold speech in *Barnaby Rudge*. Such a comparison is justified on many points. For one thing, many recent critics of Dickens (like Orwell, Wilson, and Zabel) persistently compare the two novels as wholes. Furthermore, both books are "historical novels" that deal with some event in the distant past; and the event, in both cases, involves insurrection in the form of mob violence.

When we come to the two speeches, we find that, in *A Tale of Two Cities,* Dickens throws rose-water vaporings over the possible meaning of the mob scenes by giving us Carton's notorious "It is a far, far etc. etc." But, in *Barnaby Rudge,* he gives us the speech of the criminal Hugh, bastard son of a nobleman who has deserted his mother, who in her turn had been hanged, on this very scaffold, for petty forgery and theft. The theme which Dickens' imagination has been illuminating throughout the novel—by means of getting behind the reader's evasions so as to make him see that Barnaby's view of the world and Dickens' own are, in matters of official and unofficial violence, the same view—is the direct relation which exists between the gallows and the criminal. As in the most effective parts of *Oliver Twist* (i.e., the early chapters that deal with the parish workhouse), Dickens follows the created vision of his imagination with explicit comment. And here is Hugh's speech on the scaffold, a choral comment if there ever was one:

"That gentleman yonder"—pointing to the clergyman— "has often in the last few days spoken to me of faith, and strong belief. You see what I am—more brute than man, as I have been often told—but I had faith enough to believe, and did believe as strongly as any of you gentlemen can believe anything, that this one life would be spared. See what he is!—Look at him!"

Barnaby had moved towards the door, and stood beckoning him to follow.

"If this was not faith, and strong belief!" cried Hugh, raising his right arm aloft, and looking upward like a savage prophet whom the near approach of Death had filled with inspiration, "where are they! What else should teach me—me, born as I was born, and reared as I have been reared—to hope for any mercy in this hardened, cruel, unrelenting place! Upon these human shambles, I, who never raised his hand in prayer till now, call down the wrath of God! On that black tree, of which I am the ripened fruit, I do invoke the curse of all its victims, past, present, and to come."

The deepest power of this speech derives from the fact that it has emerged directly from the imaginative vision which has preceded it. It does not contradict—it confirms—the vision of official antihuman violence which the young Dickens has achieved, through the fusing of a madman's absorbing eye with the mad world which it sees, in this great and neglected novel.

Perhaps the most interesting feature of Dickens' imagination in this early book is its ability to show how commonplace notions of reality contain within themselves the seeds of a reality deeper and stranger than themselves, so that, when the details of everyday reality are seen from a certain point of view, or placed in juxtaposition with disturbance and social upheaval, they themselves vanish and reveal the essential reality of nightmare underneath. There are seeping wounds and cracks in the minds of the most ordinary men, wounds that suppurate under the pressure of mob violence or internal psychological pressure. This is the kind of insight into one aspect of reality that obsessed Dostoevsky (not only in his fiction, but also in his periodical writings, collected in *The Diary of a Writer*, where he endlessly examines *Don Quixote* in the attempt to determine the relation between the fantastic and the ordinary). And when we wonder what it is that Dostoevsky revered in Dickens, we can find one answer in *Barnaby Rudge*.

For Dickens' eye can penetrate to the absurdity or the nightmare that may lie behind the most ordinary appearances. In *Barnaby Rudge*, the artist's imagination looks through the eye of a madman, and what it sees is very finely suggested by a poem of Emily Dickinson:

> Much madness is divinest sense
> To a discerning eye;
> Much sense the starkest madness,
> 'Tis the majority
> In this, as all, prevails.

Assent, and you are sane;
Demur,—you're straightway dangerous,
And handled with a chain.

Or with a board. Or with a Bumble. Or with a Sowerberry.
Or with a Dennis. All of whom are weapons.

The Mystery of Edwin Drood
An Afterword

The Mystery of Edwin Drood is the last of Dickens' novels. In accordance with his practice, it first appeared in six monthly parts from April to September in 1870; and it was first published as a volume in the same year. The first three parts were issued by Dickens himself before his death, and thereafter the remaining parts were issued by his friend and biographer John Forster. Although there have been occasional speculations about the possible length of the completed novel, the testimony of Forster and others indicates that Dickens planned to finish it in twelve monthly numbers. It is true that the novelist had not always been averse to changing his plans right in the middle of a novel. For example, he interrupted the course of *Martin Chuzzlewit* by sending his hero to America, because the regular issues of the novel were not selling enough copies to satisfy Dickens, and he wished to capitalize on the popularity of his previous writings on the United States. He also modified the plan of *Master Humphrey's Clock* in such a way as to produce *The Old Curiosity Shop* and the reader can see that amazing and neglected novel taking shape before his very eyes. However, both *Martin Chuzzlewit* and *The Old Curiosity Shop* are comparatively early works, written during the years when Dickens' methods of composition, for all their astonishing fertility, were

From Charles Dickens, *The Mystery of Edwin Drood* (New York: New American Library, Signet Classics, 1961).

still more or less improvisatory. By the time he came to write *Edwin Drood*, he had learned to plan and to control both the plots and the imaginative visions of his novels from beginning to end. And there can be no doubt that Dickens, of all people, would have ended his novel within the limits which he planned, and that his conclusion would have been as imaginatively audacious as the first half, that haunting and broken vision which we possess.

The vision, of course, is one of the most tantalizing of all Dickensian attractions. There is the rather obvious attraction of the mystery-plot concocted by a master who lives just long enough to ask all of the most tempting questions and then dies at the very moment when, in the ordinary course of things, he would have begun to present the answers. But the book is attractive—one might almost say seductive—in other ways, too. The meaning which it promises and never quite has time to reveal is not only the mechanical solution to a mystery. It is also a meaning of a poetic or imaginative kind. It is this second meaning which is able to speak to those of us whose interest in the book may not depend on a taste for mystery stories in general.

Nevertheless, the problem of the plot itself remains important. After all, the novel is a mystery story, a popular kind of writing in which Dickens became interested largely through his association with Wilkie Collins. Dickens and Collins had collaborated on a few literary projects; and Dickens published, in his own magazine, several of Collins' mysteries, notably *The Woman in White* and *The Moonstone*. His interest in the craft of the mystery story is only another manifestation of the fact that Dickens was a popular writer in the strict sense of the word. His concern for the response of his public is always an essential fact about him, however one may wish to interpret it. I turn, then, to this popular mystery story itself, in order to see what its mechanical problems are, and how they might have been solved if Dickens had lived long enough to dazzle his audience at the conclusion with some peculiarly Dickensian combination of story-telling virtuosity and poetic insight.

Traditional discussions of the plot and attempts to unravel it have involved such problems as the following: the fate of Edwin Drood; the identity of Datchery, that "stranger who appeared in Cloisterham" after Drood's disappearance; and the identity of the opium-peddling hag, sometimes called the "Princess Puffer," who administers the narcotic to John Jasper and then pursues him in sinister fashion at times when he is not even aware of her. Further problems rise with regard to the mechanical relation between these various characters, in terms of the bare solution of the plot itself.

A number of subsequent authors have written their own continuations and solutions of *Edwin Drood*. I suppose this sort of thing was to be expected. Such continuations do not seem to me worth discussing at any length. I do not mean to imply that I think them arrogant. Dickens himself, as I have said, was a popular author, and I doubt if he would have objected to a widespread technical interest in a plot which he himself had tried so hard to make interesting in the first place. On the other hand, I do not believe that the continuations of the novel possess any interest beyond the merely technical one. And technique, taken alone, is trivial. What matters in Dickens' novel, as in the works of any great author, is the illumination of meaning which the technique is made to serve.

There have been more responsible Dickensians, however, among those whose concern is to understand, if possible, just what it was that Dickens himself intended to do with his half-finished plot. Noteworthy among such investigators has been Mr. W. Robertson Nicoll, who in 1912 published his book *The Problem of 'Edwin Drood': A Study in the Methods of Dickens*. In this careful and scholarly work, Mr. Nicoll gathered together all of the relevant external evidence (in the form of remarks made by Dickens to his associates and to members of his family, testimony by his illustrator, and so on) which might contribute to a solution of the plot. He also succinctly reviewed the most intelligible and probable suggestions for a solution. Other scholars, in the responsible tradition of Mr. Nicoll, have been at work on the novel more or less constantly since Dickens' death. This is not the place to review their work. But I wish to settle on the most remarkably important result of that work: the conclusive identification of John Jasper as a criminal.

Now, the kind of criminal Jasper turns out to be is the occasion for long and difficult research, the chief results of which have been brilliantly summarized by Mr. Edgar Johnson in his distinguished biography, *Charles Dickens: His Tragedy and Triumph.* Jasper is a murderer. He has murdered Edwin Drood and, perhaps, concealed the body somehow in the Sapsea monument. Datchery, the stranger with the stagey white hair and the fluttering ill-concealed hands, is generally conceded to be the fearless and resourceful Helena Landless. The exact identity and function of the opium-dispensing Princess Puffer is not clear, and it will probably remain forever a matter for speculation, whether scholarly or amateur. A friend of mine recently told me of a medium who claimed to have been in touch with Dickens during a seance. When she asked him what sort of thing he did to while away the time over there, he answered, in an acutely uncomfortable voice, that he was still trying to solve the complete mystery of Edwin Drood.

But whether or not the mystery itself can be solved, I think that the very identification of John Jasper as a criminal is a matter of the greatest significance. For it was not the mystery itself, conceived as the mere unravelling of a plot, that engaged the attention, as it were, of Dickens' entire poetic imagination. It is characteristic of Dickens throughout his career that he is able to use a variety of literary conventions for the fulfillment of some deeper imaginative intention, whether he is adapting the convention of the sporting-story (as it was written by Surtees) in order to arrive finally at *Pickwick* or the convention of the mystery-story in order to arrive at the character of John Jasper. Remarking on Dickens' ability to shape popular conventions toward his own artistic ends, I wish to quote a passage from an article that appeared in the *Pall Mall Magazine* in June, 1906, some thirty-five years after Dickens' death. The article is called "Edwin Drood and the Last Days of Charles Dickens, by his younger daughter Kate Perugini." After summarizing the external evidence for the view that Edwin Drood is murdered by his uncle John Jasper, Mrs. Perugini writes the following:

> If those who are interested in the subject will carefully read
> what I have quoted, they will not be able to detect any word or
> hint from my father that it was upon the Mystery alone that he
> relied for the interest and originality of his idea. The originality
> was to be shown, as he tells us, in what we may call the psycho-
> logical description the murderer gives us of his temptations,
> temperament, and character, as if told by another . . . I do not
> mean to imply that the mystery itself had no strong hold on my
> father's imagination; but, greatly as he was interested in the
> intricacies of that tangled skein, the information he voluntarily
> gave to Mr. Forster, from whom he had withheld nothing for
> thirty-three years, certainly points to the fact that he was quite as
> deeply fascinated and absorbed in the study of the criminal
> Jasper, as in the dark and sinister crime that has given the book
> its title. . . . It was not, I imagine, for the intricate working out
> of his plot alone that my father cared to write this story; but it
> was through his wonderful observation of character, and his
> strange insight into the tragic secrets of the human heart, that
> he desired his greatest triumph to be achieved.

It seems to me that Dickens' daughter, one of the most
intelligent as well as one of the most audacious and indepen-
dent of his many children, has placed the emphasis where it
belongs. It is true that Dickens was interested in the intricacies
of his plot in *Edwin Drood;* but this is just a way of saying that he
was Dickens. The man was probably capable of being in-
terested in anything whatever; and that is one reason why he is
so precious to us, for he is capable of explaining to us, with
incomparable intensity and humor, just why it is that the
chimney pots on the London roofs are more fantastically
strange than the wildest minarets in the most dreamed-of Ori-
ents, and why and how it is that an ill-clothed and vicious
ragamuffin like Deputy is actually a poetic genius, and how it
comes about that a meanly skilled pickpocket and cutpurse like
Jack Dawkins in *Oliver Twist* has a more intelligent and more
generous grasp of human justice than has any living official
interpreter of the whole British Constitution. It is always

Dickens' capacity for being interested that leads him to his greatest artistic illuminations. His American biographer Mr. Johnson tells us that, though Dickens was not a "glittering conversationalist," he was "better than a brilliant talker, he was a brilliant listener, who stimulated others to their best, filled everyone with the conviction that Dickens delighted in his company, and allowed no man to be a bore." And just as this genius for being fascinated by other human beings leads Dickens to the creation of a multitude of characters whose extent and variety staggers the imagination, so the same powers of interest led him from his initial concern with the intricacies of a mystery-plot per se to a deeper concern with the more profound and genuinely terrible intricacies of his chief character, John Jasper the criminal.

Jasper's being a criminal, a murderer addicted to the habit of opium, is a fact of both psychological and social significance. Both meanings are related to the equally important fact of his being a highly respected citizen of his community, an admired organist in the Cloisterham cathedral. Dickens had always been deeply absorbed in the phenomena of crime and criminals, both in his travels and in his fiction. In one of the letters which he wrote to his friend Forster during his first visit to America in 1842, he speaks of visiting a prison in Pennsylvania, and reflects with horror and fascination on the supposed meditations of the prisoners who are compelled to undergo solitary confinement. Again, during the time when he was meditating himself upon the opening chapters of *Edwin Drood*, he escorted some visiting friends through some dangerous criminal haunts in London, and did not neglect the opium dens. As for his exploration of criminal themes in his fiction, a number of characters come to mind at once: Bill Sykes, whose ghastly murder of his mistress Nancy in *Oliver Twist* Dickens was reading to large audiences of hysterical women at the very time when he was working on *Edwin Drood;* Jonas Chuzzlewit, whose flight from the police in the closing pages of *Martin Chuzzlewit* is very nearly hallucinatory (to use Taine's term) in its dreadful intensity, which is rarely surpassed by Dostoevsky himself. And there are the gloomy scenes in Fleet Prison, following the trial

59

scene, in *Pickwick Papers*. Even though that first of his works is justly considered to be pervaded by sunlight, it nevertheless contains the awareness of crime, the peculiar Dickensian darkness which is a feature of his work from the beginning to the end.

And Jasper himself is a man who embodies the Dickensian darkness perhaps more thoroughly than any previous character had done. I have said that the mere fact of his being a criminal has an interest that is both psychological and social. That is, Jasper is simultaneously a solid representative of his society and a rather bitter critical comment upon it.

The psychological interest of his character has to do with his division within and against himself. Jasper is the respectable church-organist in a perfectly respectable English cathedral town. The very opening lines of the book mention "an ancient English Cathedral tower." Immediately there is the question, "how can the ancient English Cathedral tower be here!" Then, within a few more lines, Dickens evokes a world of nightmare, and we realize finally that we are not in the midst of one of those charmingly picturesque little places, so often and mistakenly associated with the name of Dickens, in which Scrooge is perpetually handing out Christmas turkeys to the Deserving Poor and the Cheeryble Brothers are forever frightening children out of their wits by throwing money at them; no, we are placed in the nightmare more directly at the beginning of Edwin Drood. Without wasting a single breath, Dickens has mentioned the cathedral town and then plunged us into one of its deepest meanings. We are in the opium nightmare of the cathedral organist. When next we see Jasper, he is perfectly in control of himself, and he enjoys the regard of his fellow townsmen. But the secret is out. Or, rather, we are in it; and, as far as the book, we ourselves never quite escape from the divided darkness of Jasper's nature.

It seems to me of crucial importance, moreover, that we should note Jasper's sincerity of feeling. That is, he is not a hypocrite. If he had been a mere liar, an actor whose feeling for his nephew Edwin Drood was only a pretense assumed for the benefit of the public, then Jasper would be nothing much.

What makes him remarkable is not only the sincerity, but the almost inexpressible intensity, of his feeling for Edwin and for everything else. And if his love for Edwin is as genuine as we have every right to believe, then the murder becomes a kind of suicide also—as perhaps all personal murders are. Oscar Wilde's startling lines are appropriate to Jasper's case: killing Edwin, he had certainly killed the thing he loved, "and so he had to die." Thus divided against himself, Jasper is always searching for ways to forget and lose that self, and he never succeeds. He tries music, opium, love: and all three lead him further into terror. Perhaps his inner division has become so intense and unbearable, that it has reappeared in his external actions; perhaps he has himself reappeared in the external world as two distinct persons. It is a weird speculation, but Dickens himself has given us the hint. In the third chapter of the novel—where Dickens is describing, of all things, Miss Twinkleton's Seminary for Young Ladies—there is the following sentence:

"As, in some cases of drunkenness, and in others of animal magnetism, there are two states of consciousness which never clash, but each of which pursues its separate course as though it were continuous instead of broken (thus, if I hide my watch when I am drunk, I must be drunk again before I can remember where), so Miss Twinkleton has two distinct and separate phases of being." Perhaps Miss Twinkleton is not the only one.

And perhaps Jasper also is not alone in his self-division. If he is a representative of his society, then that society is also divided against itself, so that often there is no sane relation between its words and its actions. And indeed Dickens' novel bears out such a reading. The first example who comes to mind is the terrifying philanthropist Mr. Honeythunder. There is no point in quoting him. He would shout me down in any case. In addition to this monster, however, there are less obvious instances of division between word and action, between deeds of light and deeds of darkness. For example, there is the Dean's refusal to offer further sanctuary to the persecuted Neville Landless. There is the almost literally insane epitaph which Mr. Sapsea composed for his wife's tomb—an epitaph which is indeed as stupifyingly funny as Chesterton says it is, and which is also one of the most frightening evidences of spiritual blindness and cruelty ever recorded. The entire book, or what we have of the book, is riddled with these pretenses and divisions. Dickens' opening evocation of the opium den, with its nightmare of character embodied in Jasper himself, establishes both the tone and the meaning of his artistic vision with entire mastery. Jasper himself is English society, the society for whom and to whom Dickens wrote. It is a society capable of much feeling, even of love sometimes; but it is also divided against itself, it hides its indifference to women's feelings under fantastic self-adulatory words, it shouts about philanthropy through the voice of Mr. Honeythunder while the small ragamuffins stone the drunken Durdles home after dark. Through what Jasper is and what he does, Dickens might have been speaking to his public in the words of the Apocalypse: "Thou sayest, I am rich; I have everything and need nothing; but thou knowest not that thou art miserable and poor and beggarly and blind and naked. . . ."

Meditations on René Char

1.

The American writer John Peale Bishop once said that a poet is a man to whom writing is more difficult than it is for other people. That is strong encouragement from a good man. I can think of three kinds of people who might draw nourishment from this reminder that difficulty is blessed. One is a poet, who needs to be reassured sometimes that his miserable scratchings on paper are the truest evidences of his craft. Another is the reader, who needs to be reminded that the effort to understand the writings of a great poet is successful only so far as it effects a transfiguration: and transfiguration is naturally painful and difficult to the person transfigured. One cannot grasp the poetic structures of Shakespeare or Tolstoy without being born again; and everyone knows how hard that can be. The second birth is as agonizing as the first. The third person who ought to be relieved at Bishop's reminder is the translator. For convenience, I can think of two translators: the thoroughly bilingual one who, if he likes, can translate a poem without much effort; and the one to whom the poet's original language is inescapably strange. The first of these is likely to be the more capable and trustworthy. He will hear the overtones of the poet without having to strain his ears. But the second translator is

From *René Char's Poetry: Studies by M. Blanchot, G. Bounoure, A. Camus, G. Mounin, G. Picon, R. Ménard, J. Wright* (Rome: Deluca, 1956).

the more fortunate. He cannot hear the overtones without straining his ears. He is trapped by his own ignorance into one of the most terrible difficulties in life—that of seeking a complex poet in that poet's strange language. Not a single word of the original can elude him because of its familiarity. For nothing is familiar. The translator's very ignorance gives him a new and painful sense of the poet's marvel. Surely, of all the translators of the great poet Char, I must have the poorest knowledge of French. But I am not mocked into humility by such ignorance. It is true that, to gain a sense of the poet's meanings, I had to carry his poems about with me for days on end; I had to get up at night sometimes for the sake of trying to capture his sounds and images in some true way for my native language; I had to wrestle and wrestle; I had to fight. But I do not feel mocked. For the difficult way—the way of pain and the discomfort of having one's consciousness driven forward to a wider inclusiveness—is the only way to read any great poet. And certainly, whether a translator be a linguist or only an amateur reader of French, he cannot really hear the music of Char's meanings without living for days on end with his book. Let this celebration of difficulty be the defense of my ignorance.

2.

In the introductory note to his two illuminating essays on the poetry of Char, M. René Menard strangely tells us—as though he were apologizing—that his friendship with the poet has clarified the efforts of criticism. I trust that the tone of apology is only an echo of M. Menard's modesty. As for the admission of friendship with the poet, it really amounts to a lucid recognition of some important facts about Char. The fact is that one needs to read his poems as though one were his companion. Writing of *To a Tensed Serenity,* M. Menard notes the form of that work, the evolving of its aphorisms, and the special demand which the form makes on the reader. "Its unity is organic; one perceives it as successive readings become contemplation." At first sight, this is a technical problem of the critical reader. But as one lives in companionship with Char's poems, one passes inevitably from a perception of the form to a sense of the man. One of my friends has called Char an abundant man; and one can learn of this abundance by reading the poems. Another friend has told me that Char is a giant—a real physical giant; and one could learn of that kind of abundance only by meeting him. Yet what harmony there seems among the poet (or what one can learn of him), and the form of his poems, and the subject of friendship to which he so often turns. One can see all of these things fused to perfection in what must surely be one of our great poems. (*Our* poems. Char is a lover of his native landscape, but he is not the exclusive expression of nationalists.) It is called "Anguish Volley Silence." In that lament for his dead friend Roger Bernard, Char addresses the dead, and offers directions through the world: "Do not look in the mountains; but, a few miles away, in the Oppedette gorges, if you meet the lightning and it has the face of a schoolboy, go toward it, yes, approach it smiling, for it must be hungry, hungry for friendship." For this poet, nature, so richly presented, is yet incomplete without man. Char has called himself a humanist. But the meaning of the poem is not to be found in a prose commentary. It is somehow to be found in the lightning's weeping face. It is a healing friendship for the things that are terrible and beautiful, and it is the very loving dirge for the dead friend.

3.

When *Hypnos Waking*, the English translation of Char's poems, was first published, I wrote to a friend that my part in the work frightened me a little. I did not know quite how to behave in the company of that force. And I said that his work ought to be the really seminal one for poets of the next half-century. I did not mean something formal. I was thinking of the meaning of the war diary, *Leaves of Hypnos*, and its theme of human generosity in the center of political anguish. But the remark could apply as well to Char's love poetry—particularly to the prose poem called "Magdalene Waiting." It is a love poem within a poem about poetry. The poet, so like Spenser, creates and presents for us a whole and concrete scene. Then he suddenly remembers that he had already written a poem about this very love-encounter, and he concludes by refusing to be surprised that his celebration of love produced not only a poem but a meeting with the living beloved. I cannot express fully enough my pleasure in the poet's strategy, his showing us the real woman, and how she emerged after the poem was written. Here again is the discovery—marveled over in the poem itself, and indeed filling out its skeleton with the beloved heart and flesh of love—how the wildest imagining turns out to be true, and how there is for the creating mind no such thing as an irrelevancy. This poet Char is always reaching out, including, learning the relationship between the poem and the beloved. And after the fullness of the experience, the poet supplies us with his evaluation of it: "Reality, noble, does not refuse herself to the one who comes to prize her, not to insult or take her prisoner." It is one of the wisest poems I know. It makes me think of Shakespeare's Pompey, the miserable pimp in *Measure for Measure*, who, forced to announce his profession, replies, "Truly sir, I am a poor fellow that would live."

4.

My friend Robert Mezey wrote me a perceptive little discussion of Char among the poets whom we call surrealists. Mezey, searching for the meaning of these men, marks between them and Char a distinction which I think important and instructive: "A technique may be discarded in any poem, technique (form) in none. Because the intellect of these men has not exerted its constant voluptuous pressure on the walls of their heart, their heart has leaked instead of streamed, and blurred their pages with indistinguishable passions. Char is a magnificent poet because the sentinels of his mind have never forgotten their duties." That is widsom for reflection and pleasure as well as for use. Char's poems have laws, but they are, aesthetically speaking, laws of his own organic creation. Thus we find him refusing, theoretically and actually, refusing to be lacerated by uncontrolled feelings or frozen by frigid controls. "To escape the shameful constraint of choosing between obedience and madness," says Char in *The Rampart of Twigs*, "to dodge over and over again the stroke of the despot's axe against which we have no protection though we struggle without stay: that is the justification of our role, of our destination and our dawdling." If the purist objects that here Char is talking about politics, and not about poetry, I reply that he can speak of both at once, and that his ability to do so is, like his ability in "Magdalene Waiting" to theorize on poetry while he sings his love poem, one more sign of his greatness. It is even more than a sign. It is a demonstration of the kind of greatness involved, the genius of inclusiveness and fusion, of reconciliation among man's vital concerns rather than destruction of his very fertility.

5.

Char has written a book—perhaps his best single work, his war diary *Leaves of Hypnos*—which deals with a political occasion, and scattered through his poems one finds a kind of political attitude—that is, his search for the human individual and the individual's various triumphs and escapes. Lest a reader think of Char as primarily a political thinker, even in *Leaves of Hypnos,* one ought to note the quality of his thought in the diary, and the numerous suprapolitical positions which he seems to take in the other poems. One can see his contempt for the political panaceas which characterize our age: "Life should begin with an explosion and end with a peace-pact? That is absurd." His political attack, as far as his poetry is concerned, is, like that of any good writer, an attack on triteness, on the clotting of the mind by outworn language. "Clear their heads, relieve them, toughen them, make them supple, then convince them that beyond a certain point the importance of conventional ideas is extremely relative and that in the end this "matter" is a matter of life and death and not of subtleties to be made to prevail in a civilization already so shipwrecked it may not leave a trace on the ocean of destiny: that is what I am struggling to persuade those around me to believe." It is true that Char has participated in war—he fought the Nazi horror—but he retained his ability to see and define the exact nature of war in this age: "I see man ruined by political perversion, confusing action with expiation, giving the name of conquest to his own annihilation." In such analysis, Char is at one with two writers whom he resembles in other ways—Hermann Hesse in *Steppenwolf* and Franz Kafka in "In the Penal Colony." Behind the delighted suicide of our wars lies our terror at reality. And Char's major theme is one with his human effort: the search for reality, the desire to embrace it without taking it prisoner. One sees this theme best in his poems about love and nature.

6.

As Char does not compose a work on the aesthetics of the love poem without evoking the true fleshed body of the beloved for confirmation of his technique, so he does not write a poem about nature without evoking the physical body of the landscape for the confirmation of his song. His imagery is so laden with the natural world and its details, that it would be silly to discuss only one poem. But I am perfectly willing to be silly for the sake of my affection for one poem. It comes in *Leaves of Hypnos*. "Le peuple des pres m'enchante," he begins; and we know that, once again, the strategy of the poet will be one of inclusion. One goes far in Char's poems before one can find outcasts; and, if they are found, they are directly seen gathered into the loving metaphors. So here: "The field mouse and the mole, somber children lost in the illusion of the grass, the green snake, son of glass, the cricket more than a little sheeplike, the grasshopper who clicks and counts his linen, the butterfly simulating drunkenness, annoying the flowers with its silent hiccups. . . ." It is vain to list them all. One is tempted to commentary on details. Actually, one need only point to them.

These details, so strangely gathered together and so inevitably related to one another, remind me of the apology for his life which the poet makes a few pages later: "My ineptness in *arranging* my life comes from the fact that I am faithful not to one only but to all with whom I find myself in serious relation." That remark reminds me of Walt Whitman; but the trouble is that Whitman's poems do not hold together as well or as often as Char's do; and it is the very triumph of inclusiveness—the discovery of new vital relationships within an intellectually mastered form—that I find remarkable in Char. Perhaps Tolstoy is a better suggestion for analogy. Char is like Tolstoy in his capacity for love; he is also like him in intellectual mastery.

7.

It is delightful to compose these meditations in prose, for in them I feel no need to erect any theory whatsoever. However, the haphazard nature of association in which I indulge here may strike the reader as fortuitous and irresponsible. Let me assure him that I have an intention, which I proceed to state.

Criticism, as I think of it, ought to have two functions. It ought to direct a reader to the work of the artist who is under discussion; and, once the reader is there, criticism ought to illuminate the work. To achieve these ends, a critic is justified in doing anything. I mean anything: except build a theory so large and involved that both reader and critic forget the original work, as a child looking for his parents at a carnival might forget them in the self-mirroring distortions of the fun house.

Char is difficult. He is not difficult to read sentence by sentence, for the most part, because he has saved his critical abilities for the composition of his poems, instead of writing bad books about other people. What makes him difficult is the fact that his themes are the great ones; they are the themes that are easy to see but hard to grasp, as God was for Holderlin. I think one might find the experience of love a good analogy for the experience of reading Char's poems. Friendship is another good analogy, which I used earlier in these meditations. Both experiences are pretty easy to fall into. It is so easy to be flattered by a superficial friend or delighted momentarily by a beautiful girl. However, it is not very easy to endure the sometimes shocking truths which good friends can point out to us, especially when those truths are concerned with our own selves. And it is not very easy to tolerate the pain that the beloved person can give us. Without either of these experiences, however, human life is nothing. The pain they offer is instructive. One cannot really realize that his heart beats unless he learns that the hearts of other human beings beat also. And one cannot really understand Char's poems without, in some sense, becoming a better person.

This invitation and warning to prospective participants in the work of a great artist is not new. Rilke's old torso of Apollo warns its beholders that—headless and limbless though it be—there is not one bit of its surface that does not see them, through the skin to the bone and through the bone to the heart. And, says the great Rilke, you cannot bear this vision by staying as you are: "Du musst dein Leben andern."

Theodor Storm

Foreword

1.

One of Theodor Storm's best friends at the law school in Kiel, Germany, in 1843, was a young man named Theodor Mommsen. They published, with Mommsen's brother Tycho, a little book that, at the time, they probably intended to be little more than a gesture of friendship. In fact they called it *Liederbuch drier Freunde*. I have never seen a copy, but it is pleasant to think about its publication. The affectionate dignity of the occasion reveals something about both Storm and Mommsen: a willingness to transform private devotions into public strength. Each was a human being whose character revealed itself with increasingly impressive clarity: each was blessed with intelligence, with an awareness of human society as a vital fact in the most secret and private lives of its members, and with a generous capacity for the true love, which Meister Eckhart shows to be a method of understanding as well as its end. Storm and Mommsen went their ways. The latter became, of course, one of the most distinguished historians of modern Europe. Theodor Storm also figured in the public life of his time, by continuing in the legal profession. He also became something of a historian, though the ancient worlds he sought to pene-

---

From Theodor Storm, *The Rider on the White Horse*, tr. James Wright (New York: New American Library, 1964).

trate, and explore, and grasp, and explain were more immediate and more external than Mommsen's.

Storm gave a handful of flawless poems to the great tradition that extends from the age of Walter von der Vogelweide to our own time. As recently as 1959, learned historians of German literature—J. G. Robertson, Edna Purdie, W. I. Lucas, and M. I'C. Walshe, for example—have confirmed the place among the masters earned by the respectable Frisian jurist; and the living influence that his work still is able to exert on contemporary literature is given both testimony and illustration by Thomas Mann's beautiful essay on his work (written and first published as the introduction to a handsome edition of Storm's *Collected Works* and later reprinted as one of Mann's formidable *Essays of Three Decades*).

2.

Hans Theodor Woldsen Storm was born September 14, 1817, on the west coast of the disputed duchy of Schleswig, in the little seaport town of Husum. The ancestors on his father's side were from Germany; those on his mother's, the Woldsens, were Frisians—those tall, enormously strong, taciturn, and powerfully poetic builders of dikes.

The Woldsens were prominent merchants, many of whom had served for generations in the civil administration of the community. Storm's father was an attorney, and is said to have been widely regarded as a model of authentic respectability. The poet's background remarkably resembles that of another artist from the northern part of Germany, the sorrowful and courageous Gustave von Aschenback, of whom Thomas Mann writes: "He was the son of an upper official in the judicature, and his forebears had all been officers, judges, departmental functionaries—men who lived their strict, decent, sparing lives in the service of king and state." From the beginning we can see Storm receiving from his forebears the burdens of public responsibility and laboring to carry the honorable skill of those burdens for the rest of his life.

After attending the Latin School of his native town of Husum and the secondary school of nearby Lubeck (where, incidentally, Thomas Mann was born), Storm studied jurisprudence at the University of Kiel, in the capital of Schleswig-Holstein, and later at Berlin. He practiced law at Husum from 1843 to 1853; during this decade, he seemed to have established himself as firmly and comfortably as he could have wished. Perhaps it was his happiest time. He was at home, and he always wanted to be at home. His parents were both still alive and strong, and he was surrounded by loving brothers, sisters, and other relatives. The routine comforts of life inspired in him a taste for the social pleasures. At one point, he even founded a musical society, which grew from a gathering of pleasant amateurs to a public organization whose performances met with considerable success.

In the autumn of 1846, Storm married his cousin Constanze Esmarch, a beautiful woman whose stabilizing influence on the somewhat nervous poet and jurist cannot be overemphasized. This was an influence he welcomed. He is said to have remarked of her, "When she came into the room it always seemed to me as if it grew lighter." Three sons were born to them during the coming few years, and they seemed settled for life.

However, in 1853 the German element in Schleswig openly revolted against the government of Denmark; and Storm, as one of the most vociferous of the Germans, lost his license to practice law. He went into exile that year, and entered the Prussian judicial service. For the next three years he held the position of *Assessor* (associate judge) in the circuit court at Potsdam. He broke out of Potsdam's somewhat oppressively pedantic atmosphere by traveling to Heiligenstadt in Thuringia, where, until 1864, he served as *Kreisrichter* (district judge). In this small village in the mountains, he was able to feel a little more at home, and it was here that he turned with an intense seriousness to his own writings. A good deal of wandering and rootlessness was in store for the poet before his final homecoming.

3.

During February, 1864, the allied armies (Prussia and Austria) invaded and successfully occupied the two duchies of Schleswig and Holstein. It requires no special knowledge of political history to understand how the citizens of these provinces must have felt in those days, at the very faintest beginning of the spring season, one hundred years ago. A substantial number of the inhabitants were German in background, in patriotic sympathy, and—a small but intensely significant detail—in language. For a great many years, they had been forced to carry on their daily lives in an atmosphere rendered constantly tense and uncomfortable by the potential or actual presence of Danish authority. Indeed, it is conceivable that, whatever the highest officials of the Danish government may have thought, the lowlier clerks, policemen, ministers, tax collectors—those Danes assigned specific tasks in the civil administration of the two provinces—were fully as relieved as their German contemporaries, merely to see the controversy over civil jurisdiction settled one way or the other.

By their mere presence, the troops canceled the officially elaborate orders, issued earlier in Copenhagen, for "encouraging" the use of Danish in the civil government of a people whose pride in their own German tongue had elaborated even its local dialects into a treasure of thrilling poetry. It must have been a strange time: the Prussian troops arriving in the company of friendly but unfamiliar Austrians and other southerners, united in their common and joyous duty as ensigns and ambassadors of poetry and of the very spring.

Perhaps it was the realization that the spring season and the Prussian-Austrian liberators could not reasonably be expected to arrive simultaneously on more than one occasion between the glacier and the insects, which persuaded Theodor Storm to resign his office and hurry back to Husum.

He came home with the spring. *Leben und Liebe,* he had once curtly sung, *wie flog es vorbei.* He was immediately appointed, by spontaneous acclamation, to the office of *Landvogt* (district magistrate) in his native city. He was responsible for the administration of civil order and civil justice; that is, he somehow got away with one of the most incredible feats of survival in all the long and idiotic history of the relationship between the poet and society. Theodor Storm, one of the finest German lyric poets of the nineteenth century, returned to his home and effortlessly assumed powers of great civic importance.

The few true poets in this world have sometimes displayed interesting complexities of character. Their behavior has ranged from the demonically comic to the frighteningly respectable. Storm's homecoming was a strange one for a poet.

One may doubt if Hart Crane and Francois Villon in cooperation would have thought of assuming simultaneously the powers of mayor, judge, and police chief in their respective home towns.

4.

Accounts of Storm's life and work, no matter how automatically pedantic or encrusted with fear of the imagination, contain in his homecoming a fact so absorbingly strange that even one hundred years of academic repetition has not succeeded in killing its powers of evocativeness. He dropped everything for the sake of getting back home. A man who has struggled against unusually adverse circumstances and achieved distinction in his chosen career cannot reasonably be scorned for deciding in favor of enjoying the benefits of his honestly earned success. But Storm decided to treat just such benefits as if they were literally nothing but a temporary inconvenience. Indeed, it is probably more accurate to say that his decision had been made beforehand. Storm understood that the main thing was not to make a successful career, but to live one's life. This successful jurist also wrote some fifty long stories and a solid handful of poems; and in his writings he says, as clearly as anyone can, that there is no such thing as success, that even the failures are forgotten, that the influential persons whom one seeks in his youth to impress themselves grow old and die, and that the main thing is not to get on in the world but to get home.

His fellow townsmen shared this knowledge, for they welcomed him home by asking him to accept the highest position of civil authority in their community. The city of Husum needed a mayor who could maintain order. But they preferred a man whose public abilities were based upon private devotion to the city itself. For once, such a leader was found. Storm had for many years demonstrated his qualifications for the position. He served satisfactorily until 1866, when the Prussian liberators annexed Schleswig-Holstein. But Storm's tenure of office, however brief, reveals his artistic and judicial mastery developed and deepened side by side throughout his life.

5.

Storm was no sooner solidly established as *Landvogt* than, in 1865, his wife Constanze died after the birth of their seventh child; seeking necessary rest after such shock and pain, he spent a short vacation at Baden-Baden, which Thomas Mann has beautifully described in his essay on Storm. An invitation had come from a temporary resident there, one who admired Storm as one of the masters of fiction. It was Turgenev. Above and beyond his gratitude for Turgenev's personal considerateness in a time of painful trouble, Storm must have been vividly conscious of his own poetic nature during those two weeks, and of the nature of his fame beyond the borders of Husum—a fame based on his power of dealing through poetry with mysterious forces of the most universally recognizable kind: the sea, the loss of children, the inability to speak glibly, or the inability, when it matters most, to speak at all.

But is was characteristic of Storm to return to the duties of public life. After the annexation, he entered the juridical service again at Husum, in the office of *Amtsrichter* (district judge). In 1875 he was promoted to *Oberamtsrichter* (judge of the Court of Appeals) and in 1879 to that of *Oberantsgerichtsrat* (chief justice of the Court of Appeals). In 1880 he was given a pension, and he retired to the little village of Hademarschen in southern Holstein. There, in July of 1888, he died, and was buried at his native Husum.

6.

I do not believe we can understand Storm's art without realizing that even his life as a public official was not really typical. He was invited to assume important public functions in Husum during a time of grave crisis, partly because the city fathers of Husum knew him a capable administrator. And yet those burghers, those solid citizens—themselves the very types of the "bankers, schoolmasters, and clergymen," the philistines of Yeats' immortal phrase—were well aware that Storm was an artist. His public life and his art are obviously related, and yet the second cannot be understood simply as a direct expression of the first. His art had its own formal tradition, in which he served his apprenticeship and to which he aspired to contribute.

Storm wrote some fifty stories in the genre called the *Novelle,* which had been adapted by Storm's artistic predecessors from the tales of Boccaccio and the "exemplary novels" of Cervantes. By the time Storm began to write, the *Novelle* had been developed to a high degree of sophistication. He labored for many years to create the form, and thereby the meaning, of his own artistic vision. Just as surely as the history of legal precedents was the basis of his own life as a magistrate, the conventions of the *Novelle* formed the basis of his art. Frank Kermode[1] has lucidly explained the importance of learning the language of any artist's conventions:

> We see what . . . tradition enables us to see. Thus the representation of reality is a task for two, artist and spectator, the latter enabled to read the signs of the former. . . . The whole problem of symbolism in the arts is illuminated by patient exploration of the simple truth that all communication involves prior understanding between transmitter and receiver. . . .

The *Novelle* as a literary *genre* has been fully described by the late distinguished scholar E. K. Bennett.[2] Having explained that in all literary compositions traditionally called "epic," the reader is "aware of that which is told and of the teller of it," and that in such compositions "the relationship between the two is of course capable of infinite variations and modifications," Professor Bennett proceeds:

> The *Novelle* is an epic form and as such deals with events rather than actions; it restricts itself to a single event (or situation or conflict), laying the stress primarily upon the event and showing the effect of the event upon a person or group of persons; by its concentration upon a single event it tends to present it as chance ("Zufall") and it is its function to reveal that what is apparently chance, and may appear as such to the person concerned, is in reality fate.

Theodor Storm's *Novellen* display considerable variety of form and intensity. The eight selections in the present volume should indicate something of his range within the limits of the form. I will mention two examples which seem to be sufficiently striking.

Immensee is one of the earliest, written before Storm was twenty years old. It has been widely read in the United States by students of German, and consequently has created the widespread impression that Storm's significance depends upon this one very youthful and tentative effort. *Immensee* is pervaded from beginning to end by a rather hazy mood of melancholy and resignation, and is thereby characteristic of Storm's earliest *Novellen*, which again and again involve characters who remain passive in adversity. In his early work Storm tries to create the artistic effect that his predecessor Otto Ludwig called "poetic realism." "The characteristic of Poetic Realism," writes Professor Bennett, "consists in the manner in which it describes reality, which is not one of analysis, investigation, examination from the standpoint of some philosophico-moral or sociological theory, but is content to be pure description." In actual practice, the poetic realists attempt to describe the prosaic, ordinary settings of every middle-class life in clear and minute detail and to create an atmosphere that they called *Stimmung*—a certain luminosity of descriptive language intended to express the author's emotional attachment to the objects and persons described. Storm's *Immensee*, whatever its intrinsic worth as a work of art, is historically interesting as an almost perfect illustration of these technical and emotional concerns. Storm clearly states his early artistic intention in some remarks quoted by Felix Lorenz:

> My art as a writer of Novellen developed out of my lyrical poetry and at first yielded only "Stimmungsbilder" or such individual scenes, in which the incident to be presented seemed to the author to contain a particular stimulus to poetical presentation. Connecting links woven in as allusions gave the reader the opportunity to picture to himself a larger complete whole, the whole destiny of a human being with the causes that set it in motion and its course to the end.

However, he soon came to understand the inadequacy of the attempt for his own deeper artistic purposes. After the completion of *Draussen im Heidedorf*, he remarked,

> I think that I have given proof therein, that I can write a Novelle without the atmosphere of a definite Stimmung: an atmosphere which does not develop itself of its own accord for the reader out of the facts narrated . . . but is contributed to the story by the author *a priori*.

Just as *Immensee* reveals Storm's early reliance on the conventions of Poetic Realism, so *The Rider on the White Horse* (*Der Schimmelreiter*), the very last of his works, shows how far beyond those conventions his own artistic imagination eventually forced him to reach. By the time he came to write *The Rider on the White Horse*, Storm had resolved the unavoidable conflict between his own personal imaginative impulse and the constricting literary conventions within which he had learned his art. Like his character, Hauke Haien the Dikemaster, he broke the old form while planning and building the new. In a letter to the Swiss author Gottfried Keller (August

14, 1881), Storm described his most adventurous dream of what a *Novelle* could be:

> The Novelle, as it has developed in modern times more es-
> pecially in the last decades and as it now appears in individual
> works as a more or less finished achievement, can deal with the
> most significant subject matter, and it only depends upon the
> poet for the highest achievements of poetry to be attained even
> in this form. The Novelle is no longer what it once was, "the
> succinct presentation of an event, which attracts by its unusual
> nature and reveals an unexpected turning point." The Novelle
> of today is the sister of the drama and the severest form of prose
> fiction. Like the drama it treats of the profoundest problems of
> human life; like the drama it demands for the perfections of its
> form a central conflict from which the whole is organized and in
> consequence the most succinct form and the exclusion of all that
> is unessential. It not only accepts but actually makes the biggest
> demands of art.

Whether or not Storm justified his artistic hopes is for his readers to decide. The eight *Novellen* in this volume represent, in the translator's opinion, a fair selection of his fiction. Turgenev and Mann admired Storm as a master. The reader is merely requested to remember that they read these stories in German, and that Storm is not to be held responsible for his translator's infelicities.

Dr. Wilhelm Bernhardt writes that Storm devoted a good deal of time during his last years to "the cultivation of his flower garden, the superb roses of which were objects of interest and admiration to tourists and florists from far and near." The words summon up the image of a successful dignitary who had established himself at home at last. And yet I find myself strangely troubled by the thought of the loneliness and homesickness that haunt his stories, and wonder if perhaps, surrounded by the admiration of all those "tourists and florists from far and near," he did not whisper secretly to the roses themselves some message akin to the words which the immortal Hafiz murmured to a certain rose of his own:

No one has seen your face, and yet a thousand are
   watching;

O rose, you are only a bud, and yet a hundred
   nightingales are in love with the rose.

NOTES

1. Frank Kermode, "What is Art?" *The New York Review of Books,*
February 20, 1964.
2. E. K. Bennett, *History of the German Novelle,* 2nd rev. ed. (London and New York: Cambridge University Press, 1961).

A Note on Trakl

In the autumn of 1952, I wandered into the wrong classroom at the University of Vienna. According to my instructions, the professor was supposed to be a German, whose name I forget. I also forget what course I had expected. But the lecturer who actually appeared was a short swarthy man; and he spoke soft, clear German, clinging to his Italian accent. His name was Professor Susini. The only other persons in that unheated room were a few old men, who resembled Bowery bums in America.

He stood still, peering into the dusk where we sat. Then he read a poem called "Verfall," the first poem in Georg Trakl's *Die Dichtungen*. It was as though the sea had entered the class at the last moment. For this poem was not like any poem I had ever recognized: the poet, at a sign from the evening bells, followed the wings of birds that became a train of pious pilgrims who were continually vanishing into the clear autumn of distances; beyond the distances there were black horses leaping in red maple trees, in a world where seeing and hearing are not two actions, but one.

I returned to that darkening room every afternoon for months, through autumn and winter, while Professor Susini summoned every poem out of Trakl's three volumes. I always went back to that strange room of twilight, where Susini

From *Twenty Poems of Georg Trakl*, tr. James Wright and Robert Bly (Madison, Minn.: Sixties Press, 1963).

peered for long silences into the darkness until he discovered the poem he sought; and then he spoke it with the voice of a resurrected blackbird.

His entire manner was one of enormous patience, and he read Trakl's poems very slowly. I believe that patience is the clue to the understanding of Trakl's poems. One does not so much read them as explore them. They are not objects which he constructed, but quiet places at the edge of a dark forest where one has to sit still for a long time and listen very carefully. Then, after all one's patience is exhausted, and it seems as though nothing inside the poem will ever make sense in the ways to which one has become accustomed by previous reading, all sorts of images and sounds come out of the trees, or the ponds, or the meadows, or the lonely roads—those places of awful stillness that seem at the center of nearly every poem Trakl ever wrote.

In the poems which we have translated, there are frequent references to silence and speechlessness. But even where Trakl does not mention these conditions of the spirit by name, they exist as the very nourishment without which one cannot even enter his poems, much less understand them.

We are used to reading poems whose rules of traditional construction we can memorize and quickly apply. Trakl's poems, on the other hand, though they are shaped with the most beautiful delicacy and care, are molded from within. He did not write according to any "rules of construction," traditional or other, but rather waited patiently and silently for the worlds of his poems to reveal their own natural laws. The result, in my experience at least, is a poetry from which all shrillness and clutter have been banished. A single red maple leaf in a poem by Trakl is an inexhaustibly rich and wonderful thing, simply because he has had the patience to look at it and the bravery to resist all distraction from it. It is so with all of his small animals, his trees, his human names. Each one contains an interior universe of shapes and sounds that have never been touched or heard before, and before a reader can explore these universes he must do as this courageous and happy poet did: he must learn to open his eyes, to listen, to be silent, and to wait patiently for the inward bodies of things to emerge, for the inward voices to whisper. I cannot imagine any more difficult tasks than these, either for a poet or for a reader of poetry. They are, ultimately, attempts to enter and to recognize one's very self. To memorize quickly applicable rules is only one more escape into the clutter of the outside world.

Trakl is a supreme example of patience and bravery, and the worlds which these virtues enabled him to explore, and whose inhabitants he so faithfully describes, are places of great fullness and depth. His poems are not objects to be used and then cast aside, but entrances into places where deep, silent labors go on.

A Note on Cesar Vallejo

Cesar Vallejo is the greatest modern Peruvian poet. I think Vallejo is one of the greatest modern poets in any language with which I am familiar at all; and it seems to me he is great for reasons which are quite clear, though rare for us to think of. In his poetry, he draws strength from every kind of reverence which he knows, including his reverence for his own life; and he uses his strength in order to confront and to overcome the most cruel difficulties of the twentieth century. He overcame them in the sense that he sought them out, wrote of them and in them with uncompromising clarity, and saved his own soul alive. He never flinched away from a struggle against any threat to human life—his own life or the lives of other human beings. His most profound source of imagination is his courage.

He rejoiced in his own determination to go on living in the face of every kind of death, from the vicious jealousy of university professors in Peru, when his first book (*Los Heraldos Negros*, 1918) was published, to the unsettled life of cold and hunger that he endured in Paris.

No one has yet written a full biography of Vallejo, and there are not very many external facts to guide us through his life. He was born in Santiago de Chuco, Peru, in 1893. He died in Paris in 1938. His home town was small and provincial, with an

From *Twenty Poems of Cesar Vallejo,* tr. James Wright, Robert Bly, and John Knoepfle (Madison, Minn.: Sixties Press, 1963).

ancient and living tradition of large, affectionate families who were of necessity mobilized, as it were, against the physical and spiritual onslaughts of death in its ancient and modern forms: disease, undernourishment, and cold on the one hand; the officials of the tungsten mines on the other. From his childhood and youth in Santiago de Chuco to his manhood in Europe, we see Vallejo continually reaching out into more and more profound regions of thought and action. But it would be a mistake to see his expansions as so many steps where, each time, he left a little of his life behind. On the contrary, his journeys from his home town to the city of Trujillo, and thence to Lima, and thence to Paris, and to Madrid, and back to Paris again, are not renunciations of his provincial life, but spiritual as well as physical journeys during which he gains a little more illumination of his own home, his own family, his own soul. His poems cover a great range of experience, both external and internal; but he is always returning to poems about his family, poems which in their intensity and daring are more beautiful than any other poems on the subject that I have seen.

The beauty of Vallejo's poems should itself be adequate justification for publishing a translation of them. Despite the work of H. R. Hays and a few others, we in North America do not know much about this great poet. We scarcely know of his existence. A reader may ask however just what a poet in the United States may hope to learn from Vallejo. Current poets in the United States seem to be perishing on either side of a grey division between century-old British formalism on the one hand and a vandalism of antipoetry on the other. In Vallejo we may see a great poet who lives neither in formalism nor in violence, but in imagination. He had the courage and stamina to bring his poetic imagination to bear on many different kinds of reality—the natural reality of hunger and pain, the immorality of fascism, the inner real world of the soul—and to make whole poems out of this confrontation. This is why I think he is an important poet.

Translator's Note on Herman Hesse

Few American readers seem aware that Hesse was a poet. In the seven volume German edition of his works, there are some 480 pages of poems, *Die Gedichte*. Some are very fine, and it goes without saying that a fine short poem can have the resonance and depth of an entire good novel. Readers of Hesse's novels are already aware that they contain many passages of literal verse. His *Novellen*, that peculiarly German form which Goethe first mastered and which contains some of the most profoundly beautiful and illuminating bodies of feeling in the literature—Keller, Eichendorff, and Storm come to mind, not to mention the very master of them all, Thomas Mann—are lyrical in themselves; and one of them, *In the Pressel Summerhouse (Im Presselschen Gartenhaus)*, is itself a story about poets. It deals with the young Morike's visit to the aging Holderlin. It is a story by an artist about an artist who is visiting another artist, in this case a master, and it bears some resemblance to Morike's own prose masterpiece, *Mozart on the Way to Prague (Mozart auf der Reise nach Prag)*.

I don't intend here to offer more than an implicit judgment of Hesse's work. I like his poems very much, or I would not have tried to translate some of them. But I should say something about the poet's theme. Both his curious erudition and his own writings make clear his abiding concern with art as a

From Herman Hesse, *Poems*, tr. James Wright (New York: Farrar, Straus and Giroux, 1970).

way of searching for knowledge. Whether or not the strange and haunted old man ever learned anything worth knowing is a matter still open to question. It has been argued by scholars and artists alike. All I wish to do is to offer a selection of Hesse's poems which deal with the single theme of homesickness.

I suppose the word, like love, is simple enough at first glance. If somebody else is in love, love looks charmingly silly. If somebody else is homesick, we chuckle. The poor fellow hasn't grown up. But his struggle, his growth itself, is a serious theme, and Hesse has touched this theme with a traditionally endearing delicacy.

During the recent proliferation of translations which have brought so many of Hesse's works to the attention of American readers, and particularly to the attention of the young, there has been a need to identify him, to describe his limits. Otherwise, he might go the way of a fad, as so many things—and not all of them worthless, either—have a way of doing in America. To my mind, the best criticism of this indispensable kind has been provided by the brilliant American novelist Stephen Koch. He is particularly qualified to warn against the inflation of Hesse. Quite aside from Mr. Koch's own mastery of lyrical prose, and quite aside from his learning, he is himself a young man who has written profoundly in defense of the distressed, assaulted new generation in this country. So, in his penetrating review of Hesse's *Narcissus and Goldmund* (*The New Republic,* July 13, 1968), Mr. Koch describes Hesse's limitations, and thereby, I think, reveals his true powers:

> Like everything else in his work, Hesse's thought is irretrievably adolescent, so that in his chosen role of artist of ideas, he is invariably second-rate, although unlike the other prophets of the New Age, he is never *less* than second-rate. His thought is never cheap, never trashy, but neither is it ever intellectually exalting, the way the professorial, unfashionable Mann so often is. Almost without exception, Hesse's ideas are derivative, school-boyish, traditional to the point of being academic, influenced by all the right people, and boringly correct. . . . So it goes, book after book, the Great Ideas chasing the Terrific Experiences home to their all-too-obvious destinations. Flawed

though it sometimes is, Hesse's aesthetic sense is different and better than this; *it* does sometimes rise to extraordinary levels, does transform itself into "something else," as the kids say. The final third of *Steppenwolf* is one of the great moments in modern literature, a moment original to the point of being in a class by itself, and one with an importance to future art which is not to be patronized.

I think that Mr. Koch has caught the nature and value of Hesse's art so beautifully in this passage that it remains only to offer yet another few lines, taken from the closing pages of *Steppenwolf*, which I have followed as my guide in selecting and translating some of Hesse's poems. The lines I mean do indeed appear in the final third of *Steppenwolf*. I have abbreviated them; but they provide what I take to be Hesse's best and noblest expression of his artistic theme. In this passage, the girl Hermine is trying to explain to the forty-year-old Harry Haller why his life is nothing, and yet not nothing:

"Time and the world, money and power belong to the small people and the shallow people. To the rest, to the real men belongs nothing. Nothing but death."

"Nothing else?"

"Yes, eternity."

"You mean a name, and fame with posterity?"

"No, Steppenwolf, not fame. Has that any value? And do you think that all true and real men have been famous and known to posterity?"

"No, of course not."

"Then it isn't fame. Fame exists in that sense only for the schoolmasters. No, it isn't fame. It is what I call eternity. The pious call it the kingdom of God. I say to myself: all we who ask too much and have a dimension too many could not contrive to live at all if there were not another air to breathe outside the air of this world, if there were not eternity at the back of time; and this is the kingdom of truth. The music of Mozart belongs there and the poetry of your great poets. The saints, too, belong there, who have worked wonders and suffered martyrdom and given a great example to men. But the image of every true act, the strength of every true feeling, belongs to eternity just as much, even though no one knows of it or sees it or records it or hands it down to posterity. . . . Ah, Harry, we have to stumble through so much dirt and humbug before we reach home. And we have no one to guide us. Our only guide is our homesickness."

That is what I think Hesse's poetry is about. He is homesick. But what is home? I do not know the answer, but I cherish Hesse because he at least knew how to ask the question.

Frost

"Stopping by Woods on a Snowy Evening"

Robert Frost's little poem "Stopping by Woods on a Snowy Evening" is an awesome presence to my mind. It would be easy to be clever, and to proceed by deliberately building up a little verbal charm, for the purpose of translating the awesome presence of the strangely silent poem itself into a multitudinous plurality of other presences, themselves sufficiently awesome. They are the presences of Frost's critical interpreters, already awesomely numerous, forbiddingly articulate. I do not mean to imply that most of Frost's critics have published their commentaries with the intention of frightening the poet's readers away from the presence of his poems. As a matter of fact, among the several peculiarities that distinguish Frost individually among the other major poets of our century, surely one of the most noteworthy is his power of inspiring in so many professional critics of diverse philosophical persuasions the same singular and beautiful desire: to read the poet's poems with an intelligent love worthy of the nobility embodied in his several masterpieces. There are a number of good reasons why this generally sympathetic relation between Frost and the literary critics should give us pause. For one thing, unless my present reader is himself a professional student of literature, he might well be comparatively unfamiliar with the by no means predictable responses that some of the great poems have evoked from even the ablest literary critics of their time.

From *Master Poems,* ed. Oscar Williams (New York: Washington Square Press, 1967).

As Mr. James M. Cox has remarked, Frost "seems to have gathered his forces deliberately and bided his time until he was sure of not launching himself too soon." And when at last he did launch himself, at thirty-nine, his power of attracting serious critical admiration displayed itself almost immediately. Mr. Cox further notes, "when *North of Boston* appeared, both William Dean Howells, the aging patriarch of American letters, and Ezra Pound, the eccentric and rebellious exponent of the new poetry, reviewed and praised it." These two early reviews signify a good deal more than mere variety of critical response. Both reviewers belong to the small handful of American periodical editors who have regarded the editorial position as a serious critical responsibility while many of their fellows have modestly accepted the same position as some kind of sordid reward for services rendered, through an infernally long and murky intellectual lifetime, to some nebulous "great tradition of spiritual values" or other. It is utterly astonishing, and bottomlessly fascinating, to witness the same strange critical drama in a performance as recent as Frost's eighty-fifth birthday dinner on March 26, 1959. Mr. Lionel Trilling, the principal speaker, displeased many persons, apparently because of his having spoken of Frost as a "terrifying poet." The most spectacularly publicized expression of this displeasure was a column in *The New York Times Book Review* (April 12, 1959).

Mr. Trilling, in the course of the speech in question, confessed his "partisan devotion" to what he called the "essential work that is done by the critical intellect"—that is, "to create around itself the intensity and variety that traditionally characterize the intellectual life of the metropolis." One may disapprove of this critical viewpoint; but I believe one is bound to recognize in it a spirit akin to Pound's own in praising Frost: a disillusioned realism; a resignation to the self-conscious gracefulness of a deliberately studied style of prose whose very real simplicity is a severe achievement earned by labor and not snatched by spontaneous luck; and, finally, a stubbornness, almost a pigheadedness, in claiming a place for the urban intellectual in the life of the nation's spirit. I privately suspect that it was this sort of claim that Mr. J. Donald Adams in his column found as shocking as anything else in Mr. Trilling's speech, and that made him feel sincerely hurt. Our respectful sympathy belongs to any man whose intellectual vision of his country's ideals has been abruptly shaken and perhaps even flawed forever, even though it may be a vision in which the Founding Fathers brood, dreamy and immortal, above one another's quill pens on the frieze of a postage stamp, looking for all the world like plump and snuff-stained temperance fanatics whose ill-designed dentures have tortured their shrivelled gums into those heart-tugging little smiles of cruelty and despair. But it is unprofitable, and fortunately unnecessary, to subject Mr. Adams' critical powers to unkind scrutiny. He is a lover of Frost's poetry, which he wished to vindicate from what he thought an attack.

In effect, Mr. Trilling deplored (once and for all, it seems to me) the widespread attempt to castrate Frost's poetry by means of the intricate psychological tactic that we all are aware of by now: startled by the terrifying presence of a genuinely tragic imagination stubborn enough to cast its searchlights upon the most hysterically cherished of our American false pieties—our nostalgia for a personal and national childhood that never was, our cold-blooded hatred of man's intellectual life cunningly displaced and disguised as a modest, gentle affection for our virtuous great-grandfathers in rural areas—many literary journalists have praised their own lying public image of Frost, and denied his fierce greatness by lavishing upon him an unprecedented popularity. They have tried to flatter him into drowsing while they shear his locks. What Trilling did was to cry out to the poet in the very company of his flatterers, "The philistines be upon thee!" The poet woke, and was not blind.

The best thing a reader can do at this moment is to follow Mr. Trilling's example by applying its principle to the reading of Frost's individual poems. They will respond to our intellectual respect by yielding up rich treasures of pleasure invisible to flatterers blinded by their own refusal to grant Frost his own poetic intelligence. The famous little poem "Stopping by

Woods on a Snowy Evening" offers an occasion for putting these introductory speculations to the test. The poem is as appropriate an example of Frost's poetic power as one can imagine; and, if we are willing to grant the poem the intellectual respect that all of Frost's work deserved, I believe we can clearly identify at least one source of his power: his fantastic and yet self-concealed mastery of traditional lyric forms, and the secret boldness of his formal inventiveness.

I suspect that "Stopping by Woods on a Snowy Evening" is more widely known and loved than any other single poem in the English language at the present time. Grade-school children copy it into their notebooks for Nature Study. The late Prime Minister of India, Mr. Nehru, kept the poem on his desk as a kind of secret reminder, an emblem of steadfastness, during the last days of his life, when he realized perfectly well that he would have to carry his appalling burdens of public responsibility without relaxing for an instant, right up to the death itself. The poem privately nourished the energy of the late President Kennedy. Even the most vigorously self-assured of Frost's detractors during the thirties, Mr. Malcolm Cowley, chose "Stopping by Woods on a Snowy Evening" as a characteristic example of Frost's political and social irresponsibility. According to this reading, the poet is criticized for his habit of loitering for his mere personal pleasure at the edge of the dark woods and then blithely urging his little horse on toward home; whereas any really mature, responsible person would have dismounted and undertaken an exploration of the woods, which represent the sinister realities of American life, both inward and external. (What was Frost supposed to find in those dark woods, I wonder. A hobo jungle? A snowman? The tar-paper hideout shack of some American equivalent of Lenin's mother, ladling out mulligan stew to fugitives from the Federal Writers' Project?) The interpretations and misinterpretations of this one short poem are as numerous and varied as its readers. They all testify to its singularly powerful hold on its reader's emotion.

I invite the reader to disregard, for a moment, the usual tendency to view the poem either as a moral exhortation to fulfill one's private duties or as a politico-social allegory. I point to its lyrical craftsmanship, to its mastery of traditional form, and, finally, to the hidden skill with which the poet has combined two traditional lyric devices in such a way as to create something entirely new.

The devices I mean are devices of sound, or rhyme. Consider the first of these: the rhyme scheme of the individual stanzas. It is pleasing in itself, and even mildly odd: instead of sustaining the promise of simplicity in rhymed couplets, the poet gently surprises us in the fourth line of each stanza by sidestepping his third-line rhyme and returning to the rhymes of his first two lines: this is the first pattern. It is in the first line of his second stanza that the musical secret is fully confessed. What seemed at first a mere pleasant deviation from a strict and simple couplet pattern suddenly becomes itself a principle of pattern, fully as strict as the first and, at the same time, more complex: for the first pattern simply joined together the two lines of the couplet, whereas the second pattern joins together two entire stanzas. The poet creates his interlocking pattern by returning to the end of his third line and transforming what seemed an accident of sound, left abandoned in midair, into the very principle of pattern, a rhyme scheme whose principle is not simple repetition, as in a couplet, but development, as in—in what?

Why, in the *terza rima* of Dante's *Divine Comedy,* no less.

Stanza by stanza, Frost's brief poem, so modest in its diction, so obvious in its setting and action, so unambitious in its pattern of sound, turns out to be a devastatingly rich combination of two great traditional lyrical devices: the stanza form of the *Rubáiyát of Omar Khayyám* and the *terza rima* of Dante combined into a new harmony. The fourth line of each stanza of the *Rubáiyát* rebels against the couplet pattern into which it is being forced, and, instead of meekly completing the imperious sound of its syntactical counterpart in the third line, abandons that sound to fend for itself, and becomes a pathetic echo flowing constantly back to repeat the fulfilled rhymes of the first couplet. The effect of the sound in the *Rubáiyát* is to make one's ear constantly aware of a gentle yet persistent tugging, almost a faint undertone of yearning toward what is already perfected, already fulfilled in pattern, and already past. The principle of rhyme in the *terza rima* is, of course, just the opposite: the ear of the reader, after hearing at least one completed pattern of rhyme at the beginning, naturally listens with specially alerted interest to the sound of a new word introduced at the end of any line that in itself does not fit into any already established pattern of rhyme, and concentrates its listening attention in the only direction from which the fulfillment of a rhyming pattern can possibly come. That is the direction of the future: the next line, perhaps, or the line after the next.

So Frost in his poem combines two irresistibly strong currents of sound, one toward what is past and fulfilled, the other toward what may yet come into its own fulfillment; the two undertones of time become a single current, and the listener's yearning back toward the one flows into his yearning forward toward the other. These movements of rhyme give lyrical embodiment to two inescapably serious kinds of human music: the music of pathos that sings of our yearning to return, and the music of present energy that sings of our need to waken and discover, or even to create, what is alive and new. Frost has fused the two distinct principles of the elegiac and the philosophical lyric into a new lyrical principle, which he sings in a voice unmistakably his own. His syntax is so colloquial, his tone of voice modulates itself so casually back and forth between the murmur of speech and the humming of a solitary sleigh driver poised—for an eternal, absent-minded instant—between snowfall and nightfall—that his poem seems to record that strange moment when time pauses, whispers, and miraculously renews itself.

A Master of Silence

One afternoon a few months ago in New York City, my wife and I joined a small group of people—I suppose there were about thirty of us—to hear a reading of poems by David Schubert. We weren't acquainted with more than half a dozen people at the gathering, and we all of us, strangers and friends alike, draped ourselves as comfortably as we could all over whatever sofas, hard-backed chairs, and spaces of the floor that we could find.

Even before the reading began, I was struck by the strangeness of the occasion and of ourselves. Who were we? What were we doing there? I could answer for myself, of course. All three of the readers were particularly dear friends of mine, and I cared not only about them but also about their own devotions. David Schubert's exquisite wife was also there, and I thought for a moment that all the other people in the room, strangers to me, were simply other friends of hers, come to honor her by paying respects to the work of her husband. Yet it turned out that she was personally acquainted with as few members of the audience as I was. People of all ages were present. Even some small children sat plumped up among the overstuffed cushions.

I think the small size of that audience haunts me to this very moment because of the sense it gave me of a vastness, a full-

---

Excerpt from a lecture given at the University of Delaware, Newark, Delaware in the fall of 1978.

ness, an authenticity. The vastness I have in mind has nothing to do, of course, with sheer numbers of people. Like anyone else in our modern age who has thought about the problem at all, I have more than once found myself among crowds numbering in the thousands, troubled by the sense that no one was really there. But thirty of us were present to listen to the poems of David Schubert, and our presence was vivid to us because we were paying attention. Attentiveness is also a fullness. That afternoon in New York, I thought of Thoreau's remark that he had never yet met a person who was fully awake. How, Thoreau wondered, could I have looked him in the face? But we were probably as awake as we could be. And we were genuine. We all of us valued the person who can speak truly. We had come to do something else, something in a way even more difficult. We wanted to shut up, so that we could, for once, listen, and listen truly. Whether or not we succeeded is not for me to say, but I do know, as I believe the others know, that we had found the proper moment in the proper place.

On an afternoon in New York City in the year 1978, we had come to listen and save ourselves from noise. We were damned as a matter of course to be children of distraction, confused by a world characterized by noise. And I believe that it is vain to hope that noise is merely the opposite of silence. One can obliterate the sound of a television set, but it is no help. The commercials go on in their screaming dumb show. We gathered to hear the poems of David Schubert, and we learned something about the art of listening truly. For this poet, our teacher in the art, is a master of silences. One of the most remarkable of his gifts is his power of gathering and preserving silence in the midst of noise. One of the purest and most serene of his poems, which I'll come back to later, deals with one of the noisiest and most distracting occasions I can imagine, and the poem, "It Is Sticky in the Subway," is a little miracle of genial silence:

> How I love this girl who until
> This minute, I never knew existed on
> The face of this earth.

                                   I sit opposite
Her, thinking myself as stupid as that
Photograph, maudlin in Mumford, of
Orpheus.

          A kinkled adolescent
Defies the Authorities by
Smoking a butt right next to me. He is
Of Romeos the least attractive who
Has played the role.

                    He
Smirks, squints, glues his eyes to her
Tightly entethered teeth, scratches
His moist passion on some scratch paper.

          Her eyes
Accuse Plato of non-en
Tity. Most delightful creature of moment's
                              above-ground.

When I call David Schubert a master of silences, I think it is
only fair to say something about noise. Just as silence is not the
mere absence of sound, and in fact can be the world where we
hear voices most distinctly, so noise is not the mere presence of
sound. It goes without saying that noise can include sounds
that cause pain. The subway stop at 86th and Central Park
West in New York is sometimes so loud that to hear it is a kind
of ecstasy of the deep. And the voice of Barbra Streisand has
given me such pain as I scarcely dreamed of experiencing on
this side of the ultimate pit, a sort of glittering hopelessness,
the atoms of the inner ear banging their heads together for-
ever and ever. But there is a dumb noise also. It is noise be-
cause its nature and function, what it is and what it does,
amounts to a distraction from reality. Now, David Schubert is a
listener, a most discriminating listener. His power of listening
is the power of paying attention, a rare power in our contem-
porary world of distraction, rare among us all and rarest of all
among our poets. The master of silences is our best ally against
noise, against distraction. It seems to me that this matter has an
importance beyond plain physical comfort. Of all guides

through the world of distraction, perhaps Jose Ortega y Gasset faces it most helpfully:

> Take stock of those around you and you will see them wandering about lost through life, like sleep-walkers in the midst of their good or evil fortune, without the slightest suspicion of what is happening to them. You will hear them talk in precise terms about themselves and their surroundings, which would seem to point to them having ideas on the matter. But start to analyse those ideas and you will find that they hardly reflect in any way the reality to which they appear to refer, and if you go deeper you will discover that there is not even an attempt to adjust the ideas to this reality. Quite the contrary: through these notions the individual is trying to cut off any personal vision of reality, of his very own life. For life is at the start a chaos in which one is lost. The individual suspects this, but he is frightened at finding himself face to face with this terrible reality, and tries to cover it with a curtain of fantasy, where everything is clear. It does not worry him that his "ideas" are not true, he uses them as trenches for the defense of his existence, as scarecrows to frighten away reality.
>
> The man with the clear head is the man who frees himself from those fantastic "ideas" and looks life in the face, realizes that everything in it is problematic, and feels himself lost. As this is the simple truth—that to live is to feel oneself lost—he who accepts it has already begun to find himself, to be on firm ground. Instinctively, as do the shipwrecked, he will look round for something to which to cling, and that tragic, ruthless glance, absolutely sincere, because it is a question of his salvation, will cause him to bring order into the chaos of his life. These are the only genuine ideas: the ideas of the shipwrecked. All the rest is rhetoric, posture, farce. (From *The Revolt of The Masses*)

Ortega's words have the general force of their context, where he is attempting to analyze what he calls nobility and inertia, or barbarism. His shipwrecked man is his noble man. But his words have a particular force for me also. He might have been describing the noble spirit which I find embodied in the poetry of David Schubert. For that poetry expresses a deep power of attentiveness, and a refusal to be scattered apart by the world of distraction.

To associate David Schubert with Ortega's phrase about the shipwrecked man calls for a few words about the poet's life. The little I know about the external facts comes from notes by Theodore Weiss, printed at the end of Schubert's most important collection, *Initial A,* published by Macmillan in 1961, and from the note, written presumably by the editor James Laughlin, which precedes the group of poems called *The Simple Scale,* included in *Five Young American Poets* and published by New Directions in 1941. Mr. Weiss' note is succinct:

> David Schubert was born in New York in 1913. After a poverty-stricken childhood and youth in which he usually had to rely on his own resources, he found his way to Amherst College, where his promise was soon remarked, and he was befriended by people like Professor Theodore Baird and Robert Frost. But he left to complete his undergraduate work at the College of the City of New York. He married Judith Ehre and, living in Brooklyn, attempted various employments, from waiting on tables to library and editorial work: but his chief, almost exclusive preoccupation was his own writing. For a time he attended the Columbia Graduate School in English and its school in library work. Briefly, he arranged lectures and exhibits in the Brooklyn Museum. . . . The rigors of the age, however, and of his own life, one passionately devoted to poetry, now began to overtake him, and even as he was readying his poems for book publication, illness and a complete breakdown led to his death in April, 1946.

Mr. Laughlin's note of 1941 contains essentially the same information, and he adds a short passage which I want to include here because it points so vividly to my notion of the poet as one of Ortega's shipwrecked men. Mr. Laughlin writes, "Schubert was homeless from the age of 15, working as a busboy, soda jerker, waiter, farm hand, and various other jobs. At one time he did a turn in the CCC. All in all it was anything but an easy life."

The details are grim enough, God knows. It is bad enough to be broke when other people have money, at a moment like our own, when custom-tattered blue jeans, once rancid with the sweat of coal miners and factory workers who welcomed brief holidays by shedding their blue jeans like dead skin, have become the unmistakable sign of comfortable leisure, the synthetic rags of an expensive poverty. But it is another thing to be broke when everyone else is broke, to know that despair is not a fashionable term from a philosophy class but the plain condition of breathing. Many people were lost in despair when David Schubert was a boy during the Depression, and he knew well that, in those days, you did not have to be a poet to be desperate. His knowledge of this plain fact of life is recorded for us in his poem "Lighthouse Mission," which may be the best poem about outcasts that we have:

> For men like this there is the sound
> Of feet forever drawing near,
> Withdrawing in the ground.
>
> After the rain like leaves blown
> Tissue paper, damp, discolored;
> They fall from a tree of air, sown
> By some peasant, centuries lowered.
>
> It means always, "Move, move on!"
> They rise and creep below,
> Above, under, on—
> Never face the sun.
>
>   Snow
> Means charity at this Lighthouse floats,
> Anchors the angels. Paper sown
> Between their skins and thin coats
> To keep them warm.
>
> War and hand grenades are
> Listening at the corners, noon.
> All night they hugged the hungry bone,
> And sealed the lips and broke the stars.

I say that this poet knew despair face to face. In our brief moment, when despair retains a certain modish fascination, and when even suicide has become a sure way of entering certain chic literary circles, it seems to me important to take Dr. Johnson's advice and to clear our minds of cant. David

Schubert, struck down at the age of thirty-three by severe poverty and illness, a young man thoroughly familiar with despair, as well acquainted with the night as the great Frost ever was, this poet is a happy poet. His gift to us is the gift of gaiety, as he moves musically among his silences in our world of distraction and noise. He wrote "A Short Essay on Poetry" to introduce his 1941 collection *The Simple Scale;* and the essay is so marked by his own eloquent reticences and touches of happiness, that I want to quote it all:

> A poet who observes his own poetry ends up, in spite of it, by finding nothing to observe, just as a man who pays too much attention to the way he walks, finds his legs walking off from under him. Nevertheless, poets must sometimes look at themselves in order to remember what they are risking. What I see as poetry is a sample of the human scene, its incurably acute melancholia redeemed only by affection. This sample of endurance is innocent and gay: the music of vowel and consonant is the happy-go-lucky echo of time itself. Without this music there is simply no poem. It borrows further gayety by contrast with the burden it carries—for this exquisite lilt, this dance of sound, must be married to a responsible intelligence before there can occur the poem. Naturally, they are one: meanings and music, metaphor and thought. In the course of poetry's career, perhaps new awarenesses are discovered, really new awarenesses and not verbal combinations brought together in any old way. This rather unimportant novelty is sometimes a play of possibility and sometimes a genuinely new insight: like *Tristram Shandy,* they add something to this Fragment of Life.

David Schubert miraculously found his critic after his death. I am thinking of the poet and highly intelligent critic Mr. David Galler, who wrote in *Poetry: A Magazine of Verse* (vol. 99, no. 6, March 1962, pp. 379–83) about Schubert's 1961 volume called *Initial A.* I do not know what happened to David Galler, but in the confusion and silliness of current criticism, I miss his writings. He says of the poetry of David Schubert that the poet "breaks through the stench of confession they (i.e., some modish poets) have broken through to, (and) arrives at splendors other than self-pity." Galler further writes this of Schubert's most characteristic work:

> Descriptive rhetoric, external projections of the self, have vanished; Catullan fragments, rapid changes of forms, have taken over to express the exact conditions of what, in the earlier poems, was a diffuse loneliness. . . . Midway through Part III the poems begin to depend for their very existence upon 'the meetings of Climatic moments.'

I would add that these climatic moments are those in which the poet's art is so patient, so lucid and reverent, that he gives substance to the very voice of silence itself.

The Work of Gary Snyder

I

Gary Snyder is an original man. He has written a poetry which is quite unusual and very different from most poetry written in the last years.

The poems take place "In the woods and at sea." In the woods and at sea, Mr. Snyder has been able to enjoy and praise the physical life. The movements of all physical things are not abstract or intellectualist, of course, and Mr. Snyder sees that all growing, physical things are in a sense like women, who have "a difficult dance to do, but not in mind."

Mr. Snyder's first book was published in 1959 by Cid Corman, called *Riprap* (Origin Press, 1959). In an appendix to the Grove Press anthology, Mr. Snyder made some remarks on *Riprap:*

> I've recently come to realize that the rhythms of my poems follow the rhythm of the physical work I'm doing and the life I'm leading at any given time—which makes the music in my head which creates the line. Conditioned by the poetic tradition of the English language and whatever feeling I have for the sound of poems I dig in other languages. *Riprap* is really a class of poems I wrote under the influence of the geology of the Sierra Nevada and the daily trail-crew work of picking up and

---

Published under the name "Crunk" in *The Sixties* 6 (Spring 1962).

placing granite stones in tight cobble patterns on hard slab. "What are you doing?" I asked Roy Marchbanks. "Rip-rapping," he said. His selection of natural rocks was perfect— . . . I tried writing poems of touch, simple, short words, with the complexity far beneath the surface texture. In part the line was influenced by the five- and seven-character line Chinese poems I'd been reading, which work like sharp blows on the mind.

The human voices and persons who sometimes rise in Mr. Snyder's poems are always distinguished by this dignity. For example, in a poem in *Riprap* called "Hay for the Horses," we see a man arrive at a barn with a load of hay. Suddenly, at lunch time, his voice breaks out with his broodings:

> He had driven half the night
> From far down San Joaquin
> Through Mariposa, up the
> Dangerous mountain roads,
> And pulled in at eight a.m.
> With his big truckload of hay
>   behind the barn.
> With winch and ropes and hooks
> We stacked the bales up clean
> To splintery redwood rafters
> High in the dark, flecks of alfalfa
> Whirling through shingle-cracks of light,
> Itch of haydust in the
>   sweaty shirt and shoes.
> At lunchtime under Black oak
> Out in the hot corral,
> —The old mare nosing lunchpails,
> Grasshoppers crackling in the weeds—
> "I'm sixty-eight," he said,
> "I first bucked hay when I was seventeen.
> I thought, that day I started,
> I sure would hate to do this all my life.
> And dammit, that's just what
> I've gone and done."

Snyder is not the man to make some complacent moralistic observation on the driver's words. This sense of worth in the lives of all human beings is not shared by very many recent American poets. But it recalls Whitman, with whom Mr. Snyder has other powers in common. For example, there is the presence of the poet himself as a living figure in nearly every poem. I mean here much more than the mere grammatical first person: I mean the pervading presence of the poet who simultaneously shares in the processes of life and reveals some of its meaning through his actions. Another power which Snyder shares with Whitman is his occasionally humorous awareness of himself in situations that challenge conventional pride. Give or take a few differences, Whitman might have written Mr. Snyder's poem "Cartagena":

Rain and thunder beat down and flooded the streets—
We danced with Indian girls in a bar,
     water half-way to our knees,
The youngest one slipped down her dress and danced
     bare to the waist,
The big negro deckhand made out with his girl on his lap
     in a chair her dress over her eyes
Coca-cola and rum, and rainwater all over the floor.
In the glittering light I got drunk and reeled through
     the rooms,
And cried, "Cartagena! swamp of unholy loves!"
And wept for the Indian whores who were younger than me
     and I was eighteen,
And splashed after the crew down the streets wearing
     sandals bought at a stall
And got back to the ship, dawn came,
     we were far out at sea.

This poem, in its direct description of life in impolite society, might seem a Beat poem—up to a crucial point. Mr. Snyder's difference from the Beats (to which I shall return later) is apparent in a superior sensitivity. Like Whitman before him, he brings a sense of delicacy to bear upon his treatment of other people's lives. He also has a sense of privacy, even in the most raucous life, which appears in the several meditative poems in *Riprap*. The very first poem in the book is a short poem formed out of a moment in a forest look-out station. It is called "Mid-August at Sourdough Mountain Lookout":

> Down valley a smoke haze
> Three days heat, after five days rain
> Pitch glows on the fir-cones
> Across rocks and meadows
> Swarms of new flies.
>
> I cannot remember things I once read
> A few friends, but they are in cities.
> Drinking cold snow-water from a tin cup
> Looking down for miles
> Through high still air.

This poem ends, like the previous poem, with an image of utter clarity, as of clear water—a promise of spiritual depth.

The meditative power and the privacy that characterize this brief, beautiful poem are powers which Mr. Snyder displays throughout his work. It is important to mention them, because they imply the presence behind the work of a man who has thought deeply about the body and value of existence conscious of itself. In short, I think that Mr. Snyder is a poet who might be called devout, or religious in the most elementary sense. He regards life with a seriousness so profound that he is able to experience and express the inner life without resorting to the worn-out abstractions which so often nullify the public discussions of spiritual matters.

The poems cited are from his first volume, *Riprap*. It is a beautiful book, and one of the two or three finest books of poetry of the last ten years.

Riprap was a simple collection of occasional poems, but Snyder's next book, *Myths and Texts*, is more carefully organized. It was published by LeRoi Jones with the Eighth Street Bookstore in 1960 (Totem/Corinth Paperbook, New York).

Myths and Texts is arranged in three sections: "Logging," which describes Snyder's experience as a logger in Oregon, and also develops the theme of the destruction of the forests; "Hunting," which describes with great delicacy the lives of animals; and "Burning," which describes certain steps of spiritual life and labors of transformation from one level of life to another. The theme of the book as a whole is praise of physical life. There is a struggle to overcome what the poet calls the "ancient meaningless abstractions of the educated mind."

"Get off my back, Confucius."

In the first section, Mr. Snyder is able to describe the violation of living creatures that takes place during a logging operation; he does so by leaping beyond the "meaningless abstractions." The following example is taken from Poem #8:

> Each dawn is clear
> Cold air bites the throat.
> Thick frost on the pine bough
> Leaps from the tree
>   snapped by the diesel
> Drifts and glitters in the
>   horizontal sun.
> In the frozen grass
>   smoking boulders
>   ground by steel tracks.
> In the frozen grass
>   wild horses stand
>   beyond a row of pines.
> The D8 tears through piss-fir,
> Scrapes the seed-pine
>   chipmunks flee,
> A black ant carries an egg
> Aimlessly from the battered ground.
> Yellowjackets swarm and circle
> Above the crushed dead-log, their home.
> Pine oozes from barked
>   trees still standing,
> Mashed bushes make strange smells . . .

Although the poet seems most directly concerned, in this poem, with describing a process of destruction, it is interesting to note that his vision also includes a great number of living creatures, whose lives he watches carefully and tenderly. It is this very sense of detail in lives which, in the next group of poems, gathers into such intense focus as to see beyond the literal physical lives of the animals. That is, the group called

"Hunting" moves beyond literal description into the beginnings of a spiritual evocativeness. At the end of the first poem in the section, the poet describes himself:

> I sit without thoughts by the log-road
> Hatching a new myth . . .

And it is true. Snyder is always "hatching a new myth," in the sense that he is always seeking for a way to embody his celebration of physical life in some form that will reveal its religious meanings. He never refers to the tired terms of classical mythology. They do not even seem to occur to him. He does use myths, however, not by referring to them but by re-creating them in his own poems. He has several poems dedicated to animals; and he refers to "deer" and "bear" as the northwest Indians do—not simply as single living creatures but also as spiritual forces. The result is a poetry of authentic strangeness, where the spirituality of living creatures shines upon them in the darkness. The following is a passage from Poem #6:

> The others had all gone down
> From the blackberry brambles, but one girl
> Spilled her basket, and was picking up her
> Berries in the dark.
> A tall man stood in the shadow, took her arm,
> Led her to his home. He was a bear.
> In a house under the mountain
> She gave birth to sleek dark children
> With sharp teeth, and lived in the hollow
> Mountain many years.

It is in the third group of poems, "Burning," that Mr. Snyder more frequently refers to the religious ideas of the Orient. What makes his religious meditations and descriptions in "Burning" so strong is his ability to present them in terms of the living plants and creatures which he has already described and celebrated in previous parts of his book. The following passages taken from Poem #6, Poem #16, and Poem #17 illustrate the tone of the third section:

"Forming the New Society
        Within the shell of the Old"
The motto in the Wobbly Hall
Some old Finns and Swedes playing cards
Fourth and Yesler in Seattle.
O you modest, retiring, virtuous young ladies
        pick the watercress, pluck the yarrow
"Kwan kwan" goes the crane in the field,
        I'll meet you tomorrow;
A million workers dressed in black and buried,
We make love in leafy shade.

Earth! those beings living on your surface
none of them disappearing, will all be transformed.
When I have spoken to them
when they have spoken to me, from that moment on,
their words and their bodies which they
usually use to move about with, will all change.
I will not have heard them. Signed
                    (   )
                  Coyote

        Rain falls for centuries
        Soaking the loose rocks in space
        Sweet rain, the fire's out
        The black snag glistens in the rain
        And the last wisp of smoke floats up
        Into the absolute cold
        Into the spiral whorls of fire
        The storms of the Milky Way . . .
        The sun is but a morning star.

    The theme of the praise of physical life present everywhere
in the book dominates Poem #16, "Hunting," which deals with
a birth:

        How rare to be born a human being!
        Wash him off with cedar-bark and milkweed
                send the damned doctors home.
        Baby, baby, noble baby
        Noble-hearted baby . . .

All the virtues of humor, delicacy, respect for living creatures, human and animal, patience and silence, are to be found in *Myths and Texts,* and in a more generally coherent and disciplined form than in *Riprap.* It is best to conclude this brief introduction to the second book by allowing Mr. Snyder to speak for himself. His words are quoted in the Appendix to *The New American Poetry:*

> *Myths and Texts* grew between 1952 and 1956. Its several rhythms are based on long days of quiet in look-out cabins; settling chokers for the Warm Springs Lumber Co. (looping cables on logs and hooking them to 'D' Caterpillars—dragging and rumbling through the brush); and the songs and dances of Great Basin Indian tribes I used to hang around. The title comes from the happy collections of Sapir, Boas, Swanton, and others made of American Indian folktales early in this century; it also means the two sources of human knowledge—symbols and sense-impressions. I tried to make my life as a hobo and worker, the questions of history and philosophy in my head, and the glimpses of the roots of religion I'd seen through meditation, peyote, and "secret frantic rituals" into one whole thing.

II

I have three ideas about Snyder's work as a whole that I want to bring up. First, his is essentially a Western imagination. His poems are powerfully located—sown, rooted—in the landscape of the far Western states. He is a Western writer just as, for example, Delmore Schwartz, Anthony Hecht, and Howard Moss are Eastern writers. This is the same distinction one would have made earlier between Theodore Dreiser and John P. Marquand; or between Sherwood Anderson and Lionel Trilling. These two sets of writers deal with different geographical landscapes but the distinction is deeper and subtler than that. They differ in what might be called the landscape of the imagination—which each in his way tries to discover and explore.

The Western writer feels a need to approach his characters and incidents with an imagination totally, if temporarily, freed from all concern with abstract ideas. The Eastern writer, such as Mr. Schwartz or Mr. Trilling, does not. Mr. Trilling, thoroughly aware of the existence of the West and the Midwest and of the writers from these areas, still writes of them as a philosopher would write: his imagination, for better or for worse, is so saturated with abstract ideas that it would be difficult, if not impossible, for him to prevent their existence in the forefront of his mind. Existing there, they blot out many details of physical life. The poetry of Howard Moss, Anthony Hecht, and Delmore Schwartz is similarly saturated with abstract ideas.

Mark Twain is a Western writer: that is, his imagination is most powerfully moved when he is concerned with concrete details in the lives of nonintellectual people. Of course, he examines such lives with an intellect of great force and clarity. This is also true of early Hemingway. Similarly, Dreiser remains a Westerner even when he writes of New York or Boston. I think that one major sign of these writers' intellectual power is their ability to penetrate and explore the lives of people who are invisible to the academies—the "custodian" who comes in the afternoon and empties the professor's wastebasket; the timid young man who cleans out the rest rooms after ten o'clock at night; the frightened and ambitious textbook pitchman; the farmer who works in the field nearby; the idiot hired man. To force the fact of their mere existence into the consciousness of people whose whole lives are worries over social status is evidence of a strong intellect. With this power the grasp of the writers is permanently caught in sensuous details and imaginative images fresh in themselves. At any rate, the powerful mind that expresses its understanding of life in the forms of the imagination rather than in the forms of abstraction is the kind of American mind I have called Western. Most of its greatest representatives so far have been writers of fiction. One of the most interesting features of Gary Snyder's poetry is that in him we see this "western" imagination in a poet.

The point is worth examining further: it helps to identify

Mr. Snyder's originality and it suggests a kind of American poetry that hasn't been very much explored—a kind of poetry which Mr. Snyder has been writing with freshness and dignity, which might be called a poetry of the Western imagination. The term itself doesn't matter much, except for the sake of convenience. It ought to suggest, however, certain features of poetry which are imaginative rather than rhetorical. In such poetry the forms of poems emerge from within the living growth of each particular poem and most definitely *not* in a set of conventions (such as the classical English iambic, with all its masterpieces of the past and its suffocating influence in the present). This new poetry is also marked by the presence of a powerful intelligence which does its thinking through the imagination itself, and not through repetition of the thoughts of established philosophical authorities or of classical myths which are degenerated through excessive or inaccurate use into obstructions rather than doorways to clear thought. Mr. Snyder does indeed embody certain myths in his poetry, but they are not classical myths, but "bear myths," and myths of the senses.

My second idea is that Mr. Snyder's poetry is very different from "Beat" poetry. Snyder has been associated primarily in magazines with the Black Mountain school and the Beats. His association with the latter (he is the hero of *Dharma Bums*) results from his friendship with Kerouac. Snyder's poetry is, however, immediately distinct both in imagination and in style from Beat work. A certain gentleness and care for civilization in Snyder is utterly absent in Ginsberg or Orlovsky, who are in favor, as they say, of "cat vommit." Ginsberg and Orlovsky make strong efforts to coarsen themselves, whereas Snyder does the very opposite. The Beat writers are opposed to civilization of all kinds: Snyder is not. Snyder's work everywhere reveals the grave mind of a man who is highly civilized and who, moreover, makes no pretense of denying his own intelligence.

Snyder's life is entirely different from the life of a Beat poet. Snyder took no part in the race for publicity among the Beats. Instead of merely talking about Zen, he went to Japan and entered a Buddhist monastery in Kyoto, where he still remains, learning Japanese, and undertaking serious study. The difference between his devotion to the Orient and the public exploitation of oriental religiosity by Jack Kerouac, among others, becomes immediately apparent. In order to read Chinese poets, Snyder learned ancient Chinese, a difficult language. He now makes his living translating from ancient Chinese and Japanese texts at a Zen institute in Kyoto, working in the institute in the afternoon and spending the morning at the monastery. His dedication to Chinese civilization is also shown in his translation of some ancient Chinese poems; here is his translation of a little poem by Po Chu-i:

> Tears soak her thin shawl
>   dreams won't come
> —In the dark night, from the front palace,
>   girls rehearsing songs.
> Still fresh and young,
>   already put down,
> She leans across the brazier
>   to wait the coming dawn.
>
> —*Floating World*, 3

My third idea is the reality of the oriental influence on Snyder. The influence of the Orient on Snyder is interior: it is the desire to overcome vanity and ambition. This is an influence that is not necessarily available to collectors of oriental objects and books.

The great poets of Japan and, especially, of China, are almost invariably men who pride themselves on being men who devote their entire selves to the life of contemplation and imagination. In their poems they succeed in the struggle against vanity and the desire for power.

Another oriental influence concerns the method of construction of the poem. Chinese poems are formed out of images whose sensory force strikes the mind directly, not as an abstract substitute for an experience, but as an original experience in itself. Let me quote two short poems. The first is Chinese, the second, one of Mr. Snyder's:

Sleeping a Spring Night in the Palace Annexe

The flowers hide palace walls sunk in shadow,
Birds chatter on their way to roost,
The stars shine and twinkle into the ten thousand
  palace windows,
The nine terraces of heaven lie lulled in the added
  brightness of the moon.
Unable to sleep, I listen for the turning of the
  golden key in the lock.
Because of the wind I think I hear the jade ornaments   .
  tinkle.
Tomorrow morning I have to report to the throne,
So I keep wondering how much of the night has flown.

—Tu Fu, translated by
Soame Jenyns

Water

Pressure of sun on the rockslide
Whirled me in dizzy hop-and-step descent,
Pool of pebbles buzzed in a Juniper shadow,
Tiny tongue of a this-year rattlesnake flicked,
I leaped, laughing for little boulder-color coil—
Pounded by heat raced down the slabs to the creek
Deep tumbling under arching walls and stuck
Whole head and shoulders in the water:
Stretched full on cobble—ears roaring
Eyes open aching from the cold and faced a trout.

Mr. Snyder's poem, above, contains no external reference to China or to Chinese poetry. Somebody once said that the prose of the young Ernest Hemingway resembled clean pebbles shining side by side at the bottom of a clear stream-channel; and that is the way Mr. Snyder has let the images of his poem arrange themselves into lines. There is no forcing of the imagination into external and conventional rhetorical patterns, such as have ruptured a good many poems during recent years in America. And yet Mr. Snyder's poem is not formless. It is exquisitely formed from the inside. It follows the clear rhythm of the poet's run down the hill in the hot sun, turns suddenly when he plunges his head in the cold water, and comes to a delightful close with the poet, his skin alive with the chill, gazing under the surface, face to face with a fish.

I began by noting Mr. Snyder's conscious debt to Chinese poets, and ended by admiring his ability to convey the astonishment of a fish. The two points suggest the importance of Mr. Snyder's study of Chinese. He has bypassed its biographical and historical externals, such as might be flaunted by someone who wanted to impress his readers, and has learned how to form his imagination into poems according to a tradition which is great and vital, and which is wholly distinct from the tradition of British poetry, very great in itself but somewhat inhibiting to American imaginative experience.

It is distressing to have to say it again, but few people in American literary discussion seem to take seriously the fact that what Walt Whitman accurately called "British literature" is not the only tradition from which American writers can be permitted to learn anything. It is one thing, of course, for scholars and critics to make plump careers of writing articles on, say, Pasternak, Quasimodo, Joyce, Yeats, Tagore, and even Mao Tse-tung. But American poets, with a frequency that is dismal in proportion as it seems automatic—that is, conditioned—tend either to give up all hope of imaginative precision and delicacy altogether, as Ginsberg in his "Howl" or Freeman in his *Apollonian Poems,* or to regard all deviation from the iambic rhetoric of the British tradition as an absurdity when it fails or as a crime akin to parricide when it succeeds. Whitman patiently suggested the exploration of traditions beyond the British; but, as Hart Crane complained with terrible despair in one of his greatest letters, many people won't even read *Democratic Vistas.*

Perhaps the reading of such a work, endangering as it does the trite and completely false public image of Whitman which still persists in America despite the Beats' attempt to appropriate him, requires a courage which few men are willing to assume—a courage akin to Whitman's own. In any case, Gary

Snyder has displayed a courage of similar kind, not in order to face Whitman's devastating and perhaps unsurpassed criticism of America's puritanical materialism; but in order to undertake one of the tasks of the imagination for which Whitman often felt poets in America should prove most capable: the exploration of living traditions which, shunning the British tradition, nonetheless display powers of poetry which equal and sometimes surpass that tradition; and to make this search for the purpose of claiming America itself—by which I mean literally our own lives and the people and places we live among day by day—for the imagination.

I have discussed the Chinese poets at some length in this essay because they mean so much to Mr. Snyder, and because they reveal in their own work the possibility of a further growth in American poetry which has scarcely been considered. My final impression of Mr. Snyder himself, however, does not depend on his debt to this or that writer.

What matters most to me is that Snyder has been able to live his daily life with the full power of his imagination awake to all the details of that life. A civilized and educated man, he is at his most sensitive and intelligent when he is writing about loggers, sailors, and animals. He has a poem which deals movingly with the moment when surveying the clutter of American life, he seems to decide to put off ambition and to be true to the imagination. The poem is called "Nooksack Valley." The poet has been sitting in a berry-picker's cabin, "at the end of a far trip north," and meditates on his American life so far, and on his possible future:

> . . . a week and I go back
> Down 99, through towns, to San Francisco and Japan.
> All America south and east,
> Twenty-five years in it brought to a trip-stop
> Mind-point, where I turn
> Caught more on this land—rock tree and man,
> Awake, than ever before, yet ready to leave.
> damned memories,
> Whole wasted theories, failures and worse success,
> Schools, girls, deals, try to get in

To make this poem a froth, a pity,·
A dead fiddle for lost good jobs.
                    the cedar walls
Smell of our farm-house, half built in '35.
Clouds sink down the hills
Coffee is hot again. The dog
Turns and turns about, stops and sleeps.

In this poem, as in so many others, the poet meditates alone. His recording of solitude in his poems is another striking feature of his work, one which makes it rather unusual in recent American poetry. American poets in recent years have tended to be like other Americans in shunning any experience which has to be undertaken alone.

Mr. Snyder has courage and an air of faithful patience. He keeps his voice low, not out of timidity but out of strength.

II

Some Notes on Chinese Poetry, a Sermon, and Four Interviews

Some Notes on Chinese Poetry

It is curious and haunting to me that there should be so much poetry in the world which matters so much to me, and that it is written in a language that I do not know and will probably never know. I have to leave the Chinese language to those who are competent to deal with it. Still, I am willing to accept the authority of the translators who have presented what seem to me real poems in English.

In these translations I find a pleasantness and a precision attractive in themselves. But these features don't account for the deep appeal that Chinese poetry has for me, and I believe, for many other Americans at this time.

That deeper appeal rests on at least two things: the power of the Chinese poets to record vivid human personality, both their own and that of the persons of whom they sometimes write. The first kind of expressive personality I find, for example, in the poems of Po Chu-i, most extensively translated by Arthur Waley. The second kind, which embodies and reveals another person within the poet's own poem, is most strikingly revealed in Kenneth Rexroth's translation of Lu Yi's poem, "The Wild Flower Man" (see Rexroth's *One Hundred Poems From the Chinese*, p. 103).

But the deeper appeal of the Chinese poets rests on some-

From a talk delivered at a conference on "Chinese Poetry and the American Imagination" given by the Academy of American Poets in April 1977, and published in *E.N.V.O.Y.* (Spring/Summer 1981).

thing at once more general and more particular. I would call it the capacity to feel—to experience human emotion, whether the occasion of that emotion be a great public event, a disaster, or the most intimate private event or scene. Living as we do in a time when our imaginations have been threatened with numbness and our moral beings nearly shattered by the moral ghastliness of public events and private corruptions, we turn naturally—and necessarily, I believe—to a tradition of poetry like the Chinese. However they differ in time and place, they share an abiding radiance, a tenderness for places and persons and for other living creatures. They seem to have saved their souls in the most violent circumstances. Our need to do the same is literally a matter of life and death. I turn to a poet who stated the issue as fully and truly as any poet I know:

> The subject is indeed important! For the human mind is capable of being excited without the application of gross and violent stimulants; and he must have a very faint perception of its beauty and dignity who does not know this, and who does not further know, that one being is elevated above another in proportion as he possesses this capability. It has therefore appeared to me, that to endeavor to produce or enlarge this capability is one of the best services in which, at any period, a writer can be engaged; but this service, excellent at all times, is especially so at the present day. For a multitude of causes, unknown to former times, are now acting with a combined force to blunt the discriminating powers of the mind, and, unfitting it for all voluntary exertion, to reduce it to a state of almost savage torpor. The most effective of these causes are the great national events which are daily taking place, and the increasing accumulation of men in cities, where the uniformity of their occupations produces a craving for extraordinary incident which the rapid communication of intelligence hourly gratifies. To this tendency of life and manners the literature and theatrical exhibitions of the country have conformed themselves . . . and, reflecting upon the magnitude of the general evil, I should be oppressed with no dishonorable melancholy, had I not a deep impression of certain inherent and indestructible qualities of the human mind, and likewise of certain powers in the great and permanent objects that act upon it, which are equally inherent, and indestructible . . . (Wordsworth)

A shiver goes over me when I read those words; they seem to me so shockingly true of my own time and place. All the more reason for me to turn to the Chinese poets, who have had a long history of violence and confusion, and who seem always able, come hell or high water, to keep human feeling alive and to increase its range through the imagination. Time and again these poets can deal with the most commonplace of scenes and occasions, and to fill them with clear feeling and with the light of the imagination. I will conclude with one short example, a poem at once typical and amazing:

In Passing an Old Friend's Farm

An old friend has prepared a chicken and millet dumpling
And invited me to his home in the fields.
Green trees surround his village on every side,
Blue hills slope away outside the wall.
At the open window the kitchen garden faces me.
We drink wine and talk of mulberry and flax;
Wait till the ninth day of the ninth moon,
I will come again to sample your chrysanthemum wine.

(—Meng Hao-Jan,
  translated by Soame Jenyns,
  *Selections from the Three Hundred
  Poems of the T'ang Dynasty*)

Of Things Invisible

1. The text is the ninth chapter of the Gospel according to Saint John.
   A. John is to my mind the dark lyric poet of the Gospels. Cf. the opening of his account on the word. The Word as God.
   B. Yet he is not an ornamental poet, His chs. short, his words blunt. Not blunted, but sharp.
   C. His accounts of Jesus' life, episode by episode are more brief than those of the other three who, in their way, were more skillful storytellers. Surely he could not match Luke, whom Shaw calls "the literary artist."
2. Yet in John's account there is a ferocity of swiftness, a clear mind almost pouncing in medias res upon the meaning of Jesus' most complex actions. In John, as in Jesus himself, I have always sensed something that could almost be called a contempt for false rhetoric.
   A. That is an old story. Socrates vs. the Sophists.
3. In John, nine, we come upon three human beings who share one impulse: a ferociously clear intellect, which is impatient with ornamental language, which by its nature is designed by false teachers to conceal truth, which in turn appears first as we all appear first—naked and ignorant and alone. The three are John, Jesus, and the man blind from his birth.

Notes on a sermon on the Gospel of Saint John delivered at the Methodist Church, Malden, New York on April 27, 1969.

126

4. These three, a trinity of impatient men, impatient with sophistry, all three dark and brooding thinkers, all three skeptical of abstruse toyings with plain fact, all three characterized by the power of simply being present at the event of the physical senses, share, surely, as men, the right to claim the same claim Whitman made: "I was the man. I suffered. I was there."

   A. And where were they? They were in the presence of a miracle.

Digression: The miracles of Jesus always strike me as being casual and intimate acts of personal friendship. The first was at the marriage of some young people. His mother was with him, in Cana, and she remarked, offhand, that the hosts had run out of wine. He told the servants to fill the jars with water, and so everybody had enough wine to drink. I share G. K. Chesterton's delight in this first of the miracles. The whole account, as St. John describes it, is private. Jesus made no display of performance. In fact, he remarked to the bridegroom, "Everyone else serves the best wine first and after the guests have drunk alot he serves the ordinary wine. But you have kept the best until now."

"Jesus performed this first of his mighty works in Cana of Galilee; there he revealed his glory, and his disciples believed in him."

And the final line in this account of Jesus' first miracle is perfect in tone and touch:

"After this, Jesus and his mother, brothers, and disciples went to Capernaum, and stayed there a few days."

What we have come to think of as the miracles are evidently the casual, offhand gestures of kindness which a man, sympathetic by nature, tends to make toward his intimate friends. De la musique avant tout chose. Privacy above all else.

Surely the plainest evidence of Jesus' distaste for sensationalistic advertising is his rejections of the temptations in the wilderness. He was not interested in conning the suckers.

5. "Why, who makes much of a miracle?" asked Whitman. "As for me, I know of nothing else but miracles." I think those lines reasonably suggest the attitude of Jesus toward the man blind from his birth.

   A. A miracle took place, surely. Plenty of people have

been born blind, and we have all seen them. They sit
and beg. What in the hell else are they to do? Inherit
Bloomingdales? Jesus sees the man, because the dis-
ciples have drawn the man to his attention during a
walk. And, as usual, they ask him (they were silly like
us; their gift survives it all) to give some metaphysical
discourse in order to account for a plain fact which
anybody can see with his own eyes. The disciples ask,
"Teacher, whose sin was it that caused him to be
born blind? His own or his parents' sin?"

B. I have always loved that question. It makes me feel
like a disciple. It is a silly question, the kind that I
would have asked: a question whose answer is al-
ready obvious. And time and again, Jesus' answer
has made me laugh with great delight. His powers of
sarcasm are I trust clear enough. But all he said was:
"His blindness has nothing to do with his sins or his
parents' sins. He is blind so that God's power might
be seen at work in him."

C. Then the famous miracle occurs. Jesus rubs a little
mud on the blind man's eyes, directs him to the pool
of Siloam. "So the man went, washed his face, and
came back seeing."

D. But the famous miracles are so often merely acts of
personal friendship. Again and again, Jesus seems
annoyed at the suggestion, explicit or implied, that
his concrete gestures of personal friendship be given
a rousing hullaballoo from the housetops. I suspect
he must have found such suggestions more than a
little boring. To him, a miracle must have seemed
the most natural thing in the world.

6. But there is something else in this little episode in Jesus'
ministry which is truly miraculous. It is the astonishment
of the blind man himself. And, if St. John speaks true, it
was not the opening of his eyes which astonished the man
who had been born blind. What seems to have startled him
was the reaction of the Pharisees.

A. Now, these were no Birchite illiterates. I remind you
that St. Paul, no less, had once been a Pharisee. A

man thoroughly learned in the law, and in languages. The learned men who investigated the healing of the blind man were not fools. They proceeded in a way which I can respect. I mean no sarcasm when I saw that they were plainly men who could see a good deal more than other people could see because they had studied more deeply than others had done. And they themselves, unless I misread St. John's brief chapter, are the miracle, the authentic miracle, in the present case. They could see everything except what was right in front of their eyes. The story is familiar enough, and I need not recount how the Pharisees, whose political power certainly exceeded that of Dr. Hoover, and at least equaled that of the Schutzstaffell, grilled the parents and neighbors of the blind man; how, at last, out of a perfectly comprehensible fear, everybody sent the Pharisees to the healed man himself.

7. But I want to draw your attention to the order of miracles which the blind man assigns on his own. It is clear in every text of the New Testament I have ever consulted that at the moment when Jesus healed the man of his blindness the man had no idea who it was who healed him. The text is plain.

"So the Pharisees asked the man once more, "you say he opened your eyes—well, what do you say about him?"

"He is a prophet," he answered. . . .

A second time they called him back, the man who had been born blind, and said to him, "Promise before God that you will tell the truth! We know that this is a sinner."

"I do not know if he is a sinner or not," the man replied. "One thing I do know: I was blind, and now I see."

"What did he do to you?" they asked. "How did he open your eyes?"

"I have already told you," he answered, "and you would not listen. Why do you want to hear it again? Maybe you, too, would like to be his disciples?"

They cursed him and said, "You are that fellow's disciple; we are Moses' disciples; as for that fellow, we do not even know where he comes from!"

The man answered, "What a strange thing this is! You do not know where he comes from, but he opened my eyes. We know that God does not listen to sinners; he does listen to people who respect him and do what he wants them to do. Since the beginning of the world it has never been heard of that someone opened the eyes of a man born blind; unless this man came from God, he would not be able to do a thing."

(Here, give the Pharisees' reply in the King James version, with its coiling sneer.) They answered back, "you were born and raised in sin—are you trying to teach us?"

8. They cast him out. What did they cast him out from? It was their flawless self-assurance. There is a flaming scimitar of lightning that swings from one side of Jesus' body, and it is the clear blade of comedy. He hated no man, and sinners, who are you and me, delighted him. I believe with all my heart and with all my soul and with all my mind, such as it is, that the man born blind was delighted by the blindness of the Pharisees. They are not to be scorned. But they are funny. They knew everything except what stared straight into their faces.

"I have never seen a man who was fully awake," wrote Thoreau in his Journal. "How could I have looked him in the face?"

What Jesus says to the puzzled Pharisees is plain enough:

"Some Pharisees who were with him, . . . asked him, "You don't mean that we are blind too?"

Jesus answered, "If you were blind, then you would not be guilty; but since you say, 'we can see,' that means that you are still guilty."

Here read *Paradise Lost* III, lines 1–55:

Hail, holy Light, ofspring of Heav'n first-born,
Or of th' Eternal Coeternal beam

May I express thee unblam'd? since God is Light,
And never but in unapproached Light
Dwelt from Eternitie, dwelt then in thee,
Bright effluence of bright essence increate.
Or hear'st thou rather pure Ethereal stream,
Whose Fountain who shall tell? before the Sun,
Before the Heav'ns thou wert, and at the voice
Of God, as with a Mantle, didst invest
The rising world of waters dark and deep,
Won from the void and formless infinite.
Thee I re-visit now with bolder wing,
Escap't the *Stygian* Pool, though long detaind
In that obscure sojourn, while in my flight
Through utter and through middle darkness borne
With other notes than to th' *Orphean* Lyre
I sung of *Chaos* and *Eternal Night,*
Taught by the heav'nly Muse to venture down
The dark descent, and up to reascend,
Though hard and rare: thee I revisit safe,
And feel thy sovran vital Lamp; but thou
Revisit'st not these eyes, that rowle in vain
To find thy piercing ray, and find no dawn:
So thick a drop serene hath quencht thir Orbs,
Or dim suffusion veild. Yet not the more
Cease I to wander where the Muses haunt
Cleer Spring, or shadie Grove, or Sunnie Hill,
Smit with the love of sacred Song; but chief
Thee *Sion* and the flowrie Brooks beneath
That wash thy hallowd feet, and warbling flow,
Nightly I visit: nor somtimes forget
Those other two equald with me in Fate,
So were I equald with them in renown,
Blind *Thamyris* and blind *Maeonides,*
And *Tiresias* and *Phineus* Prophets old:
Then feed on thoughts, that voluntarie move
Harmonious numbers; as the wakeful Bird
Sings darkling, and in shadiest Covert hid
Tunes her nocturnal Note. Thus with the Year
Seasons return; but not to mee returns
Day, or the sweet approach of Ev'n or Morn,
Or sight of vernal bloom, or Summers Rose,
Or flocks, or herds, or human face divine;

But cloud instead, and ever-during dark
Surrounds me, from the chearful waies of men
Cut off, and for the Book of knowledg fair
Presented with a Universal blanc
Of Natures works to mee expung'd and ras'd,
And wisdom at one entrance quite shut out.
So much the rather thou Celestial Light
Shine inward, and the mind through all her powers
Irradiate; there plant eyes, all mist from thence
Purge and disperse, that I may see and tell
Of things invisible to mortal sight.

I will ask you to close your eyes and share with me a prayer
written by a blind Irish poet, Conaught O'Riordan:

Dear God, though Thy all-powerful hand
Should so direct my earthly fate
That I may seem unfortunate
To them who do not understand
That all things follow Thy decree,
Staunchly I'll bear whate'er's Thy will—
Praying Thee but to grant me still
That none shall come to harm through me;
For, God, although Thou knowest all,
I am too young to comprehend
The windings to my journey's end;
    I fear upon the road to fall,
    In the worst sin of all that be
    And thrust my brother in the sea.

—*Come Hither*

An Interview with Michael André

Michael André: Stephen Stepanchev has described your poetry as 'deep image', that is, he feels a prime element is images which appeal to subconscious feelings. Did you think that was an accurate description?

Wright: I think it was an accurate description of some experiments that I was making for myself, at a certain time. But these experiments were related to translations I was making. A few years ago when I met Robert Bly, I felt that, for myself, a certain kind of poetry had come to an end, and I thought that I would stop writing poetry completely. Poetry has to be a possibility. Or we're dead, I think. Robert Bly suggested to me that there is a kind of poetry that can be written. People have written it in some other languages. He said it might be possible to come back to our own language through reading them and translating them, and I think that in one sense this has been the value of translation. It lead me into some areas of thought, and of rhythm also, that I hadn't tried to work out before.

M.A.: How did you meet Bly?

Wright: I was back living in Minneapolis. Robert lived and still lives on a farm in western Minnesota. I received the first copy of his magazine about the time I felt depressed about the work that I was trying to do. What I did was write him—let's see, I

Unmuzzled Ox 1, no. 2 (February 1972).

wrote him two letters. There were sixteen pages, as I recall, single space, in two days, and he just answered, "Well, come out to the farm." As soon as I got out there, it turned out that we were two of the very few people in the United States who had ever heard of Georg Trakl.

M.A.: I hadn't heard of him until I read your work.

Wright: Well, I had attended a series of lectures given by Dr. Eugene Susini at the University of Vienna a few years earlier, and I had made many notes about Trakl, and I had his *Collected Poems*, but only a couple of other people I'd met knew about Trakl, and I didn't know how to make some practical sense out of his poetry, his great original imagination. It turned out that Bly felt the same way, and we began work on our Trakl translation the very first time we met.

M.A.: That's how the traditional forms of your first two books dropped from your work?

Wright: I don't think I've dropped traditional forms. That is, I tried in some later poems to make further experiments in the formal possibilities of the American language. But I think that all poetry is formal. Images are always fairly sparing; I've never written a richly metaphorical poetry. My own ideal, which I've tried to accommodate to whatever abilities I have, is really a neo-classical one. I believe in the kind of poem which does have a single effect, and I try to subordinate whatever I know about language to one single effect, every time.

What we like about some poems, the poetry of someone like Cid Corman, is the clarity and precision of language which is able to embody something which is finally mysterious. Here is the genius of Creeley, too. The poets we continue to care about are the poets who in their poetry can embody a kind of mystery. That doesn't mean that their poems are vague. On the contrary. Cid Corman is probably the most precise and clear poet alive. His clarity is what makes him so mysteriously alive.

M.A.: Apropos other poets, you attended the University of Washington. Did you have much contact with Roethke there?

Wright: Yes, we were good friends for about four years there.

M.A.: You did your undergraduate studies at Kenyon. Did you start writing poetry before you went to Kenyon?

Wright: Oh, I had written a few things when I was in the army. I tried to write poems seriously when I was at Kenyon. I still think Ransom is a great poet and teacher.

M.A.: Do you feel Ransom influenced your work in a way comparable to Bly?

Wright: I wouldn't say he influenced it directly through his poetry—it was indirectly through his teaching. Actually, Ransom has a wonderful rhythmic imagination. He told me last spring when I went to see him—he's an old man now—that he is a great fan of Robert Bly's. And the reason for that is that Robert among other things has presented some major questions about—well, this is a work that Bly hates, but about prosody—about the rhythmical possibilities of the American language, and all the things that flow into it. American is a wonderful language because it is so open to all kinds of influence. All we need is someone intelligent enough to bring these influences to a focus, and then apply them to our lives.

You're a Canadian, aren't you, Michael? You didn't read the same kind of sentimental history books that I read when I was a boy, but in one of those books we were told the story of a man named Nolan, "the man without a country." Now, he said once, "Damn the United States. I hope I may never hear of the United States again." Today, what would I say? If you meet anyone on the street and ask him what he thinks of America, he as like as not will say to you, not "Damn the United States. I wish I may never hear of the United States again." He would be more likely to say, "Are you kidding? America sucks!"

The pungency of the language has clarified itself.

M.A.: You taught in Canada last summer. What do you think of Canadian poetry?

Wright: I think Canadian poetry is beautiful, and there are three phases of it. The French poetry, poetry like the poetry of Anne Hébert, is very clean and also very strange. It has powerful classical structure to it and the language is very precise. Also we have poets like Frank Scott and A. J. M. Smith who are also classicists. Along with this there has been a hospitality among Canadian poets like Irving Layton that has enabled them to welcome the poetry, the wonderful original poetry of people like Robert Creeley and Denise Levertov and Gary Snyder. Those poets are very popular up there, and justifiably so, and they're welcome because of the influence I think of someone like Irving Layton.

Canada is a very exciting place for poetry.

M.A.: What do you think of Confessional poetry?

Wright: Oh, I'm getting tired of people telling me about their operations. I've got enough operations of my own. Oh, not really. No, it turns into a pain in the ass after a while. "Let me tell you about my hemorrhoids."

By the way, you're going to edit this, aren't you? This is horrible. I'm bound to say a lot of ghastly things.

M.A.: You can trust me, Jim. Don't worry about anything.

Wright: Let me repeat though that in Montreal, which is one Canadian city, a considerable city, I think a great city, the students and teachers and people whom you meet throughout the town are very hospitable to poetry. This isn't always true in the United States. It seems to me that there is a more direct living connection between poetry and ordinary life in Canada than in the United States.

M.A.: What have you been writing recently?

Wright: Well, what I just finished is a new translation from the German of Herman Hesse. My son and I worked together on that. It's called *Wandering,* in German *Wanderlung.* Hesse had written a number of articles attacking the Junkers in Germany, and he was finally told—well, as Amos was told in the Old Testament by the priest Emaziah "Why don't you go elsewhere and prophesy? Go out of the country and prophesy." The book is a travel book about his experiences in Switzerland moving south toward Italy, after he was politely ejected from Germany. The book consists of water colors, prose pieces and poems.

M.A.: You also did a translation of Theodor Storm which struck me as very unlike your translations of poetry, more serious and scholarly.

Wright: Yes. Well, I'm an academic person after all. I'm very devoted to Storm. And to a certain kind of imagination that he had.

M.A.: You also expressed affection occasionally for people like Shadwell and Longfellow whom nobody reads and consequently nobody knows honestly whether they're good or not.

Wright: That's an odd question. I mean, it's an interesting statement. I must say that you haven't asked me this, but my favorite poet in the world is Edward Thomas. You don't know him? Well, you should. He's an English poet from World War I who wrote beautifully about nature—he's able to write about nature with a sense of the religious value of things, the life of the spirit. He wrote only a few poems and was killed in World War I. He is my favorite poet.

M.A.: Your The Branch Will not Break *has a most intense love of nature. Was that particularly true of that period of your life?*

Wright: Yes.

M.A.: I thought you described yourself much better than Stepanchev in your introduction to Far from the Madding Crowd, *simply a lover of natural things, which unfortunately I came upon only yesterday.*

Wright: Well, this is what the poems were about. Are you saying that you were confused?

M.A.: I was confused. I was trying to find surrealistic . . .

Wright: This is something that should be clarified in our discussion of poetry. We have been used to interpreting poetry so much that we've been in danger of losing our ability to respond to it directly. There's a poem of mine called "Lying in a Hammock at William Duffy's Farm . . ."

M.A.: A great poem.

Wright: People have been outraged by this, absolutely outraged, because they think the last line of it is immoral. The last line is not immoral. The poem is only descriptive—or as my friend from Calcutta would say, it's an evocative poem. All I did was describe what I felt and what I saw lying there in the hammock. Shouldn't that be enough? But oh no, there's your American every time—God damn it, somebody's got to draw a moral.

M.A.: Could you read the poem?

Wright: The only moral poem that I've ever read is "The Shooting of Dan McGrew," by Robert W. Service.

Actually I can tell you one thing that's behind this, because I think that our responses to nature or to anything can be educated and sharpened and refined by poets whom we've read, and when I wrote this poem, I wasn't particularly thinking about the Chinese poets, more specifically the translations of Arthur Waley, that very great man. But I can see that Arthur Waley sort of hovers over this poem and guided me, and guided me in responding to what happened that afternoon. It's simply this—

Lying in a Hammock at William Duffy's Farm
in Pine Island, Minnesota

Over my head, I see the bronze butterfly,
Asleep on the black trunk,
Blowing like a leaf in green shadow.
Down the ravine behind the empty house,
The cowbells follow one another
Into the distances of the afternoon.
To my right,
In a field of sunlight between two pines,
The droppings of last year's horses
Blaze up into golden stones.
I lean back, as the evening darkens and comes on.
A chicken hawk floats over, looking for home.
I have wasted my life.

M.A.: The last line is . . .

Wright: It infuriates people. I don't understand that at all.

M.A.: The last line is present sublimally in the earlier images, almost coded into the images.

Wright: And how are you going to describe your feelings? Let me ask you, Michael. If you're going to describe how you feel. How would you actually describe your feelings? Don't you have to reach out to the things that are around you? You can either do that or sit there and say ugh. The English were infuriated because they thought the last line of that poem was supposed to be a moral. Why have a poem with a goddamn moral in it? 'I have wasted my life'—well, that's the way I happened to feel at the moment. Actually, I haven't wasted my life.

M.A.: I was going to ask you about that.

Wright: I don't think so.

M.A.: You've written a lot of melancholy poems though.

Wright: I'm a masochist. Well—I like melancholy. Poor wicked miserable me, how miserable I am.

Annie Wright, his wife: You like suffering.

Wright: I like to suffer. You might remember W. H. Auden's wonderful little poem called "The Adolescent's Song," in *The Age of Anxiety*, and the refrain is "Poor wicked miserable me, how interesting I am."

Now, listen, you were asking me about Edward Thomas. Let me say a poem by Edward Thomas, and I'll tell you why I love him. I think you'll recognize what I meant. And I am serious about that. I'm not saying that Edward Thomas is a great poet. He's not Aeschylus, he's not Shakespeare, he's not Neruda.

Well, neither am I. Who is? And there's a sense in which one ought to be able to say, who has to be? We should be able to listen to people's music for its own sake. Shall I say a poem of his? This is a poem I love:

> There's nothing like the sun, as the year dies,
> Kind as it can be, this world being made so,
> To stones and men and beasts and birds and flies.
> To all things that it touches, except snow,
> Whether on mountainside or street of town,
> The south wall warms me. November has begun
> Yet never shone the sun so fair as now,
> When the sweet last left damsons from the bough
> With spangles of the morning storm drop down,
> Because the starling shakes it, whistling what
> Once swallows sang. But I have forgot
> That there is nothing too like March's sun
> Or April's or July's or June's or May's
> Or January's or February's great days.
> August, September, October and December
> Have equal days, all different from November.
>
> No day of any month but I have said
> Or, if I live long enough, should say
> "There's nothing like the sun that shines today."
> There's nothing like the sun till we are dead.

He wrote that in a trench in World War I, a muddy trench full of rain.

M.A.: What's it called?

Wright: "There's Nothing like the Sun." A holy man, I believe, a saintly man, Edward Thomas, without any great public reputation, but one of the secret spirits who help keep us alive. And let formal problems be damned to Hell. Edward Thomas shares a holiness with Louise Niedecker, Cid Corman, and Kenneth Rexroth. This is all we have, is it not? We have our internal life. Our external life is usually asinine, for Christ's sake.

For example, there is a ten percent surtax on imports, Hugo Black has just died, and Richard Nixon is the present president of the United States.

This is the ancient clutter of things.

Ah, but we have our inner life, do we not? We have what Virgil meant when he talked about the *lacrimae rerum,* the tears of things, the ancient pity of things. That pity is ancient. Nixon doesn't pity anything. But the inner life goes on. Poetry is absolutely essential in this age.

M.A.: I've often wondered why, since there are masses, literally masses of English students and would-be poets, why is it that Poetry, *for instance, isn't a mass magazine?*

Wright: You mean *Poetry—Poetry* of Chicago? I'm sure that I haven't read an issue of that in three years. Although I think that—no, *Poetry* has been a very important magazine, and I should say that the reason I haven't read it is that I haven't read much of anything. I read very few magazines any more. What I've been doing is reading in other languages and trying to write in my own. But the reason for that is some secret reason of my own which I suppose I myself don't understand. What has been going on in *Poetry?* You say they're only dealing with contemporary things?

M.A.: Why isn't it a mass magazine?

Wright: Well, it has tried to be, and it is, if you see it in a context of the whole world. For example, summer a year ago, Annie and I were in Yugoslavia. People are very aware of it there.

M.A.: Poetry?

Wright: *Poetry*—are you kidding? *Poetry Magazine.* Yugoslavia is a splendid place for poetry. The guy who drives you in a taxi, you know, will be a poet.

M.A.: Your own poetry seems to be emerging from an unjust neglect it suffered in the fifties and early sixties.

Wright: There was a problem at that time. People who were teaching in universities and were trying to write poetry were generally trying to write poetry which—I think it's called "the square poem." It always rhymes and so on. Further experiments in the rhythm of the language and also in the real precision of diction, and in the precision of rhythm were being carried on by people like Cid Corman, wonderful poet, very neglected. People didn't know one another. There was a restlessness in everyone in the fifties, and I suppose largely through the influence of Allen Ginsberg, who brought to poetry not only a great genius for language but a genius for human sympathy—I think under the influence of people like Ginsberg and Gary Snyder and Lawrence Ferlinghetti, who is somewhat ironic and reserved in a way but nevertheless brought to poetry a kind of welcome and sympathy, and enabled people to come to know one another and become aware of one another, I think that it enriched poetry very much. I feel much more easy and much more at home in the American language than I ever did before, just because of these people, because I got to know them.

M.A. An adjective some critics have used to describe your later poems is "relaxed."

Wright: Well, that's true in some of them, in some of them, not.

M.A.: I would have thought from your essay on Whitman which appeared in the early sixties that you disliked Ginsberg and Ferlinghetti.

Wright: No. I thought at that time that they were trying to take off from Whitman directly, and were not bringing it off, and I did not realize that there was a great deal more going on in them. Now, take Ferlinghetti—when I wrote the essay on Whitman, I didn't mention Ferlinghetti in it, but at that time I had never really read his poetry, and I didn't come to it and come really to understand it until I met him in Portland, Oregon at the beginning of one of the antiwar readings. I got a chance to hear him. And now he's become one of my very favorite poets. I wasn't able to understand his poetry until he taught me how to listen to it; that's the value of his readings and his recordings. He can teach you how to read it and then you can go on and read it yourself, and you hear what is in America a new rhythm.

I had the same kind of experience with some of the others. I like Snyder, first of all. There's a beautiful, magnificent tragic rhythm in Ginsberg, and one is not going to understand that until he comes to read "Kaddish." One can be startled by a poem like "Howl," and one can be delighted by a poem like "America," for example, but one doesn't understand the greatness of Ginsberg until he reads "Kaddish" and realizes that "Kaddish" is a much more orthodox, tragic poem than anyone can imagine. It's not merely a poem about his mother, although it is that. It's about everybody's mother. It's about everybody's despair, everybody's grief over the dead. It's a very great poem. But it takes a while to catch up to that after all, and why not? I can't help it. I love that poem, as long as I go on learning.

The split between the Beats and the academics at the end of the fifties was fruitless, but I suppose it was inevitable.

M.A.: Ginsberg and Richard Howard seem to have renewed the debate in The New York Times *last spring.*

Wright: I didn't think that amounted to much. That was just a rehash. It didn't lead anywhere. They're both intelligent men, but I don't think that the debate meant much in terms of the real poems. Do you? What did it amount to?

M.A.: Howard upheld a "poetry of excellence" whereas Ginsberg upheld a "poetry of ecstasy."

Wright: Well, Hell, they do agree that the poetry of excellence is inevitably going to be a poetry of ecstasy.

M.A.: But many important writers "of ecstasy," such as McClure, continue to be neglected.

Wright: O.K. Another is Brother Antoninus. Nobody ever gives him a tumble and yet he's a fine poet. We ought to get away from the idea of awards, and try to help one another in a really difficult way, trying to get real poetry going. The occasion was that the National Book Award was given to what's-her-name—whoever it was—and it just seemed too academic, and stodgy for Ginsberg. The value of a poet's work is going to depend on the truth of the language and the truth of his life. I think that both Ginsberg and Howard were just very much off the point in that whole argument. It's a rather asinine discussion, as I say, by two intelligent men.

M.A.: Who'd you rather be?

Wright: W. C. Fields or Herman Melville. There's your America every time. Herman Melville's wife wrote somebody, "Herman's started to write poetry but don't tell anybody." Well, here we are, they're both dead. Would you rather be dead and remembered as Herman Melville, or Richard Watson Gilder?

M.A.: Richard?

Wright: Well, that answers my question. Melville just let people go on assuming that he was dead. And yet during that time, he wrote some of his very best things, including his poetry.

It's possible through poetry, I hope, to contribute oneself to the continuity of life, and also to surrender one's own egotism to the larger movement of things. It may not even be a hope.

Edward Thomas was wounded and sent back to England and told, since he was a university man, that he could stay in England with his wound, with his wife and three daughters and write beautiful poems. He could stay there with himself.

"No," he said, "I can't stand the idea of those illiterate Cockneys in my company stumbling around in the mud of France." So he went back to be with them. Did that do any good? Probably not, unless you consider an act like that to be good in itself. And if a thing isn't good in itself, what is good?

M.A.: I keep looking for what I take to be development in your poetry . . .

Wright: I wouldn't look for it. I think I knew pretty well what I was going to do from the beginning. I was just trying to find out ways to do it. As for the different kinds of form, I call it just a continuous exploration.

M.A.: One change in content to me was, in your first two books, you tended to pick a tragic outsider for subject, such as a murderer. In your next two volumes, the outsiders were more humorous, such as the Sioux brave.

Wright: He wasn't so humorous. It really happened. You go back to Minneapolis and somebody will come up to you and say, "I am a Sioux brave." Yes. "I am a Sioux brave, can you let me have $2.50 for a cup of coffee?"

M.A.: Are those Minneapolis poems from the beginning of Shall We Gather at the River *all taken from life?*

Wright: The one in the drunk tank and "In Terror of Hospital Bills," yes, that's right. I didn't have enough money to pay a hospital bill, and it's very frightening. And the one about not being able to pay my bill at, what the Hell's name of that department store in Minneapolis? Of course, I got out of that

very easily, but I realized after their fish eye that there were a
lot of people who weren't going to go back as a professor at a
university. As Huck Finn's father said, "He was a professor at a
college." There are plenty of people who can't do that, and I
just got a flash of that, in the moment. And it's no goddamn
joke, to have people look at you like that.

M.A.: There's the great mythic outsider in "In Memory of Leopardi."

Wright: I wouldn't know how to talk about it. I'll read it. Leo-
pardi is a great romantic Italian poet, a master of the language.
He was a hunch-back. He devoted his life very intensely to
books and to his own personal grief. He was an academic, and
among the great poets, and yet there was a terrible thing that
happened in his life. He was in love with a beautiful aristocratic
woman, and she turned away from him. After he died, a young
woman who sort of worshipped him as a great poet said to the
lady, "How could you turn away from such a great man?" And
her answer was, "My dear, he stank."

He was perfectly aware of that. In his great poem "The
Song of the Aging Shepherd":

I've gone wondering out here telling my agony.

That poem is very much behind this:

In Memory of Leopardi

I have gone past all those times when the poets
Were beautiful as only
The rich can be. The cold bangles
Of the moon grazed one of my shoulders,
And so to this day,
And beyond, I carry
The sliver of a white city, the barb of a jewel
In my left clavicle that hunches.
Tonight I sling
A scrambling sack of oblivions and lame prayers
On my right good arm. The Ohio River

Has flown by me twice, the dark jubilating
Isaiah of mill and smoke marrow. Blind son
Of a meadow of huge horses, lover of drowned islands
Above Steubenville, blind father
Of my halt grey wing:
Now I limp on, knowing
The moon strides behind me, swinging
The scimitar of the divinity that struck down
The hunchback in agony
When he saw her, naked, carrying away his last sheep
Through the Asian rocks.

*M.A.: That introduction of Steubenville is the same device central to
"As I step over a Puddle at the End of Winter, I think of an Ancient
Chinese Governor."*

Wright: No, it's not a device.

M.A.: That method.

Wright: It's just an understanding. Now, look, you've read
John Keats, haven't you? Do you like him?

M.A.: Keats, yes.

Wright: All right—now, who is more alive, John Keats or Rich-
ard M. Nixon? Who is more truly alive? And this idea was
spelled out with great force in the *Summa Contra Gentiles* by
Aquinas, and Aquinas there argued and demonstrated, and I
think demonstrated with great poetic force and also with com-
plete clear logic, that time and eternity are not the same. Some-
times they intersect, and when they intersect, we get poetry
rising out of them. But they're not necessarily the same. "The
logical conclusion is not enough to prove it to you," he'll say;
then he'll say as evidence, "take the people you love, because
love is the only device of understanding."
   Who lives longer, John Keats or Mario Proccacino?
   When you talk about the length of life, the length of life is
just the assumption that life is linear. It's not necessarily linear.

It's expansive too. We know this. Time and eternity are not the same. It's possible for a man to live forever in a split second. It's possible for someone to live eighty-five years and not get a prayer of what it's about.

Now, this is a theological argument, but it's also a logical argument and a psychological argument. Hence, why not bring these people together? Where is Yuan Chen?

I ask that because Po Chui, whom I love, cared about that, and if he cared about it, I care.

M.A.: Where was Yuan Chen? Was he dead?

Wright: They were very close friends but Yuan Chen had been exiled. Po Chui was told in Chang-an that if he made it to a certain place in the town of Chu Ko, and he got on the boat, then he could go up the river and become governor. If he didn't make it and stayed in Chang-an he would get his head cut off. He made the boat in time, but the wind was blowing in the wrong direction, and he wrote a great poem about that, beautiful—

> White billows and huge waves
> Block the river crossing.
> Wherever I go, danger and difficulty.
> Whatever I do, failure.
> Just as in my worldly career,
> I wander and lose the road
> So when I come to the river crossing
> I am blocked by contrary winds.
> Of fishes and prawns
> Sadden in the rain
> The smell fills my nostrils.
> With the sting of insects that come with the fog,
> My whole body is sore.
> I am growing old.
> Time flies past,
> And my short life runs out
> While I sit in a boat at Chu Ko
> Wasting ten days.

A great man, Po Chui. He came to a place partway up there and he found a poem written on a wall by Yuan Chen, who was his beloved childhood friend, and it was directed to him. Someone had partly erased it. Po Chui, dead these many years—ah, he's not dead.

Agnew is dead.

What we've got to reach in America is some understanding of the great Chinese. I resent this goddamn country, because we keep turning great things over to trivial people—Nixon.

M.A.: Do you like O'Hara and the New York School?

Wright: Yes, I like O'Hara especially. But my favorite poet among the people who are associated there together is John Ashbery. He's done beautiful things, and I think nobody has shown proper appreciation of what he's about. He had a prose poem addressed to, of all people, John Clare. You know John Clare? One of the insane Romantic poets of the early nineteenth century—he lived up to the 1860s. He wrote most of his poems in an insane asylum and yet he is a great nature poet. You don't know John Clare? Listen you really should. These people are spiritual sources.

> I lost the love of heaven above
> I spurned the lust of earth below,
> I felt the sweets of fancied love
> And Hell itself my only foe.
> I loved, but woman fell away.
> I hid me from her faded flame,
> I snatched the sun's eternal ray
> And wrote till earth was but a name.
> In every language upon earth,
> By every shore on every sea
> I gave my name immortal birth
> And kept my spirit with the free.

John Clare, out in the woods somewhere, in a hospital, where they tried to take care of him—they didn't know quite what to do.

Now, John Ashbery, whom people think of as just an urban poet, just an exquisite poet, has a depth in him, wonderful depth. He presents himself with the mask of the Frenchified writer. And yet underneath this, every once in a while, will come something amazingly fresh and natural.

Something to Be Said for the Light

A Conversation with William Heyen
and Jerome Mazzaro

The following conversation with James Wright took place at the State University College, Brockport, New York on September 24, 1970. Discussing Wright's work with him are two widely published poets and critics of modern poetry, William Heyen (SUNY at Brockport) and Jerome Mazzaro (SUNY at Buffalo). At Heyen's request, Wright begins their discussion with a reading of his poem "To a Defeated Saviour":

Wright:

To a Defeated Saviour

Do you forget the shifting hole
Where the slow swimmer fell aground
And floundered for your fishing pole
Above the snarl of string and sound?
You never seem to turn your face
Directly toward the river side,
Or up the bridge, or anyplace
Near where the skinny swimmer died.

You stand all day and look at girls,
Or climb a tree, or change a tire;
But I have seen the colored swirls
Of water flow to livid fire

Ed. Joseph R. McElrath, Jr., *Southern Humanities Review* 6, no. 2 (Spring 1972).

Across your sleeping nose and jaws,
Transfiguring both the bone and skin
To muddy banks and sliding shoals
You and the drowned kid tumble in.

You see his face, upturning, float
And bob across your wavering bed;
His wailing fingers call your boat,
His voice throws up the ruddy silt,
The bleary vision prays for light
In sky behind your frozen hands;
But sinking in the dark all night,
You charm the shore with bloomless wands.

The circling tow, the shadowy pool
Shift underneath us everywhere.
You would have raised him, flesh and soul,
Had you been strong enough to dare;
You would have lifted him to breathe,
Believing your good hands would keep
His body clear of your own death:
This dream, this drowning in your sleep.

W.H.: Mr. Wright, that poem is an early one, isn't it, from The
Green Wall? *I've noticed in reading the volumes following it that that
same theme—the idea of a failed saviour—keeps reappearing. Some
critics might almost call it an obsession. This is an impossible question, I
suppose, but to what do you attribute the particular kind of compassion
depicted in that poem? Could you explain it?*

Wright: Well, I don't know if I would call it compassion. Maybe
it's a sort of fear. I keep thinking, what good does it do in
America, which is very much my country, to try to help some-
one else? It seems that all of our great ethical ideals always
come to grief because, at least in part, our public figures take
our language away from us, erode its meaning, so that we can't
tell whether or not to trust other people when they make some
public gesture in language. We're left sort of scrambling
around in the dark, trying to help one another, and yet, being
afraid to. As people are afraid to help one another on the
streets.

W.H.: The main character of that poem then—if I can speak in fictional terms—is the observer, the speaker. He's not as much the defeated saviour as the man he's talking about. There's nothing he can do about the pain of the man's failure.

Wright: And it's a strange kind of pain to relate to. That poem really originated many years ago, when I was a boy. My brother had a small boat. He was fishing down on the Ohio River, and some kids were swimming right off-shore, and one of them got caught in what they call—a hideous Ohio phrase—a suck-hole. A whirlpool started where people had been dredging mud out of the river. My brother was just about twelve years old, and he wasn't a strong boy. And the kids on the bank kept yelling at him to jump in and save the boy who was drowning, and he didn't know what to do. He held his fishing pole out to the kid, and the kid tried to get hold of it but missed it, and sank.

J.M.: There's a similar sense of things captured in your second book, in the poem "At the Executed Murderer's Grave."

W.H.: You create thieves and murders and similar kinds of characters in your poems; and you have a deep feeling for them. There's a real concern, it seems to me, for these sad people that are down-and-out. You return to them again and again.

Wright: Yes, and this is the sort of thing that's started to get on some people's nerves—and it's starting to get on my nerves too. I'd rather be happy.

J.M.: I think it shows in some of your later poems. They are much stronger in terms of the possibilities of rescuing.

Wright: Yes. You know, this last summer Annie and I were having breakfast in Paris. While we were drinking our *café au lait,* we could hear a young American talking to a lady. Among other things, he said to her, "only people who suffer complete despair are going to have any hope." And as I overheard this snatch of conversation, I suddenly realized, yes, and how we love to wallow down there, in despair, don't we? It made me tired of many of my own writings, in a way.

J.M.: Tell me, when you came back from the army after World War II and went to Kenyon College, did you intend to become a poet then?

Wright: I had tried to write some things earlier. But it wasn't until I met John Crowe Ransom and some other teachers at Kenyon that I tried to put together poems more formally. I never took a course in writing as such. We read some great masters in English and a couple of languages other than English, and we had a good literary time. It was a very classical and disciplined kind of education.

W.H.: On the dust jacket of your first book, The Green Wall, *I think, you said that you were trying very hard to write in the mode of Robert Frost and Edwin Arlington Robinson, that you wanted to say something humanly important instead of just showing off with language. Did you have in mind then primarily a thematic importance—I think of the "Defeated Saviour" theme in this regard—or were you concerned with the mode of expression, the language?*

Wright: Well, during the few years after I left Kenyon, I was trying to learn how to write in what I call a classical way, and I wanted to subordinate whatever devices of language I could control to a single theme in each poem. Such a statement makes me sort of wince now. It sounds like what Howard Nemerov once said about such an aim: it's a little like being against sin; everyone would like to.

J.M.: But why would someone from Ohio, writing about things midwestern go to New England poets for his models?

Wright: Well, in the first place, Frost and Robinson are very much more than just New England poets. I like to think of Robinson as being one of the great poets of the dark side of American experience. And his language is very strict and clear.

J.M.: I mentioned this because it seems that as you treat Ohio more and more you tend to move away from Frost and Robinson in your poetry— as though you're finding a voice that is uniquely yours.

Wright: Maybe Ohio has its own rhythm. It's a strange place, Ohio. It's both northern and southern; it's eastern and western; all kinds of people live there. It's literally covered with good small colleges; and yet, the people who live in Ohio seem very uneducated, in many ways brutal. I like Ohioans very much.

W.H.: Could we return for a minute to that statement of yours in The Green Wall *about wanting to make poems say something humanly important? Looking back, does it seem to you that you were a bit too insistent or perhaps shrill? I ask this because in your later works you seem more willing to let the poems speak for themselves.*

Wright: That was a sort of Puritanical statement, wasn't it? There's a certain pompousness about it, it seems to me now.

W.H.: I suppose it's a young man's statement.

Wright: Like beating against the sand, or being virtuous. At any level one would like to be so if he only knew how.

W.H.: The Green Wall *was dedicated to two Teds. I take it that one of the Teds was Theodore Roethke. Can we talk for a minute about his influence on you, both personal and literary?*

Wright: Roethke was a very liberating teacher. His knowledge of English and American poetry was fantastic, and he believed very much in getting poems by heart in the old-fashioned way. I took only one course from him—it lasted just a semester—but I knew him for about four years there in Seattle. As a person he was very complex and, in many ways, very simple. In some ways even simpleminded. He was always stimulating, and he was such a genuine poet. He really couldn't have been anything else. He was one of the chosen ones, I think.

J.M.: There's a wonderful sense that you share with him and Goethe of being able to listen to nature and hear what it is saying. Rilke had it too.

Wright: That's a wonderful combination of poets; it's flattering to be joined to such a group.

W.H.: Knowing Roethke's work as you do, where do you think the major achievement resides? Is it in The Lost Son, *as many critics have said? What do you think the best Roethke is?*

Wright: I think you have to take him whole, entire, since he moved in so many directions. He would stumble on a way of writing during a certain period. In another period he would move in another direction. The significant thing was that he had not only the ability but the imaginative courage to chance moving in another stylistic direction to its very end, or as far as he could possibly go. There are so many things he tried to do. It's hard to single out *the* major achievement.

J.M.: You are one of several poets who radically altered their styles. Roethke did, Lowell did, and your poetry changed at one point from a more or less formal form to a freer one. I don't want to call it informal, because it isn't. Your recent work does have a kind of hidden form to it, but it's no longer the kind of form that we can block out.

Wright: Well, there wasn't a truly radical change taking place between the books *Saint Judas* and *The Branch Will Not Break*. But it was just that I hadn't previously tried to discipline, to subject myself to the discipline of writing real, good free verse. I thought it was about time to do that. I wanted to—and I continue to try to—listen to as many kinds of music in our language as I could. We have so many things available to us in ours. Ironically, this is one of the reasons why it is sometimes so difficult to write. When we open our ears to what's available we find that there's so much and that it is so very much alive. So many ways of writing and so many possibilities of combination. That's a very exciting fact, I think. And, in a way, it's a dangerous one too. In the American language we have not only the possibility of a really great poetry in terms of diction and rhythm. We also have the possibility of a terrible poetry—I mean, a really bad poetry. A great deal of it does get written and published. You know, the great possibilities of the American language affect all sorts of people in various ways. I think it's very interesting the way this Vice-President Agnew has been fooling around with it. He fancies himself the wonderful baroque prose stylist. One of these days the American language is going to strike back. He's going to give a speech some day and make a slip. He'll produce some unbelievable obscenity. He'll contribute a new obscenity to the language, the way Mayor Daley does. Now Daley has fooled around with the language for quite some time. And it gets even with him frequently. He's always saying things like, "the thing that keeps people apart is their inability to get together." Suddenly the bottom drops out of the universe; you turn to someone and ask, "what did he say?" Or another, "the great city of Chicago will rise to ever-higher platitudes of achievement." That's going to happen to Agnew some day.

J.M.: Speaking about the use of language, Lowell once said about younger poets that they're not risking enough, that they're very well pleased with fine melodies and polished techniques, but they're really not risking anything. Do you find that to be true?

Wright: From the work by young poets that I have seen, I think that they are taking greater risks, probably because of Lowell's own example. After all, *Lord Weary's Castle* is certainly one of the formal masterpieces, not only of American literature but of all poetry in the English language. And yet Lowell became dissatisfied with that and moved on to try something new; this is one of the things that makes him a great writer.

J.M.: That's what I like about your poetry. You take risks all the time. Any genuine poet does—any exciting poet. You never know, when picking up a James Wright poem, what you're going to find. There's always the sense of shock, of surprise, of pleasure.

W.H.: You began writing in formal modes to, as you said, discipline yourself. Do you think this ought to be generalized into a rule, or a strong suggestion, for aspiring young poets? Wouldn't it help the many young poets who begin with free verse and, unfortunately, never attempt anything else? Do you think it's true that a fellow ought to be able to paint an apple, or render something photographically, before he goes on to abstractions? It sounds like a conscious thing in your case. It seems as though, during those years you were writing the poems of The Green Wall *and* Saint Judas, *you were consciously restraining yourself within particular forms. Why?*

Wright: Well, I felt so many energies in the language that I wanted to approach them pretty carefully. I didn't want them to swallow me alive. They sometimes *are* rather savage things to turn loose; and yet, if one approaches these energies, whatever they are, with a certain patience and, indeed, with a sense of courtesy, they will then reveal themselves.

W.H.: Do you consider yourself a rebel like, say, Robert Bly? I think of Bly now because we once talked about aspects of formalism and Bly was saying, "Let's face it. Rhyme is boring. Rhyme is dead. No one wants to hear rhyme any more, today."

Wright: That depends on who the rhymer is. I don't consider myself a rebel. I think of myself as being a very traditional writer; all of the formal devices in may later work are pretty plain.

J.M.: There are some words in your poetry that are somewhat recurrent, if we can talk about them—one of them being "dark." And it has to do, I think, with your images. Would you care to comment on that?

Wright: I don't know, Jerry, what to say about it, except that most of the things that I've written about so far do have a certain darkness to them, an emotional darkness. But again, I'm getting sort of tired of the darkness.

J.M.: What I had in mind was—well, Robert Bly uses the word "dark" quite a bit. But he does it somehow differently from you. With Bly, I think he wants the dark to remain dark and mysterious. He does not mean to eliminate it.

Wright: I don't think that I would want to eliminate the darkness from human experience entirely. But there is something to be said for the light also, after all. Again, it's the danger we fall into in America, of perhaps wallowing in pain too much.

W.H.: I think, Jerry, Robert Bly is a poet we all admire, but wouldn't you say that to a certain extent his use of the word "dark" is almost an automatic thing? You simply expect it to be there in a Bly poem. I mean it's hard, maybe impossible, to find a Bly poem without the word "dark" in it. Sometimes the words "dark" and "darkness" come up four times in two lines.

J.M.: I was going to say, it's almost as cliché as the now "old" New Critics' uses of "old" and "ancient."

Wright: This is the trouble with any poetry that tends toward realism, and it's the one very big difficulty. You can easily delude yourself into thinking that you're being very original. Maybe you're just repeating yourself or repeating someone else. The possibilities of triteness are very powerful.

W.H.: To go back to what Jerry was talking about before—this stylistic change that occurred between your second and third books. Wasn't it more than just a slight change? I recall a rather strong statement of yours, quoted on the dust jacket of The Branch Will Not Break; *it was something like, "I'll never write again if I have to write in that old style." Something to that effect. I'm still very curious as to why you felt this terrific compulsion to change your mode, to change your speech.*

Wright: I don't know exactly. I felt that I'd gone as far as I could for the time being with the book *Saint Judas,* which is very strict and careful in its form. It seemed to me that, after it was finished, it seemed to leave out so much of life. I was then thinking of just exploring other possibilities.

W.H.: Would you read at this point my favorite from Saint Judas, *"An Offering for Mr. Bluehart"?*

Wright: Fine, but let me first tell you about the original Mr. Bluehart. Mr. Bluehart was a man who had a farm in southern Ohio. He had a sign on his fence. There was an orchard on the other side of the fence, and the sign said, "Pray as you enter—shotgun law." I used to wonder, and I still wonder if he realized that this was a real invitation for small boys to climb the fence and steal the apples. He *must* have known that. If old Mr. Bluehart is listening, I enjoyed those apples very much.

An Offering for Mr. Bluehart

That was a place, when I was young,
Where two or three good friends and I
Tested the fruit against the tongue
Or threw the withered windfalls by.
The sparrows, angry in the sky,
Denounced us from a broken bough.

They limp along the wind and die.
The apples all are eaten now.

Behind the orchard, past one hill
The lean satanic owner lay
And threatened us with murder till
We stole his riches all away.
He caught us in the act one day
And damned us to the laughing bone,
And fired his gun across the gray
Autumn where now his life is done.

Sorry for him, or any man
Who lost his labored wealth to thieves,
Today I mourn him, as I can,
By leaving in their golden leaves
Some luscious apples overhead.
Now may my abstinence restore
Peace to the orchard and the dead.
We shall not nag them any more.

J.M.: That's very fine. There's a fine connection there between nature and morality. It's a connection that I've also noted in the titles of your books. Your first book was called The Green Wall, *and your second book took a religious or quasi-religious title,* Saint Judas. *The third book went back to nature with* The Branch Will Not Break, *and the fourth book, of course went back to the religious with* Shall We Gather At The River.

Wright: I think that, looking back, there is a definite pattern; but I wasn't thinking of it as an overall pattern at the time.

J.M.: Mr. Bluehart's orchard is something like the Garden of Eden.

W.H.: And Mr. Bluehart is sort of a young boy's God that has gone away too. It's a very tender and touching poem, I think. I think also that insofar as the imagery is concerned it is reminiscent of the romantic imagery of your earlier work. But technically, in the way it moves and rhymes, "An Offering for Mr. Bluehart" also reminds one of Robert Frost, wouldn't you say?

Wright: Yes, I would say so.

W.H.: Could we move to a poem from the book following Saint Judas? *Would you read a poem or two from* The Branch Will Not Break?

Wright: Let me read a poem called "A Blessing." This poem does not have any particular moral to it as far as I can tell. It's just a description.

A Blessing

Just off the highway to Rochester, Minnesota,
Twilight bounds softly forth on the grass.
And the eyes of those two Indian ponies
Darken with kindness.
They have come gladly out of the willows
To welcome my friend and me.
We step over the barbed wire into the pasture
Where they have been grazing all day, alone.
They ripple tensely, they can hardly contain their
        happiness
That we have come.

They bow shyly as wet swans. They love each other.
There is no loneliness like theirs.
At home once more,
They begin munching the young tufts of spring in the
   darkness.
I would like to hold the slenderer one in my arms,
For she has walked over to me
And nuzzled my left hand.
She is black and white,
Her mane falls wild on her forehead,
And the light breeze moves me to caress her long ear
That is delicate as the skin over a girl's wrist.
Suddenly I realize
That if I stepped out of my body I would break
Into blossom.

J.M.: I was just thinking while you were reading that, you are so much a midwestern poet, reacting to pastures and meadows and animals. Now, for the past couple of years, you have been living in New York City with your wife. I was wondering if you were finding the equivalent—in terms of the city—for those things that moved you in Minnesota and the Ohio countryside.

Wright: Well, I have written about the cities, in *Saint Judas* and *Shall We Gather At The River*. Since I have been living in New York, I have been able to write about city life somewhat. But it wasn't until this past summer, when we were in Paris and other European cities, that city poems started to arrange themselves in my mind. It was very liberating, to go to Paris. I had just finished a book and was tired of writing. I'm sure you know that feeling. The idea of writing something new is a very numbing one when you are waiting for the proofs of the book. But then, surprisingly, city poems and all sorts of poems began to appear in my mind.

W.H.: Hart Crane said on this subject that we damn sure better make the city and the machine a part of our poetics. We can't make that old division any more. It's escapism if we do.

Wright: Yes, that's true. We have our lives to deal with, and the city is so much a part of our lives.

W.H.: "A Blessing," which you just read—I'd like to talk about it for a minute. It just happens that a couple of weeks ago I typed it out because I wanted to get the sense of its movement. It seems to me to be a perfect example of what Eliot meant when he said that no verse is ever really free. It's a very tight poem. I think that it is a perfect example of how the discipline you subjected yourself to in your early works became almost second nature to you. Because of that discipline you could deal with a form like that of "A Blessing."

Wright: I think that is true—about discipline, I mean. I don't know how it would be with others. Some people have an instinctive sense of form. And of course, any poem is formal. There are different forms to choose from, but one thing a person tries to do is to discover the appropriate form for whatever he is trying to say or is saying. Writing so-called free verse is tremendously difficult because it is so easy for the language to fall apart, into banalities. It can also easily fall into bad prose.

J.M.: I know you translate European poetry; in fact, you just returned from a European conference of poets, didn't you? Is there anything special that American poets do learn, can learn, or should learn from European poets?

Wright: Well, it's important just to be in contact with them. For an American poet to be in contact with someone like Reverdy or Jacob is to force himself to get outside of the constricting American experience. Perhaps by translating or reading, by learning something about the literature of another language, one can gain new perspectives on his own. You know, we are, in a sense, so isolated in the United States; we have, in effect, only our one language.

J.M.: Auden once said that it was the vitality of American poetry that it went to Europe for so much of its inspiration. He felt that English poetry was dying because it did not look beyond the shores of England, because it was still imitating Tennyson instead of going on to the French poets.

W.H.: A short while ago I read that selection of Trakl's poems that you and Robert Bly translated. It was about 1952, wasn't it, that you were in Vienna and came into real contact with his work?

Wright: Yes.

W.H.: Reading those selections, I was thinking that the lessons of Trakl—maybe that is a bad phrase—I mean his movements, his particular sensibilities didn't make themselves felt in your poetry until the time of The Branch Will Not Break.

Wright: Well, it's strange how an influence works on one's mind. One may come in contact with a tremendous critic and reader like Susini and be moved by him in some very deep way. It may take a long time for the movement of one's own emotion to come out and make sense.

J.M.: You are one of the poets who might have been influenced by the readings of Dylan Thomas, but I don't find in your poems that rhetoric which caught up so many poets of the time.

Wright: Maybe I was afraid of it and that is why I tried to be a classicist. It is a terrible thing to fall into. Thomas could get away with the high rhetoric; after all, he came from a tradition that featured high rhetoric. We knew how to handle it because he had been taught how to handle it by his own tradition. With the American language we can start off being very high-flown; the trouble is that very soon the language somehow seems to drift away from reality. Again, we see this in the various expressions of our public men. It is terribly difficult for someone in public life to say something serious. The members of the audience he is addressing are so used to the rhetoric that they wonder if he means what he is saying. If someone were to get on television and say, "Let me make one thing perfectly clear, there is an anthrax epidemic beginning," we wouldn't rush to get ourselves innoculated. We would turn first and say to one another, "does he mean it or not?"

J.M.: I was just thinking. Pound said that it was the function of the poet to keep the language viable and alive; Ginsberg some years ago said in his Wichita Vortex Sutra *that the Washington people were inferior magicians using the language to destroy language. Ginsberg quoted instances of double-think which had become so common: like, we have to wage war to establish peace, we have to let the prices go up before we can get them to go down. We hear this sort of stuff from Washington every day, and naturally it has become a preoccupation for poets. Denise Levertov's book,* Relearning The Alphabet, *and William Stafford's new book,* Allegiances, *both focus on the idea of language gone wrong.*

Wright: Well, expressions of language in a context of power do have important consequences, always. And it seems to me just a matter of life and death for writers to pay special attention to this phenomenon and at least try to think clearly and to keep the language in close contact with reality. With a statement like, we have to wage war to get peace, we have something terrifying. It is terrifying when someone says something like this publicly and has an army behind him. It is going to have consequences and the consequences are hideous.

W.H.: I don't know if I can put my finger on it exactly, but for some reason you, Robert Bly, and William Stafford are often talked about together. It seems to me that one of the things that unites this group's thrust is that the three of you are trying to get underneath the language of convention, the language gone rotten that William Carlos Williams was always very obstreperous about. What you are trying to do is, as William Stafford puts it, leave yourself loose enough to have the world come in upon you, so that the poem creates itself and is not directed by a kind of upper, conventionalized consciousness. Stafford mentions somewhere that William Blake wanted to reach out and follow that golden string of intuition or suggestion. It seems to me that the root impulse of this is a moral thing: to get underneath the political jargon we hear all the time to something very true and real.

Wright: It's partly that. In this kind of poetry there is involved a willingness on the part of the poet to trust the language a little more, and perhaps to trust nature, trust other living things. And yet it is literally difficult for human beings to trust one another right now. To go back to the example of the people in cities, this is surely one of the ghastly things about our own time. We walk through the city and see someone lying on the sidewalk, foaming at the mouth or whatever. Anyone in New York City would certainly think twice because you don't know what's going to happen—maybe he'll bite you. Or, maybe the real fear is that you'll bite him.

W.H.: This reminds me of your poem "Saint Judas." Does my connection make any sense? I'm not sure, but the theme of the Samaritan is a peculiarly modern aspect of the kind of alienation we feel. I wonder if you'd read it and talk about it.

Wright: Well—this poem is called "Saint Judas" and it takes off from the biblical story of Judas, who placed himself beyond the moral pale, and he realized this. I've always been strongly moved by his hanging himself. Why did he do it? You would think he'd be a completely cold person. And yet, he couldn't have been to experience such complete despair. I tried to imagine what Judas was like.

Saint Judas

When I went out to kill myself, I caught
A pack of hoodlums beating up a man.
Running to spare his suffering, I forgot
My name, my number, how my day began,
How soldiers milled around the garden stone
And sang amusing songs; how all that day
Their javelins measured crowds; how I alone
Bargained the proper coins, and slipped away.

Banished from heaven, I found this victim beaten,
Stripped, kneed, and left to cry. Dropping my rope
Aside, I ran, ignored the uniforms:
Then I remembered bread my flesh had eaten,
The kiss that ate my flesh. Flayed without hope,
I held the man for nothing in my arms.

W.H.: Do you remember how you chose "Saint Judas" for the title poem of that volume?

Wright: I don't remember exactly. I had the poems arranged in a certain way and "Saint Judas" was the last. It's a short poem and sort of a summary, stylistically and thematically, of everything I was trying to do in the book. It's a book about desolation of the spirit, and so I thought that "Saint Judas" would bring everything into focus.

J.M.: May we talk about the upcoming Collected Poems *for a second? You are going to, I believe, print in book form some of the poems from the years between* Saint Judas *and* The Branch Will Not Break *which appeared in magazines in the early sixties?*

Wright: I'm not going to reprint those yet. What I'm doing presently is practically all *The Green Wall*, all of *Saint Judas*, and then there will be a section called "Some Translations." I've gotten together about thirty-five translations from around the time after I'd finished *Saint Judas*. During that time I was searching around, trying to write something new; I stopped writing things of my own then for a while and tried some translations. For me this was a good exploration. It introduced me to a world I hadn't known before; I did many translations—a great many, out of which I've chosen about thirty-five to print. And then will come *The Branch Will Not Break*, then *Shall We Gather At The River*, and then some thirty new poems.

J.M.: I do know that one of your favorite authors is Dickens. But I have yet to catch a Dickensian spirit in your poetry. Is this coming?

Wright: One of these days, I hope. When we speak of the Dickensian spirit, first of all I guess we mean the tremendous spirit of laughter to be had. But, along with that laughter comes a tremendous understanding of the dark world and people who live on the other side of the billboard.

J.M.: You do have that sense of the Dickensian lower world in many of your poems. But the sense of Dickensian laughter is different from that in your poems. Dickens is more eccentric. His characters are a little bit more eccentric than Mr. Bluehart. Is this ability to capture the eccentric what makes Dickens' humor so memorable for you?

Wright: I certainly enjoy that aspect of life, and Dickens caught that better than anyone else: the complete nuttiness of people. Santayana said people who think Dickens exaggerated are people who just don't know how to pay attention. Dickens' people are rather strange, interesting creatures.

W.H.: I think real humor comes into your poetry with The Branch Will Not Break, *but maybe it's a kind of sad humor. I'm thinking of titles like, "In Response to a Rumor that the Oldest Whorehouse in Wheeling, West Virginia, Has Been Condemned," from* Shall We Gather At The River. *And in* The Branch Will Not Break, *the one entitled "Depressed by a Book of Bad Poetry, I Walk Toward an Unused Pasture and Invite the Insects to Join Me." Read that for us, would you?*

Wright:

Depressed by a Book of Bad Poetry

Relieved, I let the book fall behind a stone.
I climb a slight rise of grass.
I do not want to disturb the ants
Who are walking single file up the fence post,
Carrying small white petals,
Casting shadows so frail that I can see through them.
I close my eyes for a moment, and listen.
The old grasshoppers

Are tired, they leap heavily now,
Their thighs are burdened.
I want to hear them, they have clear sounds to make.
Then lovely, far off, a dark cricket begins
In the maple trees.

That literally happened. Someone asked me to review a certain anthology and the poems in it seemed to me to be so bad, so trite in their hysteria that I just got sick of them. I didn't want to expose my mind to those bone-crushing banalities anymore. I wanted to hear the cricket or something.

J.M.: The poem reminded me that there is a touch of the "absurd" in your whole approach. I was wondering how profound an influence, do you think, Albert Camus has had on the writers of your generation.

Wright: I don't know how profound an influence there is, but there certainly is one. He's affected so many people. One can't escape it, and one shouldn't. He's a serious man.

J.M.: Somehow your defeated saviours are like his Sisyphus.

Wright: What a terrible myth that is.

W.H.: Unless it's read happily.

Wright: Yes. Laurel and Hardy, it occurs to me, used the same thing in moving their piano. Remember, the film will begin and they're moving their piano again. You don't know why, but you join in. They'll deliver it, get it up the hill on this concrete outdoor stairway, and pause to wipe their brows. The piano comes thundering down, crashing through about three houses.

W.H.: If I might change the ground a bit. The translations of various poets that you've done, and the ones you've done with Robert Bly, may have been a very fertile influence on your own work, and on American poetry. People talk about the wonderful kind of imagery that we get from Trakl or from certain South American poets. Can you make a distinction between what the image is for, say, Trakl, as opposed to what it was for the English and American Imagists? What is this new imagery that Bly and Wright are talking about? How is it different?

Wright: I don't know that the really effective image in any poem is different from the effective image in another, at least artistically.

W.H.: Would it have something to do with the hard conjunctioning of images? I mean, reading your translations of Trakl, I see how one image sort of leaps in almost a shocking way, into a different kind of world. Another image will then open another world. The poems are less rounded than those of the Imagists. They visit more worlds than one. There's not that consistency that we get in those 1910 Imagist poems, not that circle.

Wright: Well, the world that Trakl lived and wrote in was the same world of the British and American Imagists, but he saw it differently. His experience was quite different. I think the crucial thing in his life was that he felt a war coming. I'm sure many people did, but he understood what it would be like. He understood that war in this century was not going to be like any other war, that there was going to be a kind of war that had no redeeming qualities at all. The machine guns and the bombs and so on.

J.M.: Many people have remarked that the world wars of our century along with automation and technology have made us less human. At least they have tended to increase our tolerance for brutality. You write poetry that tries to counter this, that tries to bring us back to humanity. Is that your deliberate purpose? Do you consciously pursue that goal?

Wright: I think it is conscious, Jerry, in that I know from my own experience that perpetual exposure to violence and the representations of violence have threatened my own capacity to feel. Often, through poetry, I've tried to find a way to restore that capacity, to keep it alive. I think that all of us are threatened not only by physical violence; our very emotional lives, our moral lives are threatened. The dreadful things that have happened in Southeast Asia, that are happening in the Middle East right now, are not felt as real by many people. They have been desensitized in regard to actual violence and brutality by the constant viewing of so-called imaginative television shows like *Combat* and the many World War II movies.

J.M.: This recalls a commercial for athlete's foot medication that I see on television. In it is a comic skit which may acclimatize many viewers to chemical warfare. It's a very sinister commercial.

W.H.: Would you elaborate on that, Jerry?

J.M.: Yes, that commercial captures exactly what I believe Mr. Wright is speaking of. In that cartoon commercial there are the figures Fungus, Itch, and so forth. They launch a campaign against a human foot, and soon swarm all over that foot, making it wiggle in discomfort. They are sprayed with the athlete's foot medication; they are foiled; and the figures quickly beat a retreat, carrying their dead. One figure reports this turn of events to the general—the head Itch or whatever—and in a mock-villainous way he says something like, "Unfair! They're using chemical warfare!" The whole thing is done with such nicety that a whole generation of children, at least, may more readily accept the "normality" of chemical warfare.

Wright: Yes, and did you ever see *Hogan's Heroes?* In that weekly show you have American troops in a prisoner of war camp during World War II. And the Nazi commandant is a jolly synthetic comic figure. Everything is very jolly for everyone involved. How far from reality can you get?

W.H.: Jerry, Mr. Wright, I'm afraid our time is up. Thank you both very much.

Poetry Must Think

An Interview with Bruce Henricksen

Bruce Henricksen: Mr. Wright, you wrote a short article in Field *in 1973 in which you talked about the lack of intelligence in much contemporary poetry. I was wondering if you could comment a little bit more on what constitutes intelligent poetry.*

Wright: Well, I think that an intelligent poetry is a poetry whose author has given a great deal of slow and silent attention to the problems of craft; that is, how to say something and say it in a musical way, but I feel that ultimately any writer has to come to terms with ethical and epistemological questions about the meaning of life and of his life. It had often seemed to me at least up to a point, five years ago, that American poetry was full of discussions—endless nit-picking discussions about craft alone. And this was starting to get on my nerves. I wanted somebody to come to the point.

B.H.: Losing its ethical dimension . . .

Wright: Yes, I think that it's very significant that the poetry of E. A. Robinson is almost completely neglected, still neglected today. Nobody pays any attention to him and I think that this is because he's essentially a serious man. And I sometimes wonder whether or not we live in a serious age.

New Orleans Review 6, no. 3 (1978).

B.H.: I think you used Pound in that article as an example of an unintelligent poet. I seem to remember the phrase also that he was "aesthetically offensive."

Wright: I find his personality, his personal arrogance, aesthetically offensive and I find it morally offensive. When I criticize his intelligence I realize that he wrote and said a great many things that are helpful in the actual writing of verses, but it seems to me that in his own poetry there is a terrible, I would say, a fatal lack of wholeness most of the time. I had said something to the effect that to reject the past is to reject intelligence and you pointed out that Pound certainly didn't reject the past, and I admit that he ransacked it and he quotes people from the past all over the place. He's constantly giving you a quotation from somebody he's almost sure that you've never heard of so that he can get one up on you. But when he puts his own poems together, it seems to me that there's a failure of intelligence there, except, for the most part, when he's translating—and there he has an intellectual structure already provided for him that he can work on.

B.H.: Well, would you say that writers like Eliot and Joyce ransacked the past?

Wright: They ransacked the past and I think what gives them their crucial superiority is that they were to make wholes out of their studies of the past.

B.H.: And by "whole" you're making both an aesthetic and ethical judgment.

Wright: Yes, both an aesthetic and an ethical comment. I would say that in spite of the confusions and the mistakes and the fragments that I myself have published in my own work, still as far as I'm concerned I'm a Horatian. I believe in the "whole" of a poem and the subordination of style to some wholeness of structure and some wholeness of vision about the nature of things.

B.H.: I'd like to pursue this idea of the past and of the tradition in poetry a little bit more, although I'm not quite sure what to ask about it. How, for instance, has your own poetry been involved in the tradition? Is that something you can comment on?

Wright: I still regard myself as very much a conservative. And although after a point I started to write pieces in so-called free verse, I was simply trying to expand my understanding of what the form of poetry can be. I do not think that there is any opposition between traditional iambic verse and free verse, not any necessary opposition; they're simply two different kinds of form.

B.H.: What writers in the tradition do you feel most kinship with now? You had spoken of Robinson and Frost as important early influences. How about at this point in your career?

Wright: The authors that I feel closest to and feel most devoted to are not poets at all, right at the moment. I've been going through the works of José Ortega y Gasset again. Right now I'm in the middle of *Man and People,* his sociological study, and at least once a year I read through the complete works of George Orwell. For aesthetic wholeness and the ethical strength, I wouldn't trade his novel *Coming up for Air* for nine-tenths of the contemporary poets I've read.

B.H.: That's interesting. What about other contemporary prose writers?

Wright: Well these people aren't exactly contemporary, some of the prose writers I'm referring to. There's E. M. Forester in the essay *Two Cheers for Democracy* and the essays of Graham Greene, and Ortega always: *The Revolt of the Masses* mainly.

B.H.: The other night you mentioned Walker Percy whom you were reading lately, and I think you said that he is one of the few serious writers working today.

Wright: Yes, I say that he is serious. I mean that he answers some hunger that I feel for work that is intelligent and aesthetically significant and also has a deep ethical and even religious commitment. As far as I'm able to judge, Walker Percy, right now is the most important novelist writing with one exception I can think of; the other most serious one to me seems to be Larry Woiwode, who has published two novels. One is called *What I'm Going To Do I Think,* and a longer one that came out a couple of years ago called *Beyond the Bedroom Wall.* The latter book is a long novel in traditional form. It covers the experience of a North Dakota family through three generations. What is amazing about it is that he begins his novel simply sitting in his bedroom, closing his eyes and trying to imagine clearly and in detail every single house that was on the main street of his home town; and once he does this, he then in his next chapter immediately goes back to the experience that his father had in burying—that is physically with his own hands—burying his grandfather, and thoroughly imagines the whole past. The significance of the book is, I think, that Woiwode has the power of imagining his own life.

Richard Wilbur has a poem in his last book in which he argues, and I think very beautifully shows, that much of the time it's impossible to see what is right in front of one's own eyes without the use of one's imagination. Woiwode is a thinker, he's trying to think passionately about the true details of his own life. I think the true details of one's own life include the past.

B.H.: And that's something that you do, in your own poetry, which is very autobiographical—you've written about family, brothers . . .

Wright: Yes, it may be autobiographical in the sense that I suppose anybody's poetry is autobiographical, but I don't think it's confessional. I think confessional poetry is a pain in the ass. Most of the things that confessional poets confess are not worth confessing.

B.H.: I suppose a number of poets have written poems without ever mentioning a brother or a father or a dead grandmother. There is that sense of family, a family myth . . .

Wright: Well my own life is the only thing I have to begin with. It seems to me an aesthetically legitimate thing as well as a morally legitimate thing to try to figure out what one's own life really is. Maybe this is what draws us toward novelists like Woiwode and Walker Percy and Charles Dickens.

B.H.: In the Field *article you mentioned a couple of novelists that I hadn't heard of and one that I have since heard of—the author of* Ragtime, Doctorow. *You mentioned him and then a couple of others whose names I don't recall.*

Wright: Cynthia Ozick perhaps, who writes a beautiful prose. I'm thinking mainly of her stories. I think of her as a story writer more than anything else. She has written a novel or two, I think.

B.H.: The name Saul Bellow doesn't pop up right away in your conversation then?

Wright: Well, I admire Bellow very much. I guess I ought to mention him because he certainly is a serious man and very beautifully intelligent and sensitive. I was thinking of people who had published things in the last couple of years, maybe.

B.H.: What about this idea of criticism that you talk about again in the Field *article, the idea that each generation of poets needs its own criticism?*

Wright: I simply mean that the effort to write poetry itself at least ought to be an intelligent act, an attempt to understand language and its relationship to life. I was trying to distinguish between the criticism as merely an academic exercise for the sake of promotion and criticism in itself as a living art.

B.H.: Shades of Matthew Arnold in your considering art as criticism of life?

Wright: Partly that, but also the kind of criticism which is concerned about the efforts of contemporary poets. There ought to be a really vital relation between those two things. In this century it seems to me that some of the very best poets have been among the finest critics. T. S . Eliot is the best example and he kept insisting that he did write criticism in order to help him understand what he was trying to do in his poetry. I think that this is true and I also think that this is what made his criticism so illuminating, not only when we try to understand his poetry but also when we try to understand poetry in general.

B.H.: Does this criticism that the poets need have to come from the poets themselves?

Wright: No, not necessarily, but a great deal of good criticism does come from the poets themselves.

B.H.: Are there any examples of criticism coming from the academics that is useful to the poets? You talked a minute ago about the kind that's just done for promotion. It occurs to me that certainly there's no shortage of critical theory these days.

Wright: No, I realize that a number of academic people have been writing about contemporary poetry and I can think of four or five such people who, as far as I can tell, have begun to write about contemporary poetry, often to put it down, in the same sense that they might have begun to write articles, perhaps two or three a year, about the works of James Hogg or Martin Tupper, or if they happened to go into some other line of study, monographs about the sex life of the date palm or homosexuality in chickens. In other words, I don't think these people are essentially serious and they have nothing to do with human imagination. They're time-servers. The power struggle, as always, goes on in the academic world.

B.H.: Are there any examples of academic criticism that is useful from the poet's point-of-view?

Wright: Oh yes, and there are many academic writers, scholars, who have published things that have, I think, very great value for a poet, simply because they lucidly explain problems of poetry and have enormous knowledge behind them and a clarity of style. I'm thinking, for example, of Maynard Mack's edition of Alexander Pope's *Homer*. I think that his edition, the Twickenham Edition, in his introductory essay, has more to say about the construction of a great poem and a great translation than most book reviews I've seen.

B.H.: I've always been taken by Northrop Frye's criticism. It seems to me there's a sort of imaginative reach as well as a firm ethical sense that Frye works from.

Wright: Yes, the serious critics who may come out of the academy, serious critics who are learned and intelligent, have themselves a clear style, an imaginative style.

B.H.: It seems that everywhere you turn these days you're running into people who claim to be very knowledgeable about philosophers such as Heidegger and Godamer and Jacques Derrida. I was just reading a piece in The New Yorker *about Walker Percy's emersion in continental philosophers before his career began. Do you think there's a necessary relationship between poetry and that kind of formal philosophical thinking?*

Wright: I don't know.

B.H.: Are there philosophers that you read?

Wright: Well, I mentioned Ortega and I read him all the time. He's extremely difficult but I think he's very rewarding.

B.H.: What do you find most compelling in Ortega? Some people think he's a bit hard on the common man in The Revolt of the Masses.

Wright: I think that Ortega touches significantly on a wider range of crucial modern problems than any other author I've read, and he does so with great clarity and strength. The notion that he is hard on the "common man" derives, I think, from a misunderstanding of his terminology. One of the great excitements of reading him, in fact, is in following his long, careful distinctions of terms. In fact, he does not speak contemptuously of the "common man," but of the "mass man." The latter is not a social class—perhaps I should say he is not a member of a social class—but rather what Ortega calls a *barbarian*. Consider: in his huge effort to see life as it is, the noble man struggles with perpetual doubt. He must constantly live with the possibility that he may be in fact a fool. In this power of doubt, says Ortega, lies his intelligence. The barbarian, or mass man, on the other hand, assumes, in dealing with any problem, that the first idle thought that pops into his head represents an absolute solution. The mass man is not merely ignorant. His barbarism consists in his asserting his ignorance *as a right*. The very fact that the mass man is not merely the representative of a given social class is what makes him so terrifying. A central horror of our century is the appearance of the mass man in the very seat of authority, with all powers, including the military, at his whimsical disposal. The mass man appeared, in all his shining putrescence, in Nazi Germany. But it is idle to dispose of the mass man simply by identifying him with a temporary—though spectacularly destructive—political group in Germany. The mass man crouches sullenly within ourselves, and it is within ourselves that we had damned well better come to terms with his existence. Ortega explores these and related matters with memorable force. He is a very bracing writer, a serious guide through the tragic times in which we now have our lives.

B.H.: People talk about the stylistic changes that your own poetry has gone through. I remember the other night you talked about the response that the "Lying in a Hammock" poem got. It seems to me, if I remember correctly, that part of the controversy had to do with your changing from the more formal styles to free verse at about that time.

Wright: It seems to me that the critics who object to a poem in free verse because it's free verse, have no way of knowing whether or not a poem has a formal structure except by noticing whether it rhymes or not. Perhaps they have somebody read it aloud to them so that they can hear whether it rhymes or not. Or maybe they are deaf as well as blind.

B.H.: But your style is changing in other ways. How would you describe at this point what various kinds of things you've tried to do. What kind of changes have gone on?

Wright: Well, I've tried to understand some ways that so-called free verse could still be shaped into a genuine form, and there are all sorts of formal possibilities, the parallelism of images and sounds for example. And also I've tried to slow down and pay attention to the things that were right in front of my eyes, more closely than I had ever done before when I was trying to write in more traditional ways. This has led me to write some prose pieces.

B.H.: There's a quality in your writing that I find very attractive when you do it, and yet I think it's something you are suspicious of. Tell me if I'm right or not. It's this kind of ornate imagery that has a real loveliness to it. I think of the "Bronze butterfly" or the "Walking down hallways of a diamond," lines like that, and then, on the other hand, poetry in which you claim to be speaking in a "flat voice," as you say in one poem—just a straight conversational style, which I think in a few poems you almost present as a poetic—as though you're suggesting that this other, more ornate, style is perhaps something you've decided to be suspicious of for some reason.

Wright: I've been trying to purge it away—or trim it away, maybe I should say. I have a tendency to get too lush with sounds and I have a tendency to get lost in the confusion of certain figures of speech. Surrealism is dangerous for me and I think for everyone. I don't think that I'm intelligent enough to manage a genuinely surrealistic style. The masters of surrealism seem to me to be comedians. Genuine comedians. One reason we've had so much bad surrealism in the United States is that some American poets have seen translations of some French surrealistic poems and have assumed that they were to be taken directly and seriously. Often they are comic.

B.H.: What would be some titles of poems of your own that have a surrealistic quality?

Wright: Well, you've mentioned a couple of them: "Walking Down the Hallways of a Diamond." That's not so much surrealistic as just a sort of baroque figure of speech.

B.H.: What about the poem "Miners," where that word takes on a different meaning in each stanza. Would you describe that as surrealistic?

Wright: It's influenced by surrealism. I don't think the poem itself is surrealistic. I think it's extremely formal, very traditional. The images are all parallel to one another. It's as formal as the end of Lincoln's Gettysburg address. I don't mean it's as good.

B.H.: Did you read the piece that Stephen Spender wrote in The New York Review of Books? *It must have been shortly after your* Collected Poems. . . . *He reviewed a number of American poets. His praise of your poetry was less than complete, and I'm wondering if some of his reservations have to do with this very quality of which you have just said, you've tried to purge yourself. . . . Do you think, in other words, that as you criticize your poetry you would agree with some of Spender's? . . .*

Wright: Yes, I agree with some of what he says. I think at one point he thought that he was . . . well, he was sort of condescending to my work. He said that it had a Georgian quality in it. And he compared some of it to the poetry of Walter de la Mare. And apparently, to Spender, this was a condescending thing to say. To me it was great praise. I don't think I would trade four or five poems of de la Mare for my own work and that of Spender and all of his grandparents.

B.H.: I think he also talked about a Spanish influence. Am I remembering this right? And he argued that this made your poetry less than authentically American.

Wright: He was talking about a few poems I had written after I had translated some Spanish poems. And probably he was right. I was too heavily, too directly influenced by them. Nevertheless, I don't regret trying to write things like that because at that particular time I was trying to reach outside, rather, reach deliberately beyond the range of a certain way that I had been trying to write before. And I had to take some risks. And not many of the poems are successful. That's all right, I would gladly try it again if I had it to do over.

B.H.: But are these the same poems we were speaking of awhile ago when we were talking of "Having Lost My Sons"?

Wright: He was thinking of a poem called "To the Moon." I had said something about a panther's footprints in the snow. The moonlight throwing things like that. He said, that doesn't sound like a person who has been looking at the moonlight. . . . He's just been reading Spanish poetry. I think it was a fair statement.

B.H.: You never saw a panther in Ohio.

Wright: If I ever saw a panther I wouldn't "an-ther." No, his essay was a pretty sound and serious reading of that poem, I think.

B.H.: Has translating influenced your art in any other way?

Wright: Well, the value that translating has had for me, first of all, is that it was a way of genuinely trying to read some great poems in other languages. That's a complicated process. You can read such poems by trying to learn the language, and then read the poems as you would read poems in your own language. But actually if you try to translate them, you are forced to find some equivalents in your own language, not only equivalents of language itself but equivalents of imagination. In this way you can force yourself actually to try to understand the vision of the poet in the other language. It's bound to have an effect on you. I don't know, I wouldn't know how to describe the immediate effect. . . . I hope that trying to translate some poems by Cesar Vallejo has some effect on me just as a human being. He was a very great man and his greatness is in his poetry.

B.H.: Are you still translating?

Wright: Not at the moment. No.

B.H.: You have future plans?

Wright: One of these days Robert Bly and I are going to go back and make a new translation of the Austrian poet Trakl. We've made a few attempts at it. We don't have any immediate plans. Trakl is very beautiful.

B.H.: You included him in the selected poems. Your translations of him. . . .

Wright: One or two.

> In den einsamen Stunden des Geistes
> Ist es schon, in der Sonne zu ghen
> An den gelben Mauern des Sommers hin.
> Leise Klingen die Schritte im Gras;
>   doch immer schlaft
> Der Sohn des Pan im grauen Marmor

B.H.: Can you translate that?

Wright: On the yellow long—no—
       In the lonely hours of the spirit
       it is beautiful to walk in the sun down the
            long yellow wall of summer
          so: etc.

B.H.: That's nice. I wanted to ask you about one specific poem that you read the other night: "Lying in a Hammock at William Duffy's Farm in Pine Island, Minnesota." Because you commented on it at the end, and I think I've understood it a little bit differently from what you suggested. You talked about the final line, "I have wasted my life," as being, perhaps, a realization that more time ought to be spent lying in a hammock, as I remember.

Wright: Yes. I think that I didn't realize it at the moment, but looking back on that poem, I think that final line—I have wasted my life—is a religious statement, that is to say, here I am and I'm not straining myself and yet I'm happy at this moment, and perhaps I've been wastefully unhappy in the past because through my arrogance or whatever, and my blindness, I haven't allowed myself to pay true attention to what was around me. And a very strange thing happened. After I wrote that poem and after I published it, I was reading among the poems of the eleventh-century Persian poet, Ansari, and he used exactly the same phrase at a moment when he was happy. He said, "I have wasted my life." Nobody gave him hell for giving up iambics. You can't win.

B.H.: The line just before that describes the chicken hawk looking for home, and then earlier in the poem the farm house is empty. Those images have suggested to me that the poem is leading to a realization of a sense of lost community.

Wright: I think that's part of the mood. And the poem is, or I thought was, quite a simple poem, not an ambitious one. What I wanted to do was to record in parallel images the stage of a certain mood and not try to write something heroic, for example, but to try to find a concrete way of setting down the stages of a mood the way the old Chinese poets did sometimes.

B.H.: Your last two or three books have dealt more with European experiences than with American experiences, and I understand you're returning to Europe in December. Does this mean that the Muse is over there for good?

Wright: No, I don't think it means anything of the sort. To me it means that this is just going to Europe again. And writing about Europe is another way of trying to explore the meaning of my own life. In my last book there's a poem called, "One Last Look At the Adige: Verona in the Rain," and this poem is partly about the Ohio River and partly about the Adige River. I had never felt quite the same way about the Ohio River as I felt standing there in Verona. And there are several places in the book that reach back to my own experiences in earlier years in the United States. It's only partly about Europe.

B.H.: Can you pursue that a little more? How the European experience has modified your relationship to Ohio and to the United States. There are changed moods in those poems.

Wright: It's hard to answer. There's a prose piece about the Colosseum at Rome in which I looked at those passageways that lie under, or used to lie under, the floor of the Colosseum where the starved animals and the Christians were kept waiting, and they were kept starving too. That terrible place reminded me in some ways of the Ohio River, which was a beautiful river, but kind of frightening. I called them both a "black ditch of horror."

B.H.: The title poem in your last book, To a Blossoming Pear Tree, *returns to Minneapolis, doesn't it?*

Wright: Yes, there are two poems about Minneapolis right towards the end of that book, and they both deal with things that happened to me late at night in Minneapolis.

B.H.: I wonder if there is any special significance for the fact that that's the title poem for the book, although the book is predominantly Euro-

pean poems. With the title poem, you're returning to your native setting.

Wright: I think that the significance of that title in the poem itself is that I was trying to say that I am committed to the beauty of nature which I love very much, but that commitment in me anyway always more and more has to be qualified by my returning to my own responsibility as a human being. And the life of a human being is more complicated than the blossoming of a pear tree. It's full of pain.

B.H.: I thought immediately of Yeats' "Sailing to Byzantium" when I read it. He sets up a choice between a real world and an impossible world and chooses the impossible, whereas you make the opposite choice at the end of your poem.

Wright: Well, this is the only life I have. In many ways it's a snarled mess, but I like it. You know Stephen Crane's little poem about the man sitting in the desert land. He found the creature squatting, naked bestial who held his heart in his hand and ate of it. "'Is it good friend?' 'No,' he said, 'it is bitter, but I like it because it is bitter and because it is my heart.'"

B.H.: Are you writing any poetry right now?

Wright: Very slowly. As always I write slowly. I have about twenty-three new pieces. I think some of them are going to be published. Some of them are about Ohio and two or three are about Hawaii.

B.H.: Do you plan ahead at all? I know that you publish in journals and then bring them together in a book. But at some point as you are going along, does the book start to become a reality?

Wright: I think when I've written for a couple of years, I start to perceive some sort of dim shape for the book and work toward that.

B.H.: And is there a book that is shaping up now?

Wright: Yes . . . , well it's accumulating. Put it that way. It hasn't suggested its own shape yet. I like to give myself plenty of time. I published too much, I think when I was younger. There are many poems that I wouldn't publish now, but they're over and done with.

B.H.: The collected poems didn't include all of The Green Wall *did it?*

Wright: No, and it didn't include by any means all of the poems that I've published. There are a great many more than that.

B.H.: What journals would we be wise to look at if we want to see what you're writing right now?

Wright: Well there are going to be three new poems in *Poetry* magazine in Chicago. Let's see: there are several that are coming out in the *New Yorker*. Some have already appeared in *Ironwood* magazine, and a couple of new ones have just been printed in a broadside called the "Poem of the Month Club" in Long Island. David Ignatow is editing that. One or two poems published a month. And those two are poems about places at the edge of the water, one in Hawaii and one in Rhode Island. One is called "Entering the Kingdom of the Moray Eel." That's about swimming at night in Hawaii.

B.H.: How do we get to see these?

Wright: I don't know. They're going to be on sale in New York.

B.H.: In New York. Take a plane?

Wright: I don't have any copies on me right now. I just signed them all and sent them back to the publisher. I asked him to send me some. When he does I'll send you one.

B.H.: Oh terrific . . . thank you. The one book of yours I haven't seen is the one with the drawings.

Wright: Yes, that was sort of a chapbook with drawings. That was published by the Dryades Press in Washington, D.C., called *Moments of the Italian Summer*. Those are all prose pieces, fourteen prose pieces.

B.H.: And who did the drawings?

Wright: Her name is Joan Root.

B.H.: Which came first, the drawings or the prose pieces?

Wright: The prose pieces.

B.H.: And she did the drawings?

Wright: From the prose pieces . . .

B.H.: Was that a success, that sort of collaboration? Is that something you'd be interested in doing again?

Wright: Yes, I enjoyed it. It was a success as far as I was concerned. I liked her drawings very much.

B.H.: Did that come out as sort of a livre de luxe *before it came out for the public?*

Wright: Well, there are some copies that came out in hardback, but most of them in paperback.

B.H.: We were talking yesterday about the problems facing public education these days, and I had the impression that you might want to comment on those problems for the record.

Wright: If I have any grasp at all of our current mood in the United States, we are suffering from one of our periodic fits of outrage against Big Government, against taxes, against inflation—in short, against the difficult forces that threaten to obstruct our simple progress through our private lives. I value privacy as much as anybody does, but I can't get rid of an uneasiness about us. In our anger against stupidity and mismanagement in government—an anger by no means unjustified—we are falling into the danger of damaging, maybe even destroying, the great living tradition of public education, which has been possibly our best American achievement. What does this rage mean, this rage against taxes and inflation? I just cannot believe that the majority of Americans, even comfortable Americans, are simply to be written off as greedy and selfish brutes. That is not my sense of most of the Americans I have known, and I have known people from widely varying social backgrounds. No, there is some madness in the air. I worry about it endlessly, for our system of public education is a fragile thing, and if we destroy it, or allow it to be destroyed, it won't automatically reappear. Huge numbers of young people have got to be shown the need—not just the social need, but the personal—for an orderly life and for what Irving Howe beautifully calls a life of disciplined hope. If we do not discover the significance of an orderly life in a democratic manner, the experience of the twentieth century instructs us that somebody else will provide discipline in another manner, probably totalitarian. It is beside the point to complain that public education as it now exists is a mess. I know it is a mess, that it has got to be sustained and improved. It will take enormous effort to sustain it, much less to improve it. I believe that we are capable of such effort in America. I often wish that the Rev. Jesse Jackson, to my mind one of the finest men in public life, would run for President. Win or lose, he could draw more serious attention to these problems of public education. It's hard to speak briefly here about an issue of such terrible importance.

B.H.: I don't have any other questions written down.

Wright: I don't have any other answers written down either.

B.H.: Well, I'd like to thank you for submitting to this.

Wright: In conclusion, let me pass on to you Nelson Auburn's advice:

> Never eat at a place called "Mom's"
> Never play cards with a man called Doc.
> And never go to bed with anyone who has more
> troubles than you have.

B.H.: I'll bear that in mind, thank you. We could conclude by singing "Jr. Bird Man."

Wright: O.K. are you ready?

> Up in the air Jr. Bird Man
> Up in the air upside down
> Up in the air Jr. Bird Man
> Keep your noses on the ground.
>
> And when you hear the door bell ringing
> And you see those wings of tin
> Then you will know a Jr. Bird Man
> Has sent his boxtops in!
> B-I-R-D-M-A-N Birdman! Birdman!
> growlllll.

The Pure Clear Word

An Interview with Dave Smith

(On September 30, 1979 Gibbons Ruark and I met James Wright in his New York apartment and conducted the following interview. Wright, nearing his fifty-second birthday, appeared trim and healthy. He is a solidly built man who moves with an obvious dignity that creates the impression of forceful grace. Like the music which is so much a part of his life and his imagination, his voice and gestures reveal oscillations of exuberance, enthusiasm, sobriety, and joy which these printed words cannot well convey. During the interview, which lasted more than four hours, Wright sat before a large wall-to-wall-to-ceiling array of books. I remember clearly the sense that these books were virtually husks because Wright held all that was alive in them within his own mind. And I remember the intense, bright vitality of his eyes that flared or lulled as he spoke or was silent.—Dave Smith, November 1979)

D.S.: Because you have written much about the landscape, culture, and activities of your youth, we would like to begin with some biographical questions. Did you play high school football?

Wright: I didn't play on the high school team. I played a lot of football on a sort of semi-pro team. There was a lot of that in the Ohio River Valley, where I grew up. During the thirties and forties football was a very important activity in that com-

American Poetry Reivew 9, no. 3 (May/June 1980).

munity, all the way from Pittsburgh to Cincinnati. It was important in a way, I suppose, that it is still important to many communities in the United States. It is very difficult to say this, but I think you will know what I mean. The fall was a time when certain things began again. In nature this is the time, presumably, when things come to fruition, and it's the beginning of the end. But for people, after the long hot summer, certainly for children at school, this was a beginning again. I always felt that way myself. I loved to go back to school and it seemed to me that this was a kind of beginning with hope in it. The football season, then, was very intensely a communal activity, a communal occasion. Teams from the various towns along the Ohio River and back a little from the Ohio River met and provided a point of focus in which the members of the distinct communities would see one another. Sometimes this meeting, this confrontation with the ritualized, formalized violence of those football teams, would inspire a peculiar kind of violence in the spectators too. The game itself is formal and graceful, but people do sometimes behave very anarchically in the stands.

D.S.: Thinking, in this context, of your poem "Autumn Begins in Martins Ferry, Ohio" do you mean to protest those games or are you pointing toward certain positive qualities which may emerge from such rituals?

Wright: I think that there were positive qualities. Those games were occasions for the expression of physical grace. I still feel that any sport which is well played has a terrific aesthetic appeal. In high school I devoted most of my activities to track, and I still love track. I should say about football back in the Ohio Valley—Martins Ferry, Shadyside, and Bellaire, Ohio— that in the years when I was growing up there were some truly remarkable athletes. Lou Groza was on my high school team, for example, and he became one of the great placekickers among the pros, playing for the Cleveland Browns. That was the quality of sport in that valley. This has some other significance. In my home town, Martins Ferry, Ohio, people were quite strikingly separated from each other along class lines. It is difficult to talk about class in America because we have the powerful myth of the common man, the myth of the absence of any class distinction. This troubled Henry James. Some later novelists who couldn't write as well as James, like James Jones, were able to deal in their novels with class issues and all the terrific drama that can rise from class confrontations by placing their characters in the army. What a startling experience it is to be a young American conditioned, to a certain extent, to believe we have no class distinctions in American society, then suddenly to get into the army and realize, if you are an enlisted man, that an officer, even a second lieutenant, for all practical purposes and down to the smallest detail, is regarded—and you regard him—as almost a distinct species. Even if, as in some cases during the Vietnam war, officers felt certain loyalties toward enlisted men, I'll bet there was something condescending about them. Officers aren't very democratic. You can find extreme instances of that in American life. The person who is born to privilege or who somehow has managed in his particular community to have attained a position of privilege is often trying to show a common touch he does not really have. One of the most astonishing and, to me fascinating, examples of this is to be found in a photograph that appeared in a newspaper during the 1960 Presidential Election campaign. Henry Cabot Lodge, who was Nixon's running mate, was visiting Coney Island. Norman Mailer wonderfully said of him that probably no one had ever suggested to Lodge that he was not necessarily superb. Lodge knew that he was superb, but he had to contend with the fact of electoral politics in the United States. There he stood at Coney Island and his beautifully pressed white shirt had the sleeves rolled up. He wasn't wearing a necktie. Hundreds of people were standing around him and staring with great interest. He had a hot dog in his hand and he stared at it. The expression on his face revealed profound conflict, the sort of thing that Jane Austen would love. I can't think of any other way to say it: he looked at that hot dog as if it were an obscene object which he *had* to eat.

D.S.: In some respects it seems you still think of Martins Ferry, Ohio as your town. Could you speak further about that?

Wright: I have some places I feel especially devoted to. In a way some of them are in Europe, some in the United States. I have a peculiar kind of devotion to Martins Ferry, although I haven't gone back there in at least twenty-five years. I still have a brother there and I have friends from childhood who are still in the Ohio River Valley. I feel that I am stuck with it. It is my place, after all. My feelings about it are complicated. People in that place have gotten angry with me for things I've written. And I have always, when I have heard from people directly, written to them and insisted that I was simply trying to write about some times. I haven't always written about Martins Ferry but I have tried sometimes to write about the life that I knew.

D.S.: What might a sense of place mean to a writer?

Wright: D. H. Lawrence has a very beautiful essay about "The Spirit of Place." He is talking in particular of American places but I think that what he says is true of all places. There is a spirit of place. Virgil was aware of this. I think that he uses the word *imago,* which isn't simply image but is also presence. We still speak of the genius of a place. I believe James Dickey, in a wonderful poem of his which is plainly the idea for his novel *Deliverance,* speaks of a man who appears, a country person, a redneck I guess you'd call him, by the side of the Coosawattee River; he suddenly appears when Dickey and some friends in their canoes have got into some trouble. One has hurt himself, I think. They come over to the bank of the river and the man appears there. Dickey calls him the presiding genius of the place. There is such a genius of place, a presence, and because there is, people's feelings accumulate about it. You can share in that feeling when you become aware of particular historical events and the significance of monuments and so on.

The American Indians, the Sioux, had such a sense of place. Fred Manfred, a wonderful midwestern novelist, pointed this out to me, that the Sioux and other Indians as well had a sense that certain areas were holy ground. He said that more than once in writing his novels and in wandering around and doing research the way he does, not just reading old books but trying to get the feel of places he would write about, he realized that there was something special about certain areas of southern Minnesota. He later discovered the Indians considered it sacred ground. I think that this is, for some writers, an important way of participating in the life around them. I'm not saying that the value of poetry depends on writing about a place or not writing about a place, only that there is a kind of poetry which is a poetry of place. It appeals to me very much. There are so many different ways that language can come alive or be brought alive that it is silly to limit the kinds of poetry there could be. I think it is enough to say that there is, in our lives, a genius of place and so, appropriately, we sometimes value a poetry of place.

This suggests an interesting thing about poetry during the last fifteen or twenty years in the United States; leaving aside the effectiveness of it or the ultimate value of it, nevertheless there has been a willingness on the part of a great many writers, really, to deal with this fact of place. Earlier, we didn't see this so much, being an English-speaking culture which proceeded from Europe. This country has all sorts of places still to be discovered in it. With this idea has come the realization that, after all, anything can be the location of a poem as long as the poet is willing to approach that location with the appropriate reverence. Even very ugly places.

My feeling about the Ohio Valley is, again, complicated. I sometimes feel a certain nostalgia about the place. At the same time I realize that as my friend Tom Hodge, now a surgeon in California, wrote to me a few years ago our problem when we were boys in Martins Ferry, Ohio in the industrial area enclosed by the foothills of the Appalachians on both sides, near that big river, was to get out. It has become plain to me that football helped many people to get out. And many of these people come from desperately poor families.

Martins Ferry, which is right across the Ohio River from Wheeling, West Virginia, is extraordinarily interesting in another respect. Ohio was a free state and this figures in *The Adventures of Huckleberry Finn*. Jim, as he and Huck go down the river, understands perfectly well that if only he can reach

Cairo, Illinois, then he can go up the Ohio and find freedom. The Underground Railway went through the free state of Ohio. But Ohio is southern at the same time that it is northern, intensely so. What could be more intense than what happened in my own family background? One of my great-uncles fought for the Union and one fought for the Confederacy, members of the same family. I wrote about that in a poem called "A Centenary Ode: Inscribed to Little Crow, Leader of the Sioux Rebellion in Minnesota, 1862." My great-uncle Paddy Beck fought for the Confederacy. He got buried in the Old Soldier's Home in Tiffin, Ohio. He even managed to get the people, when he died, to give him a nice clean new uniform, which was a Union uniform.

Ohio is also eastern and western. I sometimes ask my students in New York how many of them have traveled across the United States. Most have grown up in New York and know the East Coast. Or some of them may have flown to California and back. I tell them they can't get a sense of how incredibly huge and varied this country is by flying; I tell them that after they graduate they might travel by bus straight across the United States, and stop off sometimes. I tell them to go and see what it is like to have a cup of coffee in Zanesville, Ohio. It is as far from New York to Pittsburgh as it is from Paris to Vienna, but when you've reached Pittsburgh you're not really yet at the beginning of the Middle West. And the Middle West is, itself, enormous. You have to go to the other side of Minnesota to start to get a hint of what the western United States is like. Then you go into the huge mountain region and on the other side of that is a vastness. Ohio is eastern and western while it is also northern and southern.

Martins Ferry, my particular town, has among its sixteen thousand people a Greek community, a Hungarian community, a Polish community, a Welsh community, a Black community, and a community of Wasps. All of these are distinct communities in one small town. Remarkably. They are communities in the sense that, for Europeans as well as Wasp Americans, the family traditions, the religious traditions, and traditions of manners were maintained quite vividly. I remember that we had a May Day celebration. I was in the fifth grade and each grade, I guess, of all the five grade schools in town were to do a certain dance. I think my fifth grade learned how to do a Hungarian dance. I remember that my teacher told our class one day that when we all met down on the football field we would dance with our opposite numbers in the same grades from the other schools. She said that we must not feel bad that our costumes, which our mothers had carefully made up of crepe paper, were not as nice as the costumes worn by the kids from the northern part of town—because their parents had brought their costumes from Hungary. It turned out to be true. Their costumes were silk and they were gorgeous. I got so excited that May Day that I puked. It was beautiful.

D.S.: Did you begin writing as a young man?

Wright: I started to write when I was about eleven years old. My friend Tom Hodge was a year younger than I was and he belonged to a family that was fairly well off. His father was a businessman. My father was a factory worker. A friend of Tom's family, who was a minister, had gone to the war. Tom got access to this man's books and he gave me a book of poems by James Whitcomb Riley and also the Complete Poems of Byron. Hell, I'd never heard of either of them. I got very excited about Bryon and I wrote a play in verse. I don't know what ever happened to that.

D.S.: What did you do after high school?

Wright: I spent two years in the army. I went in just after the war ended, and I moved around a lot in the army. I had never been out of the Ohio Valley. I went first to Fort Lewis, Washington. Then I was sent to Engineer's School at Fort Belvoir, Virginia. From Fort Belvoir I was sent overseas and was in the occupation army in Japan.

D.S.: Does Japan influence your poems?

Wright: Let me show you something. [Mr. Wright went to his bookshelf and pulled down a neatly wrapped package which, when he had carefully unwrapped it, was a book of his poems translated into Japanese.] I've been in correspondence with Professor Toshitada Iketani. He made this selection of my poems a few years ago. I've sent my last two books to him and he tells me he will do a selection from those. We were in the Japanese and the American armies at about the same time. Professor Iketani wrote to me several times before he could bring himself to admit that he had done this. Of course, I asked to see it and I am delighted with it. We were both enlisted men and we came, I suppose, within a few months of confronting one another. It could have happened. We might have tried to kill each other. I have been devoted to Japanese literature ever since I was in Japan. It seems to me there are several ways that a genuine influence can work. I have never, so far as I recall, referred in my printed writings to my experience in Japan as such. I have written about it. The Japanese spirit and the tradition of the poetry, I think, has influenced me from time to time—in the effort the Japanese writers make to get rid of the clutter of language, to conceive of a poem as something which, with the greatest modesty, is brought up close to its subject so that it can be suggestive and evocative. Japan was a revelation to me.

D.S.: Upon leaving military service you enrolled in Kenyon College. Did you do so because of John Crowe Ransom and Kenyon's literary tradition?

Wright: I had never heard of Kenyon College. It dawned on me while I was in the army in Japan, and I don't know why it didn't happen before, that I might be able to go to college. I had the GI Bill available to me. I applied to several schools in Ohio and they all said no except Kenyon College. So I went there. I did not know of John Crowe Ransom or any literary tradition. It was just a college. I think that with the family I came from, a very good people, there was no tradition of education in the family. I had one distant cousin who had gone to college but except for him no one else. My mother had to leave school when she was in the sixth grade, my father had to leave when he was in the eighth grade. He went into the factory when he was fourteen and my mother went to work in a laundry. All of my relatives were working people. Back in the thirties I would have called them working class. My older brother Ted, who is now a photographer in Zanesville, Ohio was, except for that distant cousin, actually the first one of us who ever graduated from high school.

D.S.: You speak with such respect for the "working class" that we wonder if there is a danger of sentimentalizing workers, a danger some have felt apparent in contemporary American poetry.

Wright: I don't think that human sons of bitches are limited to this or that social class. I'm antipastoral. I've worked on farms and I would never work on another one. I've got up at four o'clock in the morning and shovelled the cow manure out of the barn and bailed away the horse urine. The hell with it. I worked for two nights in the factory my father had worked in, and I quit. I thought it was too much for me to handle. I couldn't live that kind of life. It was just as hard for my father. Before that summer was over I got a job in another factory elsewhere in Ohio, the old Mt. Vernon, Ohio Bridge Company. We chipped paint off girders and painted them with red lead. Do you know Robert Hayden's poem about his father?

Those Winter Sundays

Sundays too my father got up early
and put his clothes on in the blueblack cold,
then with cracked hands that ached
from labor in the weekday weather made
banked fires blaze. No one ever thanked him.

I'd wake and hear the cold splintering, breaking.
When the rooms were warm, he'd call,
and slowly I would rise and dress,
fearing the chronic angers of that house.

Speaking indifferently to him,
who had driven out the cold

and polished my good shoes as well.
What did I know, what did I know
of love's austere and lonely offices?

The word "offices" is the great word here. *Office,* they say in French. It is a religious service after dark. Its formality, its combination of distance and immediacy, is appropriate. In my experience uneducated people and people who are driven by brute circumstance to work terribly hard for a living, the living of their families, are very big on formality.

D.S.: Would you describe your experience at Kenyon College? Were there other writers there with you?

Wright: Well, it was exciting. There were only about four hundred fifty students in the school. They flunked out about half the freshman class every semester. They shocked us. We all went there, of course, thinking we were pretty smart and we found that they were going to show us pretty quickly that we were not all that smart. We had pretty vital relations with one another. The classes were exciting. I had to take freshman English; I couldn't get exempted from it, but it was a splendid course. We read *Gulliver's Travels,* and essays by Matthew Arnold and Carlyle and Bacon. They wanted us to learn how to write critical essays, not just themes. Critical essays. I then took Ransom's course called Poetic Analysis and he was a splendid teacher, a great teacher. Anthony Hecht is writing an essay about Ransom as a teacher and it ought to be very fine. Tony had left before I got to Kenyon. He had been an Instructor there. Once when I was an undergraduate I wrote him a letter because of a superb poem of his that had appeared in the undergraduate literary magazine. I don't think he has ever reprinted that marvelous poem in any of his books. It was an elegy for the builders of European cathedrals. Tony had been in combat in Europe and he saw many of those things he loved being blown up. His brother Roger was there (at Kenyon) when I was and is still, I suppose, as close a friend as I have. There was also a very gifted man named Jay Gellens. I don't know what has happened to him. George Lanning, the novelist, was there. Edgar Doctorow was there. E. L. Doctorow, who became a good novelist. And during my last year Robert Mezey came. He was just sixteen years old then. The first time I saw him I had been working very hard on a paper and he was there for prefreshman week in the spring. He was sitting with a friend in the student lounge, which was in the basement of the building where we lived. I remember throwing back the French doors and staring straight at Mezey. I didn't know who he was. Then I shouted, "I am a transparent eyeball." And I slammed the doors. That line from Emerson stuck in everybody's craw back at Kenyon. We were always trying to figure out what Emerson meant by that. Jarrell and Lowell, of course, had been at Kenyon earlier.

D.S.: How do you now value Ransom's poetry?

Wright: His poetry, as the years go by, seems to me to be finer than I had realized. I always liked it. Ransom is in slightly bad odor right now, partly because he writes the so-called "square" poem: you can glance at his poems on the page and see that they scan. If you look a little closer, unless you happen to be as tone-deaf as some of our reviewers apparently are—I don't say that in malice, I say it as a kind of curiosity—you can hear that his poems rhyme. Furthermore, Ransom plainly shows in his poems that he is willing to let his conscious intelligence operate in the poems and this is very much out of fashion. It's ridiculous that it should be out of fashion. It is part of the terribly self-flattering, self-indulging anarchic spirit of our times, the spirit of confusion.

D.S.: What do you feel that you learned from Ransom?

Wright: I think it was the ideal, what elsewhere I've called the Horatian ideal, the attempt finally to write a poem that will be put together so carefully that it does produce a single unifying effect. I still conceive of a poem as being a thing which one can make rather than as a matter of direct expression. It is true that I have written and published a good many poems that do manage to be nothing except direct expression of my own feelings about this and that. I regard those poems as failures. The fact that I've written them and published some just means that I ought not to have published them.

Ransom was a beautiful teacher because he was a beautiful reader of poetry. I'm not talking about the sound of his voice, although the sound of his voice was charming and students loved him. We parodied him endlessly. We imitated his voice, as in one old parody which I participated in. I'm still proud of the four lines we achieved, although there was a committee of five or six people in on it. Here it is:

Balls on Joan Whiteside's Stogie

> There was such smoke in our little buggy
> and such a tightness in our car stall.
> Is it any wonder her brown stogie
> asphyxiates us all?

I went back to see Ransom when he was 82 years old. I finally told him this parody and he said he *knew* that. He knew all the gags. When I say he was a good reader, I mean he understood that humility is a necessary intellectual virtue, leaving its moral virtue aside. He tried to instill in us the recognition of how necessary it is to pay humble attention to what an author is trying to say. And behind that was his assumption about himself, that the first thought that popped into his mind was not necessarily coeval and coextensive with the mind of God. In other words, in Ortega's sense, Ransom was a noble man, as distinguished from a barbarian. He was very acute. He could be extremely funny. His genuine humility had quite a striking effect on students, in our occasional arrogance. He would let us undermine ourselves and he read poems with us and would take a long time reading them. It was marvelous because he could hear things in the poems that were there, in short.

D.S.: Did you subsequently go to the University of Washington to study with Theodore Roethke?

Wright: After I finished at Kenyon College I had a Fulbright Scholarship to the University of Vienna and I still had not decided whether I should go to graduate school. During the year I was in Vienna I did decide, finally, on something that I had thought a good deal about, that I wanted to be a teacher. Once I had decided to become a teacher, it seemed to me a serious matter to do graduate work and get a graduate degree. I was led to the University of Washington by a friend, Herbert Lindenberger. I knew practically nothing about Roethke. I didn't know his work. I had been at Kenyon College from 1948 to 1952. Roethke had not published very much at this time. I took one course from Roethke at the University of Washington, and only one course, because he got sick after that first semester and because I had literature courses to take. That was, however, a course in writing poetry. A course with Roethke was a course in very, very detailed and strenuous critical reading. Here was an assignment: he wanted us to go to the library and find ten or maybe even twenty iambic trimeter lines that had a caesura after the first syllable. He made us do that. For example, Robert Bridges' "Die, song, die like a breath." We tried. Remember that this was back in the 1950s and, though the people in that generation have been accused of being quietists, in any case it did not occur to us that our own immediate accidental opinions of things were not necessarily the everlasting truth. So, we knew Roethke was a very fine man, an intelligent and learned man, and when he asked us to do something we would do it. He was not trying to violate our psyches or something.

Of course, Roethke was only a part of my education at the University of Washington. I think that the most exciting and the most useful courses I took were medieval literature courses with David Fowler. I studied Chaucer with him and also the Pearl Poet, Sir Gawain. A few graduate students even persuaded him to give us a course in Langland and his contemporaries, so we read some middle English in a dialect different from Chaucer's. Also I had a superb course from Maynard Mack, the eighteenth century scholar from Yale, who came there and gave a course in Augustan literature. I still correspond with him. He was a great teacher. I retain a fondness for medieval literature though I haven't pursued it very much. I became very interested in the history of the English novel and it is my main academic subject. At Hunter College I'm teaching a course in the eighteenth century novel and Cervantes' effect on it. I've given courses in Dickens, Hardy, even whole courses in the nineteenth century novel.

D.S.: You have been both an ardent supporter and a harsh critic of academic life, at least a critic of some of its attitudes. Could you discuss what kinds of approaches your teaching takes?

Wright: I try to present to my students some of the necessary questions and problems of philosophical and historical background. For example, I have found that in presenting *Don Quixote* to my students it has been very important for them and for me to devote several class periods to a discussion of the philosophical terms Materialism, Idealism, the credibility of hypotheses and scientific method, Logical Positivism, and so on. I also occasionally teach a course called Poetics, the Poetic Tradition. This is an attempt to introduce students to some of the problems and techniques of traditional poetry and when we have read individual poems it has been necessary and very useful, helpful to us all I think, for me to offer some historical background. For example, consider a poem I think is a great and important poem by Marvell, the "Horatian Ode On Cromwell's Return To Ireland." It is not possible to understand what is going on in that poem without some awareness of the political and social problems which obtain in England from the reign of Elizabeth through Charles II. That's a very complicated story, one of the most exciting. And it is one of the richest historical periods for the study of literature. On the one side we have Cromwell, who Marvell in his very intelligent poem characterizes so beautifully, and on the other side we have Charles I. Marvell shows that Charles I, in spite of his reputation as a frivolous playboy, actually had a profound understanding of power, the nature of political power and its uses, which even resembles that of Queen Elizabeth herself.

In the midst of this we sometimes read Robert Herrick and it is important to point out that Herrick was a Royalist who disappeared at one point in his life for thirteen years.

Amazingly, in this period which historians as well as literary scholars have studied in such detail, nobody knows what happened to Robert Herrick for thirteen years. Then he emerges with his big book of poems—"I fain would kiss the calf of Julia's leg / Which is as white and hairless as an egg"—and at the end of his noble numbers he says "Upon his gravestone these words he'd have placed / His muse was jocund but his life was chaste." He must have known we would say, no, no. Anybody but a monster would hope that he scored.

Well, this is the way I approach teaching. Of course we try to come down and see how particular works are constructed. I am also interested at least in the history of the novel with the meaning and the function of the particular language that the individual novelist uses. It is highly important. E. M. Forster says that there is a kind of novelist who can sing and a kind that can't. That doesn't mean that one is necessarily better than the other. George Eliot doesn't sing but Emily Bronte does. And her singing in that prose, sometimes, is artistically and intellectually very important. Say in *Wuthering Heights*. And the flat regular prose of Daniel Defoe is designed to give the texture, substance really, of factuality in the world that he presents. He means for us to forget that he is making the whole thing up. We now have the weird and interesting fact that Defoe is called matter-of-fact and prosaic by some very prosaic critics whereas Virginia Woolf regards him as a person of great poetic imagination. I think he is.

D.S.: Does Dickens remain special to you?

Wright: Yes, he does. I did my doctoral dissertation on Dickens. He has an almost insane poetic imagination, a power of invention, and an enormous intelligence. He is a compulsive writer and it would be silly to say he wrote too much; if he had not written so much he would not be Dickens. He can be very, very precise. But it isn't only Dickens who is special to me. It is also the prose of other novelists and the prose of essayists. I read often for enjoyment and some of my favorite writers, modern and otherwise, are themselves expository essayists.

One of my very favorites, a writer I read for great pleasure, is H. L. Mencken. I have been reading with great pleasure the latest book of essays by Diana Trilling, called *We Must March My Darlings*. I admire Forster's essays. One of my favorite books, that I read the way some people read poetry, is Forster's *Two Cheers For Democracy*. In fact I think that among all modern writers I enjoy the expository essayist the most.

D.S.: Does this reading of prose affect the nature of your poetry?

Wright: I hope it does. What I hope to write is a poetry which is consecutive and clear. Sometimes I have written obscurely and sometimes I have written limply. But in these cases I know I have just written badly. That is not what I was trying to do or hoped to do. A valuable remark of Pound's is that a person who is going to write free verse should be careful not to write bad prose hacked into arbitrary line lengths. It seems to me, as I look around whatever little magazines are sent to me, that we are pratically inundated with bad prose hacked into such lines. Eliot, too, argued that poetry has been most vital when it has been closest to good prose and yet has been able somehow to retain its own character. I take it that its own character finally has something to do with rhythm, a regularity of rhythm or a clear variation on regularity.

D.S.: During the writing of your first collection of poems, The Green Wall, *you said in a letter to Roethke that "I work like hell clipping away perhaps one tiny pebble per day from the ten-mile-thick wall of formal and facile 'technique' which I myself erected, and which stands ominously between me and whatever poetry may be in me." Can you comment on your meaning?*

Wright: I think that quotation is confused. I would enlarge on it by saying that I was starting to feel then, and I still feel, that the writer's real enemy is his own glibness, his own facility; the writer constantly should try to discover what difficulties there truly are inherent in a subject or in his own language and come to terms with these difficulties. If he does that, then he might be able to discover something in his own mind, or in the language which is imaginative. I did not say very clearly what I was trying to think my way toward. What I was trying to suggest, trying to think, trying to realize is just that it is fatally easy to write in an almost automatic way. After you master certain gimmicks, whether in formal verse or in rhyme or in so-called free verse, then it is pretty easy to repeat them. I wrote a piece in my notebook about the purity and the force, really the great strength, of Richard Wilbur. He has always written regular verse and with wonderful purity and a beautiful music and great accuracy and clarity, and with great emotional depth. For a while during the fifties most writers were tending to write in too facile, too glib a way in regular meters and rhyme. Some of us turned away to free verse. Since then I think that whenever one opens a magazine nearly all the poems ones sees will be in free verse. More and more they strike me as being just as facile and automatic in their way as the earlier poems had been in other ways. That is, it isn't a solution to one's artistic problems just to stop rhyming.

Here is one of my favorite themes. This is what I call "trite surrealism." The French surrealists, and there are some very good ones, understood that Dadaism and Surrealism were comic reactions to certain preestablished conventions of rationality in writing. They started to be deliberately irrational. They were able to write good poems when in one way or another they were comic. Americans who have tried to follow the Surrealistic way don't get the joke. There are many bad surrealistic poems and there are horrible examples of the most automatic, unimaginable kind of thing. They are straining toward imagination and something new. They are like the Puritans in Dr. Seuss' old pocket book of boners. Some student wrote that the Puritans came to America to worship God as they saw fit and to see that everybody else did the same thing.

This matter of trite surrealism requires critical analysis. In a recent issue of the magazine *Kayak* (No. 51, September 1979, p. 38) there appears a letter by John Haines. I think he is a thoroughly admirable, serious man, one of the best poets now writing. What he says is so intelligent and important that I want to quote it at length:

> The greatest poetry has always shown abundant evidence of *mind*, of intellect directed toward a felt conclusion. The trouble with surrealism, as with many another modern mode, is that it is partial, a piece of a whole. The best efforts in our time have always been directed toward that whole, whether achieved or not. The liberation of thought and feeling granted to many modern poets through the influence of surrealism has been at its best a means to an end.
>
> One problem in all this, and it hardly needs saying, is the talent we display for trivializing everything, and by a mindless repetition, for turning even the most innovative ideas into cliches. (The trivialization applies as much to the objectivity of Williams and the ideogramic method of Pound as it does to the studied accidentals of surrealism.) It needed no great power of imagination to foresee that when a new poetry began to be written here in the early sixties, it would not be long before its characteristics would be imitated to the point of becoming just another promotional device. What we have seen, I suppose, is the domestications of Surrealism. At this point, most efforts at surrealist poems strike me as pathetic. The offerings of the unconscious are only the beginning, and whoever takes those shadows for the truth will never see the daylight.
>
> Another thing not brought out is the hidden motive, or hope, (implied anyway in surrealism) of making poetry relevant in the modern world, by claiming for it a significance we are afraid it no longer has. By taking over, in one way or the other, the material and terminology of psychology, by assuming a pseudoscientific approach to structure and meaning—by becoming finally a specialization—poetry would take its rightful place as a serious occupation. Or so, perhaps, the evidence indicates. The poet-interview, the many workshops and conferences, the solemn discussions of technique or "craft," are examples of what I mean by this, and destined perhaps to become the curiosities of an era.

D.S.: How do you feel about your early poems?

Wright: I haven't read them for a while. About three years ago I sat down and read my whole *Collected Poems*. Some of them I couldn't remember having written and some of them I didn't understand. It is true that I wrote to my publisher after *St. Judas* and said I don't know what I am going to do after this but it will be completely different. This comment, and also Robert Bly's essay on my work, has given rise to some sort of assumption that I calculated that I was going to be born again or something, that I would become a completely different person. I think that this is nonsense. There was a good essay by Mark Strand, in *Field* magazine, regarding changes in poetry. He used my work as an example and he said that the only difference, really, was that I don't rhyme so often now. I don't think that a person can change very quickly or easily. Well, there is such a thing as a conversion experience surely. William James has written formally about this in *Varieties of Religious Experience*. That change is a reality. Let me say that to change one's kind of poetry would be, in effect, to change one's life. I don't think that one can change one's life simply as an act of will. And I never wanted to. What I had hoped to do from the beginning was to continue to grow in the sense that I might go on discovering for myself new possibilities of writing.

I have written a good many prose pieces now and I did this because I liked prose and I wanted to express myself that way. I put some prose pieces in my last couple of books and sometimes these have been called poems. They are not poems. They are prose pieces. Now whether they are well written or badly written is another question. I said before, in other connections, that we sometimes have a hard time discussing writing itself in the United States because we are constantly getting bogged down in nitpicking about technical terms. The French can talk about the prose-poem and do so effectively just because they can use a phrase like that and everybody knows that people may disagree with one another about these terms. But everybody in the controversy also knows that the prose-poem is a term of convenience. They know perfectly well that Flaubert wrote prose and that Baudelaire wrote in verse, and was a poet.

With this distinction, then, they are free to go on and try new combinations of things. This is what I have always hoped for myself. The trouble with it all in the United States is that sure as hell somebody's going to say, now which is it, prose or poetry?

Yvor Winters said a valuable thing in this respect. He said, poetry is written in verse whereas prose is written in prose. That is a help because I think it allows us to drop the nitpicking and then go on and try to see what the writing in question is. Then we can try to determine whether or not there is a way to understand it and, finally, to undertake the extremely difficult task of determining whether it is any good or not.

Good in relation to what, we may ask? Literary criticism itself, I think, ought to be as Matthew Arnold said: an effort to see the thing in itself as it really is. He went on to say it ought to be an effort to make reason and the will of God prevail. T. S. Eliot remarked that there was Arnold referring to that joint firm, Reason and the Will of God. Whether or not that particular phrase of Arnold's is useful to us still, he did see that observing the thing itself as it really is, is only the first part of the task. The further task is the more dynamic one of trying to determine whether or not the thing itself was worth doing and what effect it can have—how far it is expressive, how far it is communicative, and finally whether it is any good. This requires us, as critics, to try to truly understand whether or not there is such a thing as the good or the bad. What do we mean by that? Can we make it clear? These are terrific and serious tasks for literary criticism.

I said at one point that there can't be a good poetry without a good criticism. I did not mean that there has to be a great body of formal criticism in print. I meant that a person who is writing and reading is going to be able to write better and more truly if he tries to think about language, if he tries to imagine what his own writing is going to look like and smell like and sound like to an intelligent person of good will. These are critical efforts. Or if he tries to determine what relation he has or can have to the authors whom he, himself, genuinely considers to be great and enduring. What do I have to do with

Horace? It is a question that I have to ask myself if I am a serious man. Well, I can try to understand what Horace says, many of the things that he says, for example his pieces about the art of poetry. I can try to be true to them in the immediate terms of my own work. He says valuable things. This is not to say that I have ever written anything or could write anything within a thousand miles of Horace's excellence. To know this, and to know as I do know, that the assumption of my equalling Horace, the least thing by Horace, is an illusion—this is a help to me in understanding my own limitations and my possibilities. I am a traditionalist and I think that whatever we have in our lives that matters has to do with our discovering our true relation to the past.

D.S.: Can you talk about why you wrote poems about Goerge Doty, a convicted and executed murderer?

Wright: I was preoccupied with that because it startled me for a while, the whole notion of how little we human beings understand one another. I was preoccupied with how, back in Ohio, a taxi driver named George Doty from Bellaire, drove a girl out in the country and made a pass at her, which she resisted, so he banged her in the head with a tree branch and killed her. I was convinced that he didn't really know what in the hell was happening. He had stumbled into something evil, a murder he had committed, but I don't think that he understood anything about the legal proceedings. Many people in that community thought he was terribly wicked, but he did not seem to me wicked. He was just a dumb guy who suddenly was thrust into the middle of the problem of evil and he was not able to handle it. I thought it was ridiculous to execute him and, further, I thought that murder is murder whether the state commits it or some stupid, retarded taxi driver. That is what I was trying to say. The epigraph of the second poem, "At the Executed Murderer's Grave," is from Freud. Many people thought the epigraph referred to execution. I was a little calculating about this. It is interesting to do this with critics and reviewers, to say something and see how they will go on rattling about it and will show with every damn word they write that they haven't the faintest idea of what you mean. Freud was not speaking of capital punishment there. It is taken from his book *The Future of an Illusion* and he is referring to the idea we call The Golden Rule. Freud says "Why should we do this? What good is it to us? Above all, how can we do such a thing? How can it possibly be done?" Notice how Freud, who was very precise and careful, is repeating himself compulsively. He's staggered by this idea. Knowing what he knows about human beings, it is a staggering idea to him.

D.S.: How do you respond to the assertion that "A Poem about George Doty in the Death House" has an ugly, unfeeling conclusion?

Wright: I can understand that. Some people believe that I was sympathizing with the criminal rather than with the victim. Well, I sympathize with the victim all right. As I have replied at least ten times to people from Martins Ferry who have written to me to protest that poem, I sympathize with the victim. I'm just saying that I sympathize with George Doty, too. I think what annoyed them is somehow that the person who committed this crime ought to be cut off from human fellowship; that is, they believed this and I did not believe it.

In the same sense I believe that *The Adventures of Huckleberry Finn* is a genuinely subversive book. It is subversive not because it uses bad grammar and not because it takes an ornery little boy as its hero; what is subversive about it is that it doesn't say each human being is complex and valuable. Instead it demonstrates in scene after scene, action after action, with absolute finality that the slave Jim is a complex human being with a high moral intelligence. Mark Twain makes that undeniable. And this is unbearable to a person who has to regard somebody as a thing, as property. The idea of slavery still lurks powerfully. The idea that some men are no more than things, the idea that, if you give some men bathtubs they will only fill those tubs with coal. This still lurks powerfully in spite of our liberal rhetoric. In recent years everybody in America has taken over liberal rhetoric. But the idea of slavery remains. It is not so much the racists as people who are comfortably off.

This is exactly the appropriateness of Cyril McFadden's good novel, *The Serial*. She sees that the comic imagination is required to examine the influence of Freud and psychoanalysis in the United States, an influence which has turned into a rhetoric that Americans have seized upon so that we can tell one another how neurotic we are instead of facing our genuine human tragic problems. Her novel is about life in Marin County, California and nobody can say or do anything without saying "create your own space" or "build up your karma" and so on. In one scene a child goes into the bathroom and locks itself in and turns on the water and is drowning in the bathtub. They can't get in and the kid is screaming. Instead of doing anything—they've all been divorced about five times through creative divorce—they sit there and talk about creative parenting. They hang loose in their own space.

D.S.: Was "At the Executed Murderer's Grave" a watershed poem for you?

Wright: Yes. And it was that in its language too. The previous version of it was very, very overblown and rhetorical. That version had appeared in *Poetry*. When I came to try and put it into *St. Judas* I was completely dissatisfied with it, so I sent it to Jim Dickey. He and I had had a misunderstanding and a disagreement earlier, followed very rapidly by an exchange of letters. We became good friends and have been so ever since. I sent him the *Poetry* version of the poem. It was a mess, full of mythological and biblical references and so on, very Victorian. He made comments all over it and sent the poem back. I studied his comments in Minneapolis. Then I had to go up to Seattle to defend my Ph.D. dissertation, which I did, and on the way back, on the train, I didn't have his comments with me but I remembered them. I didn't have the poem either. So I sat there and rewrote it without looking at the previous version, from the beginning, and rewrote it as straight and direct and

Robinsonian as I could make it. That is the way it came out. It was important to me. I felt as if I had shed something.

D.S.: Have you forgotten this (showing a poem to Wright) earlier, first version which was published in Botteghe Oscure?

At the Executed Murderer's Grave

Reflective calm, you tangle, root and bone,
Fang, fist, and skull, that huddle down alone.
Sparrows above him, sneaking like police,
Peck at the lawn, the hedge, the careful trees.
Man's wild blood has no heart to overcome
Vengeance and summer and the lily's bloom.
Henceforth, so long as I myself shall live,
Earth will be torn, the mind be fugitive.
My shadow flees me over mattocked stone:
Father and citizen, I killed this man,
This man who killed another who might kill
Another who might slay another still
Till the tall shadows of mankind are cast
Bodiless on the empty stars at last.
Rage and destruction trouble me, and fade.
The casual flocks of sunbeam round my head
Flutter away to dusk, and I am dark,
Peering between the granites for his mark.
Slow hills away, the milch-cows pause and yawn,
Wondering when day will go, and man be gone:
That one man, angry at the heart's release,
This brutal pastoral, this unholy peace.

Wright: Well, I'll be damned. This is still pretty rhetorical. It was a stage. What I would do today would be to just keep that in my notebook. I know Robert Bly feels that the third, finished version that is in *St. Judas* is very much a failure. I don't think that one is a failure. I think it is clearly what I wanted to say. Robert feels that it is a failure, I believe.

D.S.: What good is a poem, finally?

Wright: I don't know. A poem is good because of the pleasure that it provides us. Samuel Johnson argues in his preface to the 1765 Shakespeare that a work endures if it gives pleasure but then, very acutely, he says that there are different kinds of pleasure. Some are more frivolous and occasional. There is nothing wrong with that, except such pleasure wears out. There is a deeper pleasure we can find in trying to see the truth, by which Johnson means to imply something about the tragic complexity of life. Shall I state Johnson's remark? He says it with such force.

> Nothing can please many or please long but just representations of general nature. Particular manners can be known to few, and few only can judge how nearly they are copied. The irregular combinations of fanciful invention may delight a while by that novelty, of which the common satiety of life sends us all in quest, but the pleasure of sudden wonder are soon exhausted and the mind can only repose on the stability of truth.

Johnson is, of course, as thoroughly aware of the multiplicity of truth as Shakespeare is. But there is a difference between the truth to be found in what T. S. Eliot very brutally calls birth, copulation, and death, and what Johnson means. There is more pleasure, Johnson says, in being able to understand those tragic complexities than there is to be found, say, in concrete poetry. Thom Gunn said the same sort of thing a few years ago while reviewing a book-length poem. He said, "This must be the first full-length *Waste Land* that I have read in a couple of years."

D.S.: You have said that when your own work fails it does so because of a lack of clarity. What do you mean by clarity and why is it difficult?

Wright: I would like to write something that would be immediately and prosaically comprehensible to a reasonably intelligent reader. That is all. That is all I mean by being clear, but it is very difficult for me. This is a Horatian idea. It is the attempt to write, as one critic said once of the extraordinarily and beautifully strong writer Katherine Anne Porter, so that "every one of her effects is calculated but they never give the effect of calculation." We read a story like her "Noon Wine" and it is what we call seamless. It is almost impossible to pick that story apart and find her constructing a beginning, middle, and end. When you read the whole thing you do realize, and not just with your feelings but with your intelligence, that what you have just looked at is a living thing. It has a form. She hasn't written in bulk, never in such bulk as, say, Edward Bulwer-Lytton. And yet, her work has a certain largeness about it because it is so alive. I think that she has thought very clearly and carefully about the need to make things clear to a reasonably intelligent reader of good will. As for other kinds of readers, well there are fools in the world, and bastards.

D.S.: You said this once: "One thing a person tries to do is to discover the appropriate form for whatever he is saying." What do you mean by form?

Wright: I don't mean form in the abstract. I mean what anyone would mean when he talks about true rhetoric. I mean the proper words in the proper places. That's all. We have mentioned Robert Creeley's idea that form is no more than an extension of content. I think I follow what Creeley is saying and as far as I follow it, I think it is sound. Beyond a certain point, however, it gets confusing and starts to sound vague. It is easiest to talk about such matters when one is dealing with comic poetry because there, as Auden pointed out, the form is predominant and the joke comes out of discovering in the following of certain strict forms. This is true even when one writes a parody in free verse like that one in William Harmon's *Oxford Book of American Light Verse,* which is a wonderful parody of Whitman in long-line Whitmanesque catalog form. There is a housewife present and her husband is drunk and comes in singing, "We won't get home until the morning" and at the end of this long line, which takes about five lines of print, the husband is finally inside and the parodist says "He inebriate, chantant." And consider Whitman's great bad line, one of the great bad lines in the world, I think, and yet like some lines in Dickens only Whitman could have written it. It's this: "How plentious, how spiritual, how resume." Isn't that nice? It reminds me of Dickens. David Copperfield, after he's gotten hung over, knows that the pure Agnes Whitfield has seen him drunk, so he goes and asks her forgiveness. She forgives him and he says . . . it is just staggering. A mediocre writer could never have written this. It has the whole of Victorian taste in it. He says, "Oh Agnes, you are my good angel, beast that I am." Isn't that fine? I know it is horrible, but it has genius in it.

D.S.: Would you speak about your life in Minnesota, after you had left Seattle?

Wright: I taught at the University of Minnesota for six years and at Macalester College for two years. I was not given tenure at the University of Minnesota, so I was invited over to Macalester. I taught there for two years and then I felt I had been in Minnesota long enough. I had a Guggenheim Fellowship that next year and this enabled me to look around. I finally found a job in New York and I have been here since.

D.S.: Would you speak about Allen Tate and John Berryman, your colleagues at the University of Minnesota?

Wright: I knew Tate pretty well. I went to his house many times and we were good friends. I knew his wife at that time, Isabella Gardner, and we are still good friends. She is in New York, too. I got along with them very well. I did not know Berryman so well, personally. But formally I knew him and admired him. I still admire Tate's poetry very much. I realize that at the moment there isn't very much discussion of it, but I believe that his best poems are good enough to survive beyond fluctuations of fashion. "The Ode to the Confederate Dead," some of the sonnets. "The Eagle"—these are wonderful. Berryman, after his death, of course, provoked all sorts of speculation, his alcoholism, and so on. I think we are going to come back to Berryman's poetry in a few years when the smoke has cleared and someone will set about making a good selected poems and will discover the work is extremely fine. He was a very rattled man. He was desperately sick and I think his achieving so much was really quite heroic, amazing.

D.S.: Was Robert Penn Warren at Minnesota during this time?

Wright: No, he was there earlier. I have got to know him somewhat, personally, since then. We have corresponded and met a couple of times. He certainly is a fine man. There is an interesting thing about Warren. In America we have a very powerfully operative myth about, and not only about, writers who burn themselves out while young. This comes to us, I suppose, from the twenties and from, or back of, F. Scott Fitzgerald. We have also still, perhaps from grade school and high school, a kind of confused notion of literary romanticism. People don't express this so openly and directly, but I believe that it is somehow in the air. It is the notion that it is actually very desirable for a young person to create a big hullaballoo and die very young. But we have also had, in America, the extremely fine possibility of the writer who continues his search and is steadfast. He continues his effort to learn how to write well and to be true to life as he understands it. This is the writer who in spite of his steadfastness may occasionally write clumsily, but who nevertheless is not dull. This is the writer who in his advanced age is able to bring so many of his good-hearted, I think you can use that word, goodhearted and stead-fast efforts to fruition. That is what has been happening in the work of Warren with his most recent books. If you did not know he was seventy-four years old, you would think he has the vigor and freshness of someone who is perhaps thirty.

Another author who is able to do this, who is a little plod-ding and not perhaps so startlingly gifted as Warren has ob-viously been as a novelist and as a critic and as a teacher, as well as a poet, who nevertheless wrote poems to the end of his life, poems of great beauty, is John Hall Wheelock. I told Mr. Wheelock once that I hoped he understood how much his very life meant to somebody like me and to many people my own age. I told him that Galway Kinnell agreed with me, that by being true to himself he really had given us some hope. He had demonstrated to us that to try to be true to whatever poetic gift we might have, large or small, really did mean something. It was not a stupid vain effort. Of course this is obviously not the same thing as saying we can't fail; most of us probably will fail, but the failure isn't total.

Warren right at the moment, it seems to me, is an inspiration. Another interesting thing is that he seems to have no hostility toward writers younger than himself. He will do anything to help people.

D.S.: Thinking specifically of your review-essay of Warren's Promises, *which appeared in the* Kenyon Review *in 1958, it appears that you suggested something in Warren's development that was, perhaps, also occuring in your celebrated shift of form at about that time. Can you discuss the importance of Warren's influence on your work?*

Wright: Yes. The way I see things now, Warren has been more important to me than even I realized at the time. What I take it that he was doing, what I tried to write in that essay, however clumsily, was important to me. It was important for me to write that essay and Mr. Ransom understood that. Ransom and I were corresponding and I had said that my friend Morgan Blume and I were reading Warren again. Morgan, who was a very, very close friend of mine at Minnesota, died three years ago of a stroke. A terrible loss, he was just forty-three years old. Morgan was very bright and a passionate student of literature. He wrote some poems and essays, but mainly he was a superb reader and a good critic. He and I were going through Warren. We met and talked often and we were talking about the novels, the poems, and we read a great deal in these. We were sort of speculating about the relationship between them. I told Ransom this and he wrote back and said why don't you do a piece on Warren's new poems and get Blume to do his fiction. So we did that. We wrote our essays and showed them to each other and talked about them. Then they were published in consecutive issues of the *Kenyon Review.*

I think that you can speak legitimately and reasonably and necessarily, about the craft of writing. Well, I think that Warren is as much a master of the craft as Ransom and Tate. People who have split their poems, Warren's and Tate's and Ransom's, away from emotion are just wrong. Who could be more passionate than Tate? Sometimes he's so passionate in his poems that he is almost inarticulate. He had the boldness to do this. "The Eagle," is, I think, a great poem and yet there are parts of it that are just about gibberish. But the rhythm is so powerful that it goes over you and through you.

Warren had become a technical master, a master of craft, and in *Promises*, knowing this, he tried deliberately to be craftsmanlike and constantly to reach out in terms of his rhythm and his diction. And also, by the way, in terms of place; he was trying to write a poetry of place. They are Italian poems. And all of this is what moved me, what seemed to me exciting. It seemed bold and original and also helpful. One could learn something. One could learn first the necessity of trying to master a craft and then to recognize that, as I was arguing a little earlier, that there was a danger of glibness, of an excessive facility. Then one could learn to try and keep one's language and one's rhythms open to new possibility. Of course this kind of poetry can lead to clumsiness, which is embarrassing and asinine and unintentional. I suppose that there is no escape from the charges of sentimentality and asininity so long as you are willing to try. It has seemed to me in my own life, in my own attempt to write, and within my own narrower limits—I don't have Warren's learning or range or anything like Warren's intelligence—but within my own limits it seemed to me necessary and sensible to discover new ways of writing for oneself. The discovery of such new ways surely has something to do with discovering the possibilities of one's life. It is something like Thoreau's remark. He said, I have never met a man who was entirely awake. How could I have looked him in the face?

In Warren's *Promises* language had been taken to a formal extreme only to be broken and reshaped. You could feel him doing it in the book. It is a ragged sort of book, yet it has such life in it. And where does that life consist? How can we find it?

How do we find it, if it is not in what I would call the entirely finished and polished poem? It is in his ability to show us the struggle going on as he writes, so that each poem in that book is very dramatic even if it is just a piece of straight description.

D.S.: When people speak of the change in your poems after your first two books they speak of the surrealism and often refer to "Lying in a Hammock at William Duffy's Farm in Pine Island, Minnesota" as not untypical of your change. You have said of this poem, "All I did was describe what I felt and what I saw, lying in the hammock. Shouldn't that be enough? But no, there's your American every time, goddamnit, somebody's got to draw a moral." Would you comment further?

Wright: Well, I think that the poem is a description of a mood and this kind of poem is the kind of poem that has been written for thousands of years by the Chinese poets. I can't read Chinese, but I certainly can read Soame Jenyns and Robert Paine and Witter Bynner and Arthur Wailey. And that poem, although I hope it is a description of my mood as I lay in that hammock, is clearly an imitation of that Chinese manner. It is not surrealistic. I said, at the end of that poem, "I have wasted my life" because it was what I happened to feel at that moment and as part of the mood I had while lying in the hammock. This poem made English critics angry. I have never understood what would have so infuriated them. They could say the poem was limp or that it did not have enough intellectual content. I can see that. But I hope that it did not pretend to. It just said, I am lying here in this hammock and this and that is happening.

American critics think that last line is a moral, that it is a comment which says I have wasted my life by writing iambics, or that I have wasted my life by lying in the hammock. Actually, behind everything in my general thoughts and feelings was the idea that one of the worst things in American life is waste. I think that our tendency to waste is a truly dreadful one. I have told my students that one of the most horrifying things to me is to stand, being my age, and look at a class of nineteen- and twenty-year-old people who are trying to read a passage of, say, Milton or Shakespeare and to see their faces saying it is a waste of time. They don't see how precious their lives are.

D.S.: One of your poems is called "The Morality of Poetry" and another is called "The Idea of the Good." Can you speak of the difference between drawing a moral and the ideas implied in these titles?

Wright: I only used the phrase "the morality of poetry" once and it is the title of that poem in *St. Judas*. What I meant there was that there are different kinds of forms in poetry which are possible and to try to write any of them well is a good thing. That is the morality of poetry, as far as I am concerned. "The Idea of the Good" is a very, very confused poem. I don't have the faintest idea what it means. I can't imagine how anyone could find a meaning in it. It is just badly written. I forget what I was thinking of at the time. I feel this way about almost everything in my book *Two Citizens*. The book is just a bust. I will never reprint it. Let me put it this way, I ought not to have published that book the way it stands. I should have taken possibly six poems in it and tried to wait a year, to see if I couldn't revise them and see what else I had. That is what I ought to have done and I didn't. I made an ass of myself. It seems to me a bad book because most of it is badly written. Obscure and self-indulgent, it talks around subjects rather than coming to terms with them. It is impossibly ragged. It is just unfinished. If I were ever going to reprint any of it, I would take maybe six poems and write them out again in longhand and see what might happen. I would try to think about them as thoroughly as I could.

D.S.: Do you have a specific feeling about that book's initial poem, "Ars Poetica: Some Recent Criticism"?

Wright: It has some strong possibilities in it, but it is still confused. I am not quite sure what it means. That can be a glib answer, an evasion of responsibility, but I mean that when I go back and look at it I can't quite figure out what it is about. I called it "Some Recent Criticism" because I had in mind to write the kind of poem that could not be glibly disposed of by some reviewers and critics who were interested in facility alone. I made that conscious effort. Suddenly I called it "Ars Poetica" as if to say here is a piece of raw life. I think artistically that was a mistake, but that is what I was trying to do. I meant to introduce something that would be difficult for certain glib reviewers to solve.

D.S.: Is it possible that in spite of your intention and present evaluation of that poem that it could have its own myth and meaning?

Wright: If it has those I am not aware of them. I wasn't thinking of that. You can't always tell, though. You might write something and think as clearly as you can that you have said a certain thing. Then someone else will find something in it, an intelligent person of good will, and maybe he will explain to you what is really there. There is something about language that can be very surprising, and words we use—even in conversation—sometimes can have implications, very colorful ones, that we haven't been aware of consciously. We find examples of this in our public life. I really do believe that there is, in language, something like a power to heal itself, to right itself. Language is a living thing, a part of ourselves, and, as such, I think that the notion among the evangelists of the word as flesh is a very, very complex and important living idea. I am not enough of a philosopher or critic or theologian to spell it out, yet I feel it has a certain truth.

Language can convey a meaning we were not aware of. There are staggering examples of this. One of my favorite Americans, and I have a poem about his death, was Mayor Daley of Chicago. By favorite, I mean as an example. Mayor Daley used to say to his constituents such things as: If I am reelected the great city of Chicago will rise to an ever higher platitude of achievement. He did not mean to say *that*, but he did say it. And the meaning is there. There is another example in New York's Mario Procacino. In earlier years Mario Procacino would emerge to run for mayor and then disappear. He had a pencil-thin moustache, black hair slicked down and part-ed in the middle, and somebody once said he looked like a face painted on a balloon. He did various things. Once he went to Israel and told people that he was the President of Verranzo College. Of course, there is no Verranzo College. Once when he was running for mayor he went to Harlem and met a large constituency, a big crowd. All black people. And Mario Procacino, part of whose manner was to be sort of weepy and yearning like a hack obstetrician from Martins Ferry, Ohio— oh help this woman have her baby!—said to that audience. . . . I can hardly bring myself to say this, it is so good. If it were consciously controlled, Shakespeare could have written this line, though first he would have had to create Procacino and that audience. Procacino said to that black audience: My heart is as black as yours! Now he didn't mean *that*. He didn't intend it to sound the way it sounded to that audience and to you and to me. But he said it. It is almost as if the language cried out, save me. Somebody save me. We do have a wonderful language in America and we still haven't really gotten to it. Some people have approached it.

We were speaking earlier of my poem "Lying in a Hammock at William Duffy's Farm in Pine Island, Minnesota." Let me read a parody of that poem. It was sent to me by Ron Smith, from Richmond, Virginia.

Writing the Love Boat

Over my head I see blood flecks
dropped like gnats and flies
dark in the dust webs.
Beyond the kitchen table,
the scraps from last week's dinners
follow one another out the back door
to the anthill. To my left
behind the white leg
wearing pepper-like holes
a small fire blazes up
in the overflowing trashcan.
I lie back on the cold tile
as the siren howls and comes on.

> A chicken wing hangs from the chandelier
> looking for home.
> I have wasted my wife.

Isn't that good? I love that sort of thing. Maybe Ron Smith will send a copy to Robert Bly and Henry Taylor. Robert, in earlier years out on the farm in Minnesota, had a big file-folder which was stuffed with parodies people had sent him. It was wonderful.

D.S.: What value do you place on humor in poetry?

Wright: I could not do without it. Robert Bly gets annoyed at the phrase "light verse." Nevertheless, he likes parodies. He likes silly songs. I think what he really objects to is triviality and superficiality. I feel that a great deal of what you have to call light verse is very beautiful and very exciting. I'm grateful for it, for good humor in poetry. I think, for this reason, the work of the English poet Gavin Ewart is superb. Many of his poems are straight and serious, but he has written very funny poems:

> Miss Twye was soaping her breasts in the bath
> when she heard behind her a meaning laugh
> and to her amazement she discovered
> a wicked man in the bathroom cupboard.

I think that it is a wonderful poem, and look at the word *meaning*. How would you give a meaning laugh? And there is a great poem by Ben King, of whom I had never heard. It is a knockout and I like it just as a poem. I found this in William Harmon's new *Oxford Book of American Light Verse*. Ben King lived from 1857 to 1894, a funny time for prose writers but some funny poems got in too. Here is Ben King's poem:

If I Should Die

> If I should die tonight and you should come
> to my cold corpse and say
> weeping and heartsick o'er my lifeless clay,

if I should die tonight and you should come
in deepest grief and woe and say
"Here's that ten dollars that I owe,"
I might arise, in my large white cravat
and say, "What's that?"

If I should die tonight and you should come
to my cold corpse and kneel
clasping my head to show the grief you feel,
I say, if I should die tonight
and you should come to me
and there and then just even hint
'bout payin' me that ten,
I might arise a while,
but I'd drop dead again.

D.S.: Why do you so insistently use certain words such as alone, lonely, dark, and so on in your poems?

Wright: Somebody wrote to me once and said, speaking particularly of the New Poems section of my *Collected Poems*, that anybody who used the word lonely and the word loneliness that often must not really know what the experience is. I do overuse certain words. These words all meant something to me at the time I was writing them, but how they relate to one another in different poems written over a period of years would be, as far as I can tell, accidental. They may reveal something about me that I have not been aware of consciously. I see no reason to be opposed to a word so long as it is helpful in an individual poem.

D.S.: What do you mean by the "abounding delight of the body"?

Wright: I don't know. As it stands, it is a very vague and frivolous remark. I don't know. I think behind it is the notion that I simply came to like myself much better after I met Annie. It certainly doesn't mean a rejection of American Puritanism. I think it is just a pompous remark.

D.S.: You often refer in poems to "rising." Does this have a particular meaning?

Wright: I don't know. I haven't thought it through.

D.S.: One of the changes in your poems has been a move from a formal to a more colloquial diction. It has been suggested that this is like Wordsworth's demand for a language of the common man. Is this your intention?

Wright: No. I have never been able to figure out what Wordsworth means. I don't think that one can generalize about it. It depends on the needs of the particular poet. In the arrangement of the words I would like to be very formal but I would like the effect of having a certain ease. That is the Horatian notion. I do think any language is available to poetry. My brother, who lives in California and works for IBM, told me that they fed things into a computer out there. They got a computer to translate Keats' "Ode to a Nightingale." It was nutty. But in itself, it seemed to me to make a wonderful woozy kind of poem. They translated it into other terms. They tried to clarify it. I remember Ransom reading the "Ode on Melancholy" and saying "Nor suffer thy pale forehead to be kissed by nightshade." Ransom pointed out that in the Oxford English Dictionary one of the meanings of nightshade is a night-walking prostitute. Well, the computer would get some of that made clear.

D.S.: Do you consider that there is any distinction to be made between the way you have used the image in poems and the way delineated by the Imagist poets?

Wright: I do not understand any such distinction. I am simply trying to write as clearly as I can. Sometimes I use figures of speech and sometimes I don't. I do not operate according to a set of principles or manifestos.

D.S.: You have referred frequently to the musical quality of poems. Granting that each ear may perceive this music differently, can you say what you mean by the music of poetry?

Wright: It is first of all the movement of language. This includes pauses and everything meant by timing. There is the actual sound of the words, the syllables in relation to one another. And there is something beyond that which moves literally toward the condition of music. One thing that has pleased me very much is that there are at least five composers who have set things of mine to music. It has pleased me that professional musicians would find that quality in my poems.

D.S.: Can you speak of the relationship of timing to form?

Wright: Yes. Auden says it is often the timing, especially, the rhymes, that will dictate the meaning. He says that Byron suddenly became aware of this and became a great poet in "Beppo," that wonderful piece about Venice. Also in *Don Juan*.

D.S.: Is the speaker of your poems an artificial, or created, speaker? Or is it the actual James Wright?

Wright: Sometimes it is an artificial voice and sometimes it is a direct voice. There are some poems that I have written which are more like dramatic monologues in the sense that Browning conceived of that form. Sometimes I have simply made things up. Sometimes people have called me a confessional poet. I don't see that. I feel perfectly free to make up something that never happened to me. There is not a point to point reference between the events of my books and the events of my life. Not at all. I have said that I regarded writing poetry as a curse, but that remark was a silly affectation. With me, to be as realistic as I can, I would say that writing poetry has been what one could reasonably call a neurotic compulsion. I have not made that much money from it. It is not that useful. To some extent, it has made me notorious. Notoriety makes me extremely uncomfortable. This sounds like an affectation, too, but honest to

God it is not. Poetry is not a curse. Often it is a pleasure to write but I think that I have written, as I say, sort of neurotically. I have gone on writing because it has made me feel, from time to time, more emotionally safe.

D.S.: What do you mean by the remark that "the value of a poet's life is going to depend on the truth of the language and the truth of his life"?

Wright: That is another pompous remark. I don't know what it means. It reminds me of Robert Benchley's maxim from the Chinese. He says, "It is rather to be chosen than great riches, unless I have omitted something from the quotation." A remark like mine is, I think, hot air. It sort of sounds nice though. We don't have to be bullied by our own asinine remarks that have got into print.

D.S.: Do you construct your books in a certain way? Do you think of a poem or a book as having a statemental or communicative function?

Wright: Yes, I do think of the construction in a certain way. Frost said somewhere, I have forgotten where, that if there are twenty-five poems in a book, the book itself ought to be the twenty-sixth poem. That is, in presenting a group of poems in the hope that someone will read them, one ought to be aware of a relation between the poems as well as of inner relations that exist in the individual poems. It is an idea of shapeliness that appeals to me. There are blossoms all over *To a Blossoming Pear Tree,* my latest book. And I think that this book is more tightly organized than any of my previous books. Whether or not it comes through that way, I don't know. This is what I felt, anyway.

As for the second half of your question, I think that the kind of thing that a person writes will depend partly on his own interests and concerns as a human being. Those things will come out in his poems inevitably. In the poem called "To a Blossoming Pear Tree" I am talking about addressing the beauty of Nature, which is nonhuman. It suggests to me sometimes the perfection of things and I envy this perfection of things, or at least this nonhumanity, precisely because it is not involved in the sometimes very painful mess of being human. Yet I say at the end of the poem that this is what I have to be, human. Human life is a mess. This is something I wanted to say, and I said it.

D.S.: You have said in other places that you consider yourself a nature poet. What does this mean?

Wright: I care very much about the living world, the organic and the inorganic world. It comforts me more and more to realize and to observe and to feel the great self-restoring power that the creatures in nature have while we human beings are making such a mess of things. I hope that poetry, and the poetry of nature, has a similar power. Roethke said a beautiful thing once when he talked to a class about the poetry of nature. He said that we ought to remember that there is an inner nature, and I think he was suggesting something about poetry. That, perhaps, poetry could remind us of the need for restoration through the inner nature. Also, I think that in the poetry of nature there is the willingness to approach the living creatures with the kind of attentiveness that is almost a reverence. In Robert Bly's poems about nature he is at his best and most beautiful. Many of his ideas, political or religious or whatever, are absorbed into the attention that he is paying visually and spiritually to the things he writes about. The ideas are all there in the poems about nature.

D.S.: Does poetry help to move us toward the good and away from the bad?

Wright: I think that it sometimes does. Sometimes it can. But there are plenty of poems, and good poems, that wouldn't necessarily do that. They would still be good poems. Take Gavin Ewart's little poem about Miss Twye. I feel like a better person when I read that poem because it delights me.

D.S.: Do you believe that there is such a thing as a good man and a bad man?

Wright: Yes. I can read you a passage that defines the bad man about as well as anything I have ever seen. Over in chapter fifteen of *The Adventures of Huckleberry Finn* Jim and Huck get lost in the fog and are separated from each other. A steamboat goes between them. Huck goes off in the canoe and Jim remains on the raft. Then Huck returns and shows himself to Jim. Jim was so exhausted he had fallen asleep. When he wakes up, he is very glad to see Huck and says "I thought you were dead." Huck pretends that none of this has happened, that Jim has had a dream. Then he asks Jim to interpret the dream in which all these horrible things have happened and Jim gives an elaborate interpretation of it. Then Huck points out that there is some trash, dead leaves and dirt and rocks and so on, stuck on the raft. This proves that all those things really did happen. Huck was just trying to joke with Jim and make fun of him a little bit. Well, here's what Jim does.

Jim looked at the trash, and then looked at me, and back at the trash again. He had got the dream fixed so strong in his head that he couldn't seem to shake it loose and get the facts back into its place again right away. But when he did get the thing straightened around he looked at me steady without ever smiling, and says:

"What do dey stan' for? I's gwyne to tell you. When I got all wore out wid work, en wid de callin' for you, en went to sleep, my heart wuz mos' broke bekase you wuz los', en I didn't k'yer no' mo' what become er me en de raf'. En when I wake up en fine you back ag'in, all safe en soun', de tears come, en I could 'a' got down on my knees en kiss yo' foot, I's so thankful. En all you wuz thinkin' 'bout wuz how you could make a fool uv ole Jim wid a lie. Dat truck dah is *trash;* en trash is what people is dat puts dirt on de head er dey fren's en makes 'em ashamed."

Then he got up slow and walked to the wigwam, and went in there without saying anything but that. But that was enough. It made me feel so mean I could almost kissed *his* foot to get him to take it back.

It was fifteen minutes before I could work myself up to go and humble myself to a nigger, but I done it, and I warn't ever sorry for it afterward, neither. I didn't do him no more mean tricks, and I wouldn't done that one if I'd 'a' knowed it would make him feel that way.

That is a good definition of a bad man.

D.S.: Thinking of your statement in Field *magazine about the poetic line, can it be inferred that you do imagine a principle which distinguishes a line of poetry from a line of prose?*

Wright: I do not understand much of that piece of mine in *Field*. What I was really trying to say was that I am impatient with arguments of this kind. I don't think that, in any deep sense, it makes a damn bit of difference whether or not one is writing in prose or in verse, just so he's trying to be imaginative and true to what he is hearing. But I also think there is a principle such as you suggest. It is the way a line sounds, its musical structures, the conception of a line as being a musical unit itself. Of course this doesn't mean that it has to be either iambic or noniambic because there are other metrical and musical possibilities in our American language. I don't mean that the specific pattern of the line has to be repeated either. But it has to have, somehow, a musical shape. At least that is what I have tried to achieve. I think that, essentially, a poem is distinguished from a prose piece in terms of song. A piece is to be identified and enjoyed as a poem in so far as it is closer to a song.

D.S.: Why did you include prose pieces in Moments of the Italian Summer *and* To a Blossoming Pear Tree?

Wright: I felt like trying to learn how to write a clearer prose. A better prose. It grew out of my notebooks. I found I was taking more and more pleasure in writing prose. Its rhythm and its music are different from that of my poems, really.

D.S.: You have been very strong in your condemnation of Two Citizens. *How do you feel about* To a Blossoming Pear Tree?

Wright: I feel that *To a Blossoming Pear Tree* is the best book that I have ever published. It is the best written and, whatever it says, whatever the value of the book, it is the book that I wanted to write. I wrote it over a long period of time, and carefully. I had about 500 pages of manuscript in that book. I struggled with it a lot.

D.S.: Looking back over your career, you have stated often that you were strongly influenced by Robert Frost and E. A. Robinson. Can you say a little more about that?

Wright: Yes. I meant that what I was trying to do was to learn how to write poems in a simple syntax and also to write in a musically very precise way that had some ease to it. Here I mean something like the sound of Frost, although I also like the sound of Robinson and have tried to get close to that too. The subject matter, perhaps, had closer affinities to Robinson. Robinson felt, and this is what he portrays in his poems, that there is no verifiable justification for hope in this world. And, along with this, there was his recognition, you could call it psychological or moral, that hope in human beings is absolutely necessary for us to go on living. His characters are always trying to live as if there was some hope, some kind of hope, and at the same time they know that there isn't. There they are. You don't find the same kind of thing in Frost. Although, at bottom, Frost is very much a tragic poet. Yet, I don't think he explores this kind of darkness as consistently as Robinson does. Shall I say some lines of Robinson's from "Captain Craig"? The old man says, when the young man asks him how it is that he can be old and a failure and still act happy, or as if he is happy. Isn't he aware of the terrible things in life?

> I cannot think of anything to-day
> That I would rather do than be myself,
> Primevally alive, and have the sun
> Shine into me; for on a day like this,
> When the chaff-parts of a man's adversities
> Are blown by quick-spring breezes out of him—
> When even a flicker of wind that wakes no more
> Than a tuft of grass, or a few young yellow leaves,
> Comes like the falling of a prophet's breath
> On altar-flames rekindled of crushed embers,—

Then do I feel, now do I feel, within me
No dreariness, no grief, no discontent,
No twinge of human envy. But I beg
That you forego credentials of the past
For these illuminations of the present,
Or better still, to give the shadow justice,
You let me tell you something: I have yearned
In many another season for these days,
And having them with God's own pageantry
To make me glad for them,—yes, I have cursed
The sunlight and the breezes and the leaves
To think of men on stretchers and on beds,
Or on foul floors, like starved outrageous lizards,
Made human with paralysis and rags;
Or of some poor devil on a battle-field
Left undiscovered and without the strength
To drag a maggot from his clotted mouth;
Or of women working where a man would fall—
Flat-breasted miracles of cheerfulness
Made neuter by the work that no man counts
Until it waits undone; children thrown out
To feed their veins and souls with offal . . . Yes,
I have had half a mind to blow my brains out
Sometimes; and I have gone from door to door,
Ragged myself, trying to do something—
Crazy, I hope.—But what has this to do
With Spring?

D.S.: To expand the context of your remarks slightly, does it bother you that the audience for poetry in America seems a small and an academic one?

Wright: No. I like that very much. At least I like a comparatively small audience. If indeed we can say that there is an audience for poetry. Galway Kinnell and I were sitting together at the only conference I've ever attended, the National Poetry Conference up near Grand Rapids, Michigan, about three years ago. We were going to give a little course there, to be called "The Pleasures of Poetry." But we found the students hadn't actually read anything. They reminded me of the old Pogo comic strip. Richard Hugo loves this bear, too. There was a bear in the strip and he discovered he could write. He wrote some stories, but he couldn't read. So he would take them to Albert the Alligator and he would ask Albert to read them to him. As Albert read the stories, the bear would sit nearby saying things like "I was young when I wrote that."

We had a hard time conveying to that class what we meant. We'd ask somebody to say a poem he liked and somebody would stand up and say something he himself had written. Don't you like anything by John Donne? Who? We ran into a great deal of that, a great many people who don't read. I don't think we have a very big audience for poetry. We can get big audiences for poetry readings but this is something else entirely. I am sure that people do believe that there is a greater interest in poetry in other countries, but I wonder. A few years ago in Yugoslavia, with some other writers, I spoke. The entire town of Struga turned out seated all up and down the river. Still, I'm getting suspicious of that kind of public performance and the notoriety and the celebrity that goes with it. I am sure that these are social forces and powers in themselves. What they have to do with the practice of poetry, I wonder.

We hear a lot about the great Russian audiences, but I think sometimes that the Russians like to get one up on us by telling us how much goddamn soul they have got. This is a pain in the neck. It is a way of being superior. We are told by *Time* magazine that a writer like Yevtushenko has to do nothing except appear in a town and he will have an audience of fifty thousand people. All right. I don't know what his poems look like in Russian but I've seen several translations into English, and I just hope that they don't look that way in Russian. They were ungodly awful. And not even funny.

Neruda conceived of poetry as a very popular thing and he drew great numbers of people. But this was partly due to his public recognition as a Chilean legislator and diplomat. Of course in Latin American countries the tradition of the popularity of poetry is greater and stronger than it is in the United States. I do not object to the popularity of poetry as such. In Latin America, the people actually read poetry, themselves, in privacy. This is not the same thing as being a camp follower at poetry readings. We could use more genuine intelligent readers of good will.

III

Reviews

The Stiff Smile of Mr. Warren

1.

Although it is possible, generally speaking, to discover certain
consistently developing themes in Mr. Warren's work—prose
and verse alike—it is nevertheless impossible to know just what
he will do next. In our own century he is perhaps the only
American writer who, having already established his major
importance, remains unpredictable. If anyone has noted any
similarity between Mr. Warren and, say, Dickens, I should be
surprised and delighted. But the two authors share the
power—it is a very great power, and perhaps it is the heart of
the poetic imagination—of unpredictability. A critic is right in
being a little hesitant about such a writer. But how explain the
neglect of Mr. Warren's poems when we compare it with the
critical concern with his novels? I use the word "neglect" when
I speak of the poems, simply because I have a hunch that they
contain the best seedings and harvests of his imagination.

2.

A good many reviewers of *Promises* have been taken aback by
the violent distortions of language. But one reviewer is Mr.

This review of *Promises,* by Robert Penn Warren (New York: Random
House, 1958) first appeared in the *Kenyon Review* 20 (Autumn 1958).

James Dickey, in the *Sewanee Review,* who describes and clarifies my own response to the book.

The first point concerns the distortions of language, and the critic felt that most of them were flaws: "Warren has his failings: his are a liking for the over-inflated, or 'bombast' as Longinus defines it; he indulges in examples of pathetic fallacy so outrageous that they should, certainly, become classic instances of the misuse of this device. Phrases like 'the irrelevant anguish of air,' and 'the malfeasance of nature or the filth of fate' come only as embarrassments to the reader already entirely committed to Warren's dark and toiling spell." I think this is a pretty fair description of the kinds of awkwardness that frequently appear in *Promises.* However, the really curious and exciting quality of the book is the way in which so many of the poems can almost drag the reader, by the scruff of the neck, into the experiences which they are trying to shape and understand.

But this very triumph of imaginative force over awkward language is Mr. Dickey's second point, and the critic states it eloquently: "Warren's verse is so deeply and compellingly linked to man's ageless, age-old drive toward self-discovery, self-determination, that it makes all discussion of line-endings, metrical variants, and the rest of poetry's paraphernalia appear hopelessly beside the point."

Yet, so very often in this new book, Mr. Warren simply will not allow the reader to consider the rhetorical devices of language "hopelessly beside the point." That he is capable of a smoothly formal versification in some poems, and of a delicate musical variation in others, he has shown many times in the past. We are not dealing with a raw, genuine, and untrained talent, but with a skilled and highly sophisticated student of traditional prosody. In effect, a major writer at the height of his fame has chosen, not to write his good poems over again, but to break his own rules, to shatter his words and try to recreate them, to fight through and beyond his own craftsmanship in order to revitalize his language at the sources of tenderness and horror. One of the innumerable ironies which hound writers, I suppose, is the fact that the very competence which a man may struggle for years to master can suddenly and treacherously stiffen into a mere *armor against experience* instead of an instrument for contending with that experience. No wonder so many poets quit while they're still behind. What makes Mr. Warren excitingly important is his refusal to quit even while he's ahead. In *Promises,* it seems to me, he has deliberately shed the armor of competence—a finely meshed and expensive armor, forged at heaven knows how many bitter intellectual fires—and has gone out to fight with the ungovernable tide. I mean no disrespect—on the contrary—when I say that few of the poems in this book can match several of his previous single poems. Yet I think there is every reason to believe that his willingness to do violence to one stage in the development of his craftsmanship is not the least of the promises which his book contains. I do not wish to argue about any of the poems in *Promises* which I consider at the moment to be failures, though I shall mention one of them. But I think that a book such as this—a book whose main importance, I believe, is the further evidence it provides for the unceasing and furious growth of a considerable artist—deserves an attention quite as close as that which we conventionally accord to the same author's more frequently accomplished poems of the past.

3.

The distortion of language in the new book is almost always demonstrably deliberate. When it is successful, it appears not as an accidental coarseness, but rather as an extreme exaggeration of a very formal style. The poetic function of the distortion is to mediate between the two distinct moods of tenderness and horror. This strategy—in which formality is driven, as it were, to distraction—does not always succeed. It is dishonest critical damnation, and not critical praise, to tell a gifted imaginative writer that he has already scaled Olympus when, as a matter of frequent fact, he has taken a nose-dive into the ditch. The truest praise, in my opinion, is in the critic's effort to keep his eye on the poet's imaginative strategy, especially if the poet is still alive and still growing. I think that the failure of Mr. Warren's strategy is most glaring when the material which he dares to explore will somehow not allow him to establish one of the two essentially dramatic moods—the tenderness and the horror of which I spoke above. An example of this failure is the poem "School Lesson Based on Word of Tragic Death of Entire Gillum Family." The horror is stated, and the reality of horror is a lesson which everyone must learn, as the poet implies in the last line. But there is no tenderness against which the horror can be dramatically drawn, and there is no dramatic reason that I can discern for presenting the ice-pick murder of the Gillum family. Now, I am sure the reader will allow me to claim a human concern for the Gillum family, wherever and whoever they were. All I am saying is that they are *not here:* that is, their death seems to me a capricious horror; and the distorted language, in spite of its magnificent attempt to achieve a folklike barrenness and force, remains a capricious awkwardness.

My speaking of "failure" in a poet of so much stature is of course tempered by my statement of a conviction which constantly grows on me: that a failure like the "School Lesson" is worth more than the ten thousand safe and competent versifyings produced by our current crop of punks in America. I am spared the usual but boring critical courtesy of mentioning names by the fact that we all know who we are. But I am not comparing Mr. Warren's performance in *Promises* with the performance of us safe boys. I am trying to compare it with his capacities. I want to look somewhat closely at a poem in *Promises* in which the poet's exploration past facility into violent distortion ends in discovery. I suppose there are five or six fine poems of this sort in the book, but I will settle for a reading of one of them.

The poem is called "The Child Next Door." I hope that my reader will take time, at this point, to read aloud to himself the entire sequence of poems in *Promises* entitled "To a Little Girl, One Year Old, in a Ruined Fortress." Furthermore, since there can be no harm in our simply taking the poet at his word (and where else can we begin?) the reader had better read the dedication aloud also.

4.

There are two kinds of violent distortion in "The Child Next Door"—one of rhythm and one of syntax. I invite the reader to discover, if he can, some regularity of scansion in the following representative lines of the poem:

> Took a pill, or did something to herself she thought would
> not hurt . . .
> —Is it hate?—in my heart. Fool, doesn't she know that the
> process . . .
> I think of your goldness, of joy, how empires grind, stars are
> hurled.
> I smile stiff, saying *ciao,* saying *ciao,* and think: this is the
> world.

I find no regularity of metrical stresses. Now, one reviewer has suggested an affinity between Mr. Warren's new verse and the verse of Hopkins. Suppose we were to read the above quoted lines according to Hopkins' system (I quote from one of the famous letters to R. W. Dixon): "It consists in scanning by accents or stresses alone, without any account of the number of syllables, so that a foot may be one strong syllable or it may be many light and one strong." (These are, of course, Hopkins' somewhat desperately oversimplifying words to a puzzled admirer.) The system seems promising, but even this way of reading Mr. Warren's lines does not reveal a regular pattern. Playing the above lines by ear, I can hear six strong stresses in the first line, six in the second, seven in the third, and seven in the fourth. Yet I am not sure; and my uncertainty, instead of being an annoyance, is haunting. Moreover, there are eighteen lines in the whole poem, and my feeling is that nearly all of the lines (mainly with the exception of the above) can be read aloud according to a system of five strong stresses. Here, for example, is the first line of the poem:

> The child next door is defective because the mother . . .

I hesitate slightly over the word "next," but, with a little straining to get past it, I think I can find clearly strong stresses in "child," "door," the middle syllable of "defective," the second syllable of "because," and the first syllable of "mother." And so on. The regularity becomes clear only if the reader is willing to strain his senses a bit—to give his physical response to the rhythm, as it were, a kind of "body English." We find the poet like the tennis player keeping his balance and not taking a fall, and feel some kind of relief which is at the same time a fulfillment. I get this kind of physical sensation in reading "The Child Next Door," a poem in which a skilled performer is always daring to expose his balance to chaos and always regaining the balance. In plain English, the rhythm of this poem may be described as a formality which is deliberately driven to test itself, and which seems imaginatively designed to disturb the reader into auditory exaggerations of his own. Perhaps what is occurring in the rhythm of this poem is a peculiar kind of counterpoint. We have "counterpoint," said Hopkins to Dixon, when "each line (or nearly so) has two different co-existing scansions." But these words explain only a part of Mr. Warren's counterpoint. I propose the hypothesis that one can hear in the poem two movements of language: a strong formal regularity, which can be identified with a little struggle, but which is driven so fiercely by the poet that one starts to hear beyond it the approach of an unpredictable and hence discomforting second movement, which can be identified as something chaotic, something very powerful but unorganized. It is the halting, stammering movement of an ordinarily articulate man who has been shocked. The order and the chaos move side by side; and, as the poem proceeds, I get the feeling that each movement becomes a little stronger, and together they help to produce an echoing violence in the syntax.

Some of the later lines do indeed sound something like Hopkins; but that is an accidental and, I think, essentially irrelevant echo. The lines have their own dramatic justification, which I shall try to show in a moment:

> Can it bind or loose, that beauty in that kind,
> Beauty of benediction? I trust our hope to prevail
> That heart-joy in beauty be wisdom, before beauty fail.

The syntax in the earlier lines of the poem seems to be recognizably more regular:

> The child next door is defective because the mother,
> Seven brats already in that purlieu of dirt,
> Took a pill.

If the reader grants that the syntax of these earlier lines is fairly normal and regular as compared with the syntax of the passage beginning "Can it bind or loose," then I think he can identify the two kinds of distortion which I have mentioned: a distortion of rhythm, and a distortion of syntax. But each distortion, however strong, is accompanied by an equally strong regularity. And in each case the violence of the distortion is identifiable as an exaggeration of the regularity itself.

What a neat stylistic formulation! And how dead, compared with the poem!

5.

Now, to say that the sound of a poem is not identical with its sense is different from saying that the two may not exist in rhetorical harmony with each other. I believe that the exaggerated formality of sound in Mr. Warren's poem is justified by the dramatic occasion of the poem itself. Let us consider the poem's dramatic occasion by limiting ourselves, at least temporarily, to the references which we can find within it, or in the title of the sequence of which it is a part.

First, the speaker is addressing a one-year-old child. He has told us so in the title of the sequence. Moreover, the fact that in this particular poem he is not merely brooding on things in general is made clear to us by his explicitly addressing the child in the next-to-last line: "I think of your goldness. . . ." In addressing the child he first points out something that exists in the external world; then he describes his own feelings about this thing; and finally he tries to convey the significance of what he sees in relation to the one-year-old child herself. It might be objected, either to the poem or to my reading of it, that a one-year-old child could not conceivably understand either the physical horror of what the speaker points out or the confused and confusing significance which he has to extract from it. She is defended against its horror by her youth. But the speaker is also incapable of grasping what he shows the child. And he has no defense. He is exposed to an almost unspeakably hideous reality which he can neither escape nor deny.

Indeed, what makes reality in nature seem hideous is that it is both alluring and uncontrollable. Once a man is committed to it in love, he is going to be made to suffer. "Children sweeten labours," said Bacon, "but they make misfortunes more bitter." The reason is that children tear away, if anything can, a man's final defense against the indifferent cruelty of the natural world into which he has somehow blundered and awakened. The speaker in Mr. Warren's poem speaks to his own appallingly precious child about another child who seems blindly and meaninglessly lamed and halted by something in nature itself for which it is absurd to assign anything so simple as mere blame. I would find it hard to imagine a dramatic situation in which the loving commitments of the speaker are subjected to more severe tensions than this one. And conceiving, as I do, that the speaker is an *actor* in this drama, and not merely a *spectator* of it, I would say that his "pathetic fallacy" of attributing "malfeasance" to nature and "filth" to fate is his dramatically justifiable attempt to defend himself against something more horrible than malfeasance and filth—i.e., the indifference of nature and fate alike.

The speaker cannot escape the contemplation of this horror because of the very child whom he addresses. The tenderness with which he regards this child ("I think of your goldness, of joy") is the very emotion which exposes him to the living and physical evidence of the horror which man and child contemplate together, which neither can understand, but which the man is trapped by his tenderness into acknowledging.

For the horror (embodied in the defective child, the child next door) in its vast and terrible innocence of its own nature actually *greets* the speaker. He cannot ignore the greeting; for he, too, has a child—not defective, but nevertheless un-knowingly exposed to all the possibilities, all the contingencies and promises (of course, Mr. Warren knows very well, and dramatizes in this poem with surpassing power, that not all promises are sentimental assurances of a return to Eden), the utterly mindless and brutal accidents of a fallen world. So every child, in a sense which is fundamental to the loving and moral agony of this poem, is defective—and the speaker him-self is such a child. Perhaps the real "child next door" is the reader of the book.

The fallen world is chiefly characterized, in the poet's vision, by a tragic truth: that man's very capacity for tenderness is what exposes him to horrors which cannot be escaped without the assumption of an indifference which, to be sufficiently comforting, would also require the loss of tenderness itself, perhaps even the loss of *all* feeling—even the loss of hatred. The beautiful sister in the poem is not in agony, and her face is not stiff with anger, or contorted with tenderness. Her face is pure, calm. Her face is, in the most literal sense, unbearable. "She smiles her smile without taint." Without taint! To give my sense of the dramatic and human appropriateness of the poet's outburst against the maddening and untainted smile, I can only say that, if the speaker in the poem had not damned her for a fool, I would have written a letter to Mr. Warren and damned her on my own hook.

The speaker is trapped in his necessity of choice; and yet he cannot choose. Between the necessity and the incapacity the speaker is driven to a point where the outraged snarl of an animal would have been justified by the dramatic context. But this is where the imaginative courage of Mr. Warren's continu-ous explorations comes in. Instead of following the music of his lines and the intensity of his drama into chaos, he suddenly rides the pendulum back to formality—but this time the for-mality of the rhythm includes the formality of the drama, and I think that the strategy is superbly successful. Instead of snarl-ing, the speaker acknowledges the horror's greeting. He faces the horror, and his acknowledgement is a perfect embodiment of what earlier I called a severe and exaggerated formality.

Consider the emotions that the speaker must simultaneously bear in his consciousness: frightened and helpless tenderness toward his own child; horror at the idiot; rage at the calm face of the sister. His problem is like the lesson in Frost's poem: "how to be unhappy yet polite." And the speaker smiles—stiffly:

> I smile stiff, saying *ciao*, saying *ciao*.

The stiffness of that smile, I think, is what we must attend to. It is the exaggerated formality with which a man faces and acknowledges the concrete and inescapable existence of an utterly innocent (and therefore utterly ruthless) reality which is quite capable not only of crushing him, but also of letting him linger contemplatively over the sound of his own bones breaking. And the exaggerated formality is, in the sound and syntax of the poem, that violence of language which I have described, and which many reviewers of the poems have found discomforting. I admit that the distortions, which swing on the living pendulum of the poet's imagination between the sound and the sense of the poem "The Child Next Door," are discomforting. All I suggest is that they dramatically illuminate each other, and that they are therefore rhetorically harmonious parts of a single created experience: a successful, though disturbing, poem.

The Terrible Threshold

In *New World Writing No. 4*, Theodore Roethke remarks of Kunitz that "he has an acute and agonizing sense . . . of what it is to be a man in this century." This statement is true, I believe, and simply to *be* a man (instead of one more variety of automaton, of which we have some tens of thousands) means to keep one's eyes open. There is a great range of emotion in Kunitz's poetry, but this sense of agony at the helplessness of others to contend in human terms with the inhuman world of commerce is one of his central feelings. "Night Letter" is not the best poem in his book, but it contains a severe passage in which the poet wrings out of himself his own vision of the reality underneath the world of "success," advertising, and—suddenly, strangely apocalyptic—*self*-judgment:

> in the Bitch's streets the men
> Are lying down, great crowds with fractured wills
> Dumping the shapeless burden of their lives
> Into the rivers where the motors flowed.
>
> Of those that stood in my doorway, self-accused,
> Besmeared with failure in the swamps of trade,
> One put a gun in his examiner's hand,
> Making the judgment loud; another squats

This review of *Selected Poems: 1928–1958*, by Stanley Kunitz (Boston: Atlantic-Little Brown, 1958) first appeared in the *Sewanee Review* 67 (Spring 1959).

Upon the asylum floor and plays with toys,
Like the spiral of a soul balanced on a stone,
Or a new gadget for slicing off the thumb;
The rest whirl in the torment of our time.

The wasting of the spirit by commerce in this age is one of the most persistently—one might almost say compulsively—passionate themes in Kunitz's poetry, and his treatment of it defines one of his several major values, human as well as aesthetic. In "Revolving Meditation" he speaks of "the voice of the solitary / Who makes others less alone," and time and again we find him speaking of the loneliness of his fellow human victims in situations which would justify, if anything can justify, self-pity. It is the lonely man speaking out to lonely men, and trying to sow the desert for the sake of a human community. Sometimes this experienced compassion is directed to single human figures, as in "The Man Upstairs," when the poet combines, with typically condensed and explosive imagery, the isolation and fear of childhood with the despair of an old boarder:

The old man sick with boyhood fears,
Whose thin shanks ride the naked blast,
Intones; the gray somnambulist
Creaks down interminable stairs,
Dreaming my future as his past.

And Kunitz can deal with the same theme—the stupified response of the human self to the denial of its existence upon which a society of salesmen depends—by ironically denying that self, from the viewpoint of an economist who wants us to forget all these impolite morbidities and just go back to beddy-byes. The poem in question is called "The Economist's Song," and I quote its cold terrible mockery entire:

Come sit beneath the tariff walls
Among the scuttling unemployed,
The rodent pack; sing madrigals
Of Demos and the Cyprian maid

Bewildered by the golden grain,
While ships with peril in their hulls,
Deploying on the lines of trade,
Transport the future of gangrene.

Before I read that poem, it hadn't so clearly occurred to me that one of my possible destinies is to have the honor of being disposed of at so much per pound in the next gangrene rummage, and, well, you see, I don't like to think about such things very much. When Kunitz rubs our noses in our murders, he is ruthless. Let's proceed with prettier subjects.

Dear reader, forget it.

For the trouble is that there aren't any pretty subjects in this book.

Consider the love poems. Kunitz's way of contending with this subject is to take careful strategic precautions, lest the savagery and blood which are at the very source of the experience of love should escape into the multitudinous alleyways which we all contrive. In case my description should make Kunitz sound like another professional sensationalist, another flinger of blood-and-guts in the manner of Rafael Sabatini and George Barker, I hasten to point out that the ultimate achievement of the love poems in *Selected Poems* is tenderness. The delicacy of feeling which the poems record can exist *in the poems* only if the author has already run the whole course of love's experience, with its hatreds, its suicidal impulses, its secret lunge to snag the beloved's jugular vein, to bury the hatchet (inside one's father's skull), and to revolve one's children upon the spits and mandibles of adult dishonesty. In other words, the peculiar achievement of Kunitz as a love poet is his power of rescuing true human delicacy in the face of the most appalling inner realities. His drive toward self-knowledge is the highest kind of courage. He has been purified in the fires, and has made himself worthy of receiving the "absolute god" (he mentions that "god" throughout his book). In 1942, Kunitz wrote of the similarly tough and savage grace in Miss Louise Bogan's poetry: "I am persuaded that the true world of Miss Bogan's imagination . . . is 'the sunk land of dust and flame,' where an unknown terror is king, presiding over the fable of a life, in the deep night swarming with images of reproach and desire." The world of Kunitz's imagination is not, in any simple way, to be identified with that of Miss Bogan; and yet his words about her go a long way toward suggesting the magnificent fierceness of his own explorations into the underworld of love. A representative example of his power in treating this subject is the poem called "The Dark and the Fair." The poem knocks me off balance. It presents, through Kunitz's clanging and anguished rhythms, a whole drama of accusations *against* the beloved woman whom he is describing, and his odd attack reaches its climax in the beautiful line, "That furied woman did me grievous wrong." And here the poem turns and grinds on its amazing hinge, which opens the gate upon the poet's fierce secret: that the woman is beloved because of, and not in spite of, her perilousness:

> So, freshly turning, as the turn condones,
> For her I killed the propitiatory bird,
> Kissing her down. Peace to her bitter bones,
> Who taught me the serpent's word, but yet the word.

All of Kunitz's love poems are like that. To love is to effect an overwhelmingly difficult act of self-knowledge, and the reader can like it or lump it. In the hands of this poet, the subject flinches and wails. It is not pretty. It has grandeur.

The same terrible beauty attained far beyond the usual frontiers of conventional grace emerges from the surprisingly large number of poems in which Kunitz, whose character as the poems reveal it is marked by such intellectual and emotional gravity, roars out with human laughter. Sometimes he chooses the grand old manner of the formal malediction. In "The Thief," his pocket having been picked by a Roman who took him for a rich tourist, the poet rushes frustrated to his room and writes a poem of curses against the thief; and yet, as the beautiful language absorbs the comic intensity of anger into itself, the poet understands finally that the hand of the pickpocket was really the hand of his own genius:

> Now that I face the moment of my loss,
> Driven to language on the Ides of March
> Here in my blistered room
> Where the wind flaps my ceiling like a sail
> (A miracle, no doubt, to be left at that!)
> I recognize the gods' capricious hand
> And write this poem for money, rage, and love.

Kunitz's miraculous gift for transfiguring anger into laughter by charming his words into action is the burden also of his funny poem "A Choice of Weapons," in which he takes up the eternal theme of the poet's defending himself against an obtuse reviewer: "Sir, if appreciation be my lack, / You may appreciate me, front and back." But after the jokes, the poem comes true by closing on the faith so fundamental to this poet's consciousness: the poem "shoots its cause, and is a source of joy."

Kunitz blasts, rams, and generally shakes up the conventional rhythmic patterns of English poetry, until they seem always on the point of cracking with his personal tension. And then they do indeed crack, and the sound of his own voice comes through.

We may consider rhythm for a moment by looking at a poem which, with its imagery and movement, reveals yet another world of imaginative reality discovered by this poet. He has explored this world more deeply and terribly than almost any other American poet now writing, with the important exceptions of Berryman and Roethke: the world in which the agony of the isolated man, confronted with itself, becomes a prayer—ghastly, physically painful, visionary, like the prayers of Amos, Nahum, and the other prophets who saw the world fleeing from itself into the gawking chops of suicide. The poem by Kunitz which I have in mind is called "Open the Gates":

> Within the city of the burning cloud,
> Dragging my life behind me in a sack,
> Naked I prowl, scourged by the black
> Temptation of the blood grown proud.

Here at the monumental door,
Carved with the curious legend of my youth,
I brandish the great bone of my death,
Beat once therewith and beat no more.

The hinges groan: a rush of forms
Shivers my name, wrenched out of me.
I stand on the terrible threshold, and I see
The end and the beginning in each other's arms.

The rhythm is unmistakably personal, and it is doubtful if anyone could attain its power without first mastering the classical formality of English prosody. The wildness and the biblical strangeness of the imagery are defined, not in relation to irregularity of rhythm, but rather in relation to the severe formality which almost, but never quite, succeeds in holding back the soul's dark beast. One could count the number of accents in each line, but such counting would be pointless. It would reveal nothing of the thing that matters—the rhythm. In this rhythm of Kunitz—whose ancestor, I feel, must surely be the Hopkins who wrote "Inversnaid"—the words which most naturally receive the strong stress are those which inevitably rise up as the most meaningful words in the line. "I brandish the great bone of my death." How would it be humanly possible to strike one's voice on any syllables other than "brand-," "great," "bone," and "death" in that line? In short, when one reads Kunitz's lines, one irresistably *hears* them, even without moving the lips. Their rhythmic energy shivers the metronome. As for the imagery, the poem "Open the Gates" is *all* imagery, and this poet's headlong plunges into the strange world of imaginative reality reflect personal courage as well as technical mastery (and I use the word "mastery" with care, for I do not think it is the same as "skill." Any trained seal can have "skill." A master is a creator.) If the reader has not recently read the book of Amos in the King James version, let him consult it, and he will discover the living tradition of Kunitz's imagery.

Speaking earlier of Hopkins has reminded me of the image which he chose in order to describe his impression of Dryden to the doubting Bridges: the rhythm riding on the muscle and sinew of the language. The same image of a beautifully conditioned and healthy man occurs to me as an appropriate way to describe Kunitz's *Selected Poems*. They represent thirty years at hard labor, and yet the book is only 116 pages long. But they are without fat. I think that Kunitz's work has undergone comparative neglect, and yet such neglect is not nearly so important as the fulfillment which is sure to come. The book is at once an achievement and a promise. Kunitz is already one of the finest American poets of the century. But to speak of him as if his book were the work of a lifetime would be misleading. The truth is that fifty-three-year-old Stanley Kunitz is just beginning. The magnificent poems "The Way Down," "The War Against the Trees" (certainly the equal, and perhaps even the superior, of Hopkins' "Binsey Poplars"), and "The Thing That Eats the Heart" were all written and published quite recently. Through three decades of distinguished performance in an almost insanely difficult art, Kunitz has grown; and there is every evidence that he will continue to grow.

Certainly his book shudders with life, and flings seeds in all directions. He is indeed one of the masters, as Robert Lowell has said; and the publication of his *Selected Poems 1928–1958* is, I believe, an event of major importance for everyone who cares about art and human civilization in this country. The book stands on the terrible threshold of greatness.

Hardy's Poetry

A Study and a Selection

Mr. Hynes believes that "great poets need great partisans of their poetry. . . . At some point in his career the poet needs enthusiastic admiration, true-believers to enunciate and formulate his virtues." Mr. Hynes is a true-believer but not a fanatic; and he is less concerned with praise alone than with explanation of what is praiseworthy. He explores the crucial issues: diction, imagery, the "philosophy" and its meaning for the poetry, the famous awkwardness, and the relation of *The Dynasts* to the short poems. Like others, Mr. Hynes is attracted by the integrity and decency of Hardy himself, and he recognizes the poetry's power of wakening certain decencies in readers. Out of his feeling for Hardy's readers, for all of Hardy's writings, and for Hardy himself, Mr. Hynes has fashioned a book that is unobtrusively learned, confident, modest in a manner quite in tune with Hardy's own character, and sensitive to the richness of the poems. We do not have many good writers among our scholars; but Mr. Hynes is a good writer, and with this book he joins the small company of distinguished scholars whose own works are serious literature—for example, Maynard Mack, Samuel H. Monk, and B. H. Bronson.

This review of *The Pattern of Hardy's Poetry*, by Samuel Haynes (Chapel Hill: University of North Carolina Press, 1961) and *Selected Poems of Thomas Hardy*, edited with an introduction by John Crowe Ransom (New York: Macmillan, 1961) was written in 1961 and is previously unpublished.

Mr. Hynes' study is so concise that it is difficult to paraphrase. But his guiding idea is perfectly clear. He argues that there is indeed a pattern in Hardy's poetry; he explains what previous critics have found in it; he elucidates the exact function of Hardy's philosophical ideas within the poems; and he identifies and explores the "pattern" which Hardy sustains among poems written during a period of some seventy years. The pattern is "simply the eternal conflict between irreconcilables." Mr. Hynes invigorates the phrase by revealing the relevance of each of its terms to the structure, diction, rhythm, and imagery of the poems. The pattern "gives form to every aspect of substance and technique."

In explaining the pattern within the particular poems, Mr. Hynes reveals his own great sensitivity to the craft of poetry itself. Here his learning and his own native alertness support each other in ways that become extremely interesting. For example, he remarks that Hardy, far from being indifferent to metrical experiment, actually possesses a prosodic curiosity similar in kind, though not in depth and intensity, to that of Hopkins. Then Mr. Hynes writes several striking pages about the neglected William Barnes. Hardy valued the older Dorsetshire poet's philological studies as well as his beautiful poems; and Mr. Hynes, while never losing sight of Hardy himself, evokes Barnes and his theories in order to show that Hardy's admiration was justified. Such passages moved me to hope that Mr. Hynes will write something on Barnes alone. The use of knowledge to illuminate the main subject—the pattern of Hardy's own poetry—is itself one of the choice attractions of this excellent study.

I agree that it is time for Hardy's poems to be assigned their proper place. The high excellence of the best of them is no longer in question. Hardy is among the poets. But critical judgment is hindered by inadequate understanding, and Hardy has especially suffered from plain misreading. To blame obscurities on Hardy's clumsiness is beside the point. Certainly he wrote clumsy poems. He also wrote a few of the best poems in the language. Mr. Hynes recognizes both kinds; and, since the same pattern pervades both, he brilliantly discusses the bad poems in order to explain the pattern that is subtly absorbed into the good ones. In effect, Mr. Hynes has shown how to read Hardy. Anyone who follows his suggestions will find the great poems without getting lost. Mr. Hynes has written the best general introduction to all of Hardy's poetry that I have ever read.

Mr. Ransom's presentation of Hardy is of a different kind, more personal and direct. He has selected 125 of Hardy's strongest poems, and introduced them through one of his own most beautiful essays. For many years Mr. Ransom has been contemplating Hardy. It is pleasant to see this selection appearing in time to aid Mr. Hynes' purpose; to give Hardy his truest, most serious reading. Mr. Ransom's essay is the fullest of several which he has written on Hardy. He concludes by describing Hardy's place among the poets. It is Mr. Ransom's most considered statement on the poet so far. Someone should publish all of his Hardy essays in one place. They are literary criticism; but they have further interest as poetic documents in their own right. They are the reading which one remarkable poet has given another; and, as such, they resemble Coleridge's readings of Wordsworth, or the meditations on Antonio Machado by Juan Ramon Jimenez.

Mr. Ransom strengthens his sense of the poetry's art by seeing it in its living habitat. He evokes the post-Darwinian chaos of belief; the dreadful quarter-century when the rural districts of southwestern England were afflicted by a modern restlessness, when people like Jude Fawley and Clym Yeobright went prowling from country to city and back again. Moreover, in his devotion to Hardy the man, Mr. Ransom exemplifies the rarest and truest kind of literary criticism. His knowledge of external facts comes alive at every point, and illuminates the poetry through the character of the poet.

To see Hardy as a living man means to know what he knew, and Mr. Ransom is able to explain Hardy's major problem as a poet and its solution. It is the slightly embarrassing problem of finding oneself a religious poet in an age of naturalism. Any reader must sense Hardy's Christian charity. It is not a formal article of faith but rather a trait of personality. As some men are choleric, so Hardy is charitable. Not that he is nonintellectual. In fact, he intellectualizes with awful persistence. But his charity remains unarguable, a fact like a reddleman, a discontented wife, a hayrick, a Stonehenge. Hardy is trapped with it. His poems suggest a man who fully pays the price of a defenseless compassion, and who is incapable of lying himself to sleep. His charity touches even the clumsiest of his phrases. His talent for belief is curiously combined with a flair for doubt. He could find evidence only for a God ultimately mindless. The philosophical validity of his ideas is a secondary matter, as both Mr. Hynes and Mr. Ransom recognize. But the ideas themselves are facts of the first importance. The traditional elegiac mood becomes in Hardy a funeral for God Himself; and the modest lament for small creatures is no less intense than the poet's grief at the absence of God. I do not think I am distorting Mr. Ransom's reading of Hardy when I say that it implies a Franciscan man, who longs to preach to the birds but who cannot, because his very devoutness conflicts with his sorrowful honesty. He knows that the birds are properly interested in suet, not in displaced believers. But the religious emotions rise in Hardy anyway, in spite of his doubt.

This clash, so well explained by Mr. Ransom, is another version of the pattern described by Mr. Hynes: "the eternal conflict between irreconcilables." Such a conflict may be philosophically intolerable. But Hardy the poet learned to bear it. Instead of being torn apart, he accepted the conflict as a dramatic occasion for his art. It was the best he could do. Few poets have done half so much.

A great poet possesses what I might call the religious imagination. He can see local and private details within a vision of the entire creation; and the facts of his personal experience include some kind of order, some tragic pain and the courage it evokes, and some kind of glory. Perhaps Yeats is the best example of a modern master who reveals such imagination in his perpetual struggle to deepen his vision through his style. Although Hardy was more concerned with metrical experiment than is usually recognized, he is not a dramatic stylist as Yeats was. Still, he belongs in Yeats' company.

Although Hardy left no stylistic heirs, he survives as one kind of great poet: a humble workman who remained his own man come hell or high water. Within traditional forms, he wrote some poems that can bear the most severe scrutiny.

Perhaps Hardy's poetry is being increasingly admired and studied because it embodies, in a truly artistic way, his personal character. It has a homemade quality, a power of insisting on its own tone of voice, a tough evidence of true workmanship. These are the signs that a decent man has maintained his decency in the presence of the same inhumanities that threaten us. The rhetorical splendor and the transfiguring imagination are, perhaps, higher poetic powers than Hardy's, in the end. And yet, as Ezra Pound observed, Hardy has the "solid center" of genuine poetry. It is this poetic integrity—and the word should imply honesty as well as wholeness of art—which Mr. Hynes so clearly describes. Mr. Ransom's essay introduces a selection of poems which pretty fairly represent the poet's personal manner, and which often display his excellence. Of course, a reader already familiar with Hardy will wish to add a poem here and omit one there. As Mr. Ransom says of anthologists who deal with Hardy, "Rarely do two of them come out with anything like the same list of poems chosen. . . ." Perhaps one reason for such disagreement has been simply the absence of the sustained criticism for which Mr. Hynes asks. Even so, the disagreement also testifies to a power which Hardy possesses, almost alone among the best modern poets: he has the fecundity, the power of abundance. In an age often characterized by sparse poetic production, he has the old easy richness of a man who can trust the Muse as his own rustic characters depend upon the vitality of the seasons.

A Shelf of New Poets

In one of his brilliant and disturbing essays in the *Sewanee Review*, James Dickey writes the following about a poem which he admires: "It is only after the Inevitable has clamped us by the back of the neck that we go back and look carefully at the poem, and see that it is written in *terza rima*. And so, hushed and awed, we learn something about the power of poetic form, and the way in which it can both concentrate and release meaning, when meaning is present." It would be difficult to find a more lucid statement of the true relation between the form of a poem and the strange world of imaginative vision where the true form reveals itself. It would also be difficult to find a more lucid description of Mr. Dickey's own best poems, twenty-four of which appear in his first collection, *Into the Stone* (one of three collections in *Poets of Today VII*). His long poem, "Dover: Believing in Kings," is not included, no doubt because of its length. It is one of the few great poems written by an American during the past few years; it is fully equal, if not superior, to

---

Reviewed here are *Poets of Today VII*, selected and with an introduction by John Hall Wheelock (New York: Scribner, 1960); *On the Way to the Island*, by David Ferry (Middletown, Conn.: Wesleyan University Press, 1960); *Nags Head and Other Poems*, by Lee Anderson (New York: Holt, Rinehart and Winston, 1960); *White Sun Black Sun*, by Jerome Rothenberg (New York: Hawk's Well Press, 1960); and *Wage War on Silence*, by Vassar Miller (Middletown, Conn.: Wesleyan University Press, 1960). This review first appeared in *Poetry* 99 (December 1961).

W. S. Graham's "The Nightfishing," which in some ways it resembles. However, since Mr. Dickey's "Dover" is still resting in the darkness, like some beautiful and silent clipper ship poised for its launching, I will limit myself to some brief observations on the poems in *Into the Stone*.

Mr. Dickey's poems invariably embody his confrontation of some of the most difficult and important experiences that a human being can have. The experiences are sometimes public and horribly shared, like war; or they are domestic and affectionately, painfully shared, like the love a man achieves and fulfills for brother and son and wife; and sometimes they are solitary, spiritual, frightening. To all of these experiences the poet brings three great gifts: an unpredictably joyous imagination, which is able to transfigure the most elemental facts of the universe and to embody the transfiguration in an unforgettable phrase (the moon is a "huge ruined stone in the sky," the sunlight is a "great ragged angel," and, as the moonlight falls on grass, "a weightless frosted rain has taken place"); secondly, a delicate sense of music, which sometimes takes shape most beautifully in the skillful use and variation of refrains (as in the lines, "Light falls, man falls; together. / Sun rises from earth alone."); and, finally, a humane quality which is very hard to characterize, but which I should call, inadequately, a kind of courageous tenderness. Of these three gifts, the first is accidental; the poet has been touched by the capricious gods, and there is nothing anyone can do about that. The second gift is a matter of accident, in part; but it is also a matter of intelligent self-discipline; it would be easy for a writer with such a delicate ear to lose himself and his vision in a euphonious haze, but I cannot find a single phrase in Mr. Dickey's book which is not firm and clear. However, it is the final gift, the courageous tenderness, which seems to me most important, which assures us that the many remarkable talents have not been lavished on a man for nothing. Perhaps what I mean has already been stated more clearly by Mr. Dickey himself, in the few sentences which I quoted earlier: poetic form "can both concentrate and release meaning, *when meaning is present.*"

And meaning is present in these poems. I do not have

enough space to list the meanings; and, in any case, I would rather have the reader experience the joy of discovering them for himself. However, to illustrate, I might point to the poem entitled "The Performance." Here Mr. Dickey commemorates a man whose nobility expressed itself through his skill in standing on his hands. And this very man, Donald Armstrong (there is no vague "Humanity" in Mr. Dickey's poems, there are only particular men and women and children, often named and always deeply felt in their solid physical being), was later beheaded by the Japanese. The poet imagines Armstrong giving his performance in the very face of his grotesque death. Armstrong is perhaps, among other things, an image of Dickey's own imagination and skill: in the very presence of realities which are mysteries—like one's own death—the poet, like the old friend from the war, responds to the fact of personal annihilation by suddenly transforming himself into actions that are nobly graceful and that are performed for their own everlasting sake.

Reader, for your own sake, go buy this book.

Of the two other poets included in *Poets of Today VII*, Paris Leary, in my opinion, has come closer to achieving a body of good poetry than Jon Swan. Of course, the latter has virtues which are not to be cast lightly aside, and I will try to do some kind of justice to them in a moment. First let me discuss Mr. Leary.

In the first place, I think that "Addison's Walk" is a very bad poem. But it is bad in an instructive way. The very weakness which it exemplifies does something to point up the strength in several of Mr. Leary's other poems. Now, the trouble with "Addison's Walk," it seems to me, is that it is too discursive. Instead of creating Addison, or anyone else, as a dramatic character in whom the feelings of the poem could be drawn to a focus, and instead of speaking from the viewpoint of a created character himself, Mr. Leary gives us stanza after stanza of straight, prosy editorial comment. It is as though the poet had blundered upon his real poem in the midst of a strange forest, and had only circled it and circled it, without ever attempting anything to make the poem leap awake, come out of the underbrush, or reveal itself. It is the same discursive rambling, the same journalistic commenting, that weakens parts of a much better poem, "Views of the Oxford Colleges."

It is in such poems as the dramatic monologue "USAF in Oxford" and the fine poem "The Curate Crosses Vauxhall Bridge" that Mr. Leary writes most effectively. When his subjects are human and contemporary, his weaknesses vanish, and his language becomes sharp. He is a good poet who has not yet wholly freed himself from a tendency to talk about his subject instead of presenting it. And he has a marvelous subject: the human feelings of Americans caught in a strange, unfamiliar world of historical changes beyond their control or, even, their understanding.

Mr. Leary's work is informed, even in its occasional failures, by a sound intelligence. He never lets his skill sink into self-indulgent versifying. I am afraid I cannot make the same statement about Mr. Swan's poems; for they frequently strike me as having the trivial surface of light verse without the depths of wit and passionate thought which sometimes (as in the case of Swift) raise light verse into thrilling poetry. It distresses me to say that I found the book badly cluttered by exhausted subjects, depleted diction, and a habit of omitting subjects from sentences and omitting the definite article from single phrases—arch pseudo-literary devices which, as far as I could make out, serve no purpose whatever.

Mr. Swan's virtues are a talent for frankly light verse—as distinguished from archness—and a pleasing musical ear. There is one beautiful lyric in this collection. It is called "Climate," and its unpretentious diction, its simplicity and clarity of conception, and the delicacy with which its music unfolds indicate that Mr. Swan is a talented poet who has not yet been sufficiently ruthless with his own poems.

Sometimes David Ferry's poems are slightly marred, for me at least, by their dealing with rather modish subjects. I am getting tired of Adam, and Venus, and all the rest. However, I am aware that, throughout this small collection of poems by Mr. Ferry, there is a very real poetic intelligence at work, dancing, shaping, and skillfully setting to music his poetic impressions. If one compares Mr. Ferry's lyrics with those of Mr. Swan, for example, one sees immediately the essential difference between the light lyric which is nothing but froth and the light lyric which suddenly flares with poetry because of the depths of feeling which are deftly, and yet inevitably, exposed. The title poem of his collection, "On the Way to the Island," represents what I most value in his intelligent, finely molded, and often moving poems.

In the first poem in the book *Wonderstrand Revisited*, Charles H. Philbrick writes the following:

Even Cape Cod
Can recover from curio shops and motels, and from money.
Indeed, unless paleface and profiteer, both,
Learn to tread with the tribesmen, old nature
Has neither to worry about: the poisons of men
Are finally poisonous mainly to man; then the trees
Can take what shapes they please. . . .

This sort of division between human beings and the places where they live seems to me arbitrary and false. Men are evidently dismissed from this Cape Cod landscape, because they are tourists. That they seek money and profits evidently dismisses them from the poet's regard. He wants to contemplate "old nature," which seems to be something which finds human beings superfluous. In fact, it does not. It is my impression, sustained through the reading of this bad book, that Mr. Philbrick wishes to scorn the tourists and get them out of the way so that he can wallow in Nature. He cannot understand why all those ugly tourists are so horrible as to litter the beach with beer cans when he himself is so nice. It is a trivial conception of man's place in the world, and it is embodied in a language which seems to be clumsy in rhythm, pointlessly cacophonous in sound, and affected by mechanical do-it-yourself literary devices like compound adjectives that are used with almost no imaginative discrimination.

There is much truer and more intelligent sense of man's place in the natural world embodied in the latest collection by

Lee Anderson, entitled *Nags Head.* I sympathize with Mr. Anderson's attempt to write a long poem on a theme which he describes as follows: "How shall man's genius for language dissuade him from committing race suicide?" It is an important subject, and Mr. Anderson has wrestled with it manfully. I cannot agree with the jacket-blurbs that he has wholly succeeded: it seems to me that there are too many dramatic devices used in this long poem and that the scene (within the poem itself) shifts too often, without adequate preparation, for the reader to follow it. Nevertheless, we have here one more serious attempt to write a genuine long poem in America, an attempt in which Mr. W. T. Scott partially succeeded in his moving work "The Dark Sister" a few years ago. I like the intelligence and warmth of Mr. Anderson's work; and he has committed himself to his aesthetic problems with such devotion that he may yet produce something of enduring value. Meanwhile, we have the evidence of his honest effort.

An experimenter of a different kind, in many ways more interesting than Mr. Anderson, is Jerome Rothenberg in his modest pamphlet, *White Sun Black Sun.* This poet has already made something of a name for himself as a translator of modern German poets. His own poems are marked by a deeper exploration of imagery than has recently been the case among American poets. It is as though Rothenberg, having set up a simile, were giving most of his attention to the possibilities of the second term. The world of the image can be an exciting one. However, when it strays too far from the real world out of which it rises, it withers. But on several occasions, Rothenberg's poems genuinely blossom, like the memorable "A Conciliation."

I have left Vassar Miller for the last, because, with James Dickey, she is one of the two unquestionably first-rate poets in this group. Her formal conception of poetry differs from Mr. Dickey's, and her emotional concerns are narrower. But her formal sense is almost always adequate to the meaning, which in turn is to be found in the intensity of her feeling. Her lyrics, invariably brief, are religious and, sometimes, erotic; though sometimes these two related terrors meet in an embrace which, as Neruda says somewhere, makes a child leap in the bottom of the earth. It is important to note that Miss Miller, again like Mr. Dickey, belongs to no "school" whatever. If her poems on the page look superficially similar to those of the writers whom Mr. Dickey once devastatingly labeled the School of Charm, then one might say the same about the formal shape of poems by Crashaw, whom Miss Miller resembles in some other ways. As far as traditional form in poetry goes, she has no peer among the younger contemporary writers that I have read. It is just this perfect formal mastery—with a simplicity of diction that is not accidental, and that reveals the concentration of a powerful intellect—which makes especially remarkable Miss Miller's experiments in freer forms in her new volume. The book itself contains eighteen poems reprinted from her *Adam's Footprint* (1956). I think the entire book should have been reprinted. It is hard to find; and, if Miss Miller considers the other poems in that book unworthy of preservation, there is at least one reader who disagrees.

Wage War on Silence contains thirty-nine new poems, the high skill of which almost never falters. Amongst the huge clutter of bad versifying and the aimless screams that have rent the air of These States during recent years, Miss Miller's grace and reserve are very precious. They signify the modesty of a writer who possesses imaginative gifts of the rarest kind.

The Few Poets of England and America

Our age, as nearly everyone knows, is cluttered by vanity; and so it is perhaps natural that it should also be cluttered by poets. The age is also frightened; and vain men, as always, huddle together for mutual reassurance against the cold. Two signs of the time are those two anthologies, *The New Poets of England and America* [ed. Donald Hall, Robert Pack, and Louis Simpson, New York: Meridian, 1957] and *The New American Poetry*. In spite of certain ostensible differences concerning which sympathetic critics of each anthology have been rather more than sufficiently vocal, the two books are astonishingly similar in their vanity, in the general effect of dullness which they produce, and in their depressing clutter of anxious poetasters shrieking their immortality into the void.

It is my purpose here to discuss briefly the work of the few poets in the Grove anthology which I myself found to be seriously beautiful. Although the names of these writers are frequently associated with one gang (Mr. Allen Tate's wittily precise term for "generation") or other; and although it is hard to identify them in the midst of the gray fog laid down by much of the Grove anthology; still, they have produced an excellent body of work. Each is distinct from the others; and the identity of each is more easily discovered and enjoyed when it is freed

---

This review of *The New American Poetry, 1945–1960*, edited by Donald M. Allen (New York: Grove Press, 1960) first appeared in *Minnesota Review 1*, no. 2 (Winter 1961).

from the anthological prison. There are two Grove authors whose poems I enjoy; but I do not intend to discuss them here, because neither has yet published enough to justify any responsible evaluation. I am thinking of LeRoi Jones and Paul Blackburn. The rest I will leave to the kindness of Time, and silently pray the same kindness for myself.

Before I make more detailed statements about the fine poems of Robert Duncan, Robert Creeley, Denise Levertov, Gary Snyder, and Brother Antoninus, I want to note one of the most interesting similarities between the Grove and Meridian anthologies: the absence from either book of poems by some poets who are in some ways finer than any of the poets who are included. I am sure that every disgruntled reader will have favorites of his own, whose omission he resents. The omissions which I have in mind, however, are those on which I think a good many serious readers would agree; the poems of James Dickey, Anne Sexton, and John Logan. Now, I am sure that these omissions can be adquately explained. For example, the astonishing poems of Mrs. Sexton did not begin to appear in print until rather recently; besides, the editors of anthologies cannot be reasonably expected to anticipate forces of nature. The omissions of Mr. Dickey and Mr. Logan are more difficult to understand, but I will leave explanations to editors. I wish merely to record the strange sense of satisfaction that I feel concerning the three omissions. Perhaps what pleases me is that the omissions only confirm my own feeling about the poetry of these three authors: that such breadth of imaginative sympathy and generosity of intelligence are qualities which do not conveniently fit into gangs.

The work of the best Grove poets does not conveniently fit into gangs either. Let me try to release these fine poets.

Robert Creeley has now published eight books, the first of which appeared in 1952. His most recent work is to be found in *A Form of Women* (New York: Jargon/Corinth, 1959), a book which is beautiful in its purity of diction and in its expression of a real man speaking with a kind voice. Mr. Creeley is widely admired by many of his contemporaries, not only for the sensitivity of his poems but also for the integrity of his life. He has not attained a wide reading public—not in the sense that, say, Jack Kerouac, Herman Wouk, Allen Ginsberg, and other ornaments of our age have done. I would like to feel that more people are discovering Mr. Creeley's poems, but I say this for the sake of the public itself. I doubt if Mr. Creeley himself is very deeply troubled by the fact that his work as an artist has not been transformed into something like Mr. Kerouac's—that is, a consumeritem, to be considered less the work of a struggling artist than a mass-produced fantasy designed to mirror the escapist daydreams of middle-class people who despise their own everyday lives with sullen despair. There is a good deal of emotion in Mr. Creeley's poetry; but it is not sullen, and if despair appears it is the kind which the poet confronts and faces down. His poems embody the imagination of a man who is not afraid of genuine feeling in his personal struggles to live day by day in the world, and who contends with feeling in a manner invariably marked by dignity and grace. He is able to create poems out of many feelings; but perhaps the one which is most noteworthy is the feeling of love. Mr. Creeley is one of the truest and most nourishing love poets alive. I can do no better than to illustrate his skill by quoting one of his short love poems in its entirety. It is called "The Whip":

> I spent a night turning in bed,
> my love was a feather, a flat
>
> sleeping thing. She was
> very white
>
> and quiet, and above us on
> the roof, there was another woman I
>
> also loved, had
> addressed myself to in
>
> a fit she
> returned. That
>
> encompasses it. But now I was
> lonely, I yelled,
>
> but what is that? Ugh,
> she said, beside me, she put

her hand on
my back, for which act

I think to say this
wrongly.

Robert Duncan is another excellent poet whose work is measured and spare, although many of his poems are long. The diction is uncluttered, like that of Mr. Creeley; but, whereas the sound of the latter's verse is like that of a human voice speaking, Mr. Duncan's considerable talent most often assumes the form and measure of a human voice singing. He is a lyrical poet in the most traditional sense: that is, he is a musician. I do not mean that his poems, as such, need to be set to music. And I do not mean that they drip like Swinburne. At his best, he is a master of rhetoric in the Elizabethan sense of the word. Employing the simplest diction and rhythm, he can lead the reader to expect a certain pattern of sound, and then he varies it, so that the music of his verse produces a fusion of fulfillment and surprise which is one of the chief delights created by such a great lyric poet as, say, Thomas Campion. Since Mr. Duncan's poems are often longer than those of Creeley, it is more difficult to give a correct impression of his range by quoting a single one. Here are the first and last stanzas of his shorter poem, "The Temple of the Animals," which I have long admired for the restrained precision of its music:

The temple of the animals has fallen into disrepair.
The pad of feet has faded.
The panthers flee the shadows of the day.
The smell of musk has faded but lingers there . . .
lingers, lingers. Ah, bitterly in my room.
Tired, I recall the animals of last year:
the altars of the bear, tribunals of the ape,
solitudes of elephantine gloom, rare
zebra-striped retreats, prophecies of dog,
sanctuaries of the pygmy deer. . . .

I have seen the animals depart,
forgotten their voices, or barely remembered
—like the last speech when the company goes

or the beloved face that the heart knows,
forgets and knows—
I have heard the dying footsteps fall.
The sound has faded, but lingers here.
Ah, bitterly I recall
the animals of last year.

Mr. Duncan has published a good many books and is soon to have a new one. The best introduction to his work remains the *Selected Poems* (San Francisco, City Lights, 1959). However, this selection is taken only from his first four books. There ought to be another selection from his more recent work.

Denise Levertov is another of the best poets in the Grove anthology. Though still quite young, she has published four books and, more significantly, has gone through several distinct stages of development as a poet. In each of these, she has produced work of real merit. She published her first book in England, where she was born. Then (as she tells us in her modest and interesting note), after her marriage and subsequent residence in America, she began to feel "the stylistic influence of William Carlos Williams." Although some reviewers of her most recent book (*With Eyes at the Back of Our Heads*, New York: New Directions, 1959) affected to discover in her American poems a mere imitation of Dr. Williams' manner, she has actually moved beyond her amazing apprenticeship in the use of American speech-rhythms into an area wholly her own: a world where the ordinary objects of everyday American life are rediscovered and recreated from the inside, according to the spontaneously developing laws of a thrilling poetic imagination. Miss Levertov shares with Mr. Duncan and Mr. Creeley the possession of authentic imagination, in the absence of which, of course, all concern with craftsmanship is mere pedantry. However, she also shares with these others the awareness that the imagination carries its own responsibilities for craftsmanship, and therefore we find her poems to be genuine creations of a disciplined art. The music of her verse has something in common with that of Creeley: it is spare, direct, measured more according to a voice speaking than a voice singing. But such restraint allows her to speak to the reader with inflections unmistakably her own in a poetry whose recognizable charm is all the more appealing for its being based upon an imagination of tough creative force. She is nearly always excellent; and since, like Creeley's, her poems are most often brief, I can give an entire poem as a fair illustration of her vigorous work. It is called "The Hands":

> Don't forget the crablike
> hands, slithering among the keys.
> Eyes shut, the downstream
> play of sound lifts away from
> the present, drifts you
> off your feet: too easily let off.
> So look: that almost painful
> movement restores the pull, incites
> the head with the heart: a tension, as of
> actors at rehearsal, who move
> this way, that way, on a bare stage, testing
> their diagonals, in common clothes.

One of the mysteries of poetry is that there is no constant relation between the skill of a poet in his poems and the clarity of the same poet in his discussions of his craft. The poems of Mr. Gary Snyder are so unpretentious that one might expect him to decline comment on his own art. And yet he is among the most articulate of his contemporaries when it comes to explaining what he is trying to do and how he is trying to do it. In one of the "Statements on Poetics" which the editor of the Grove anthology, Mr. Donald M. Allen, has thoughtfully included, Snyder has the following to say about his way of writing: "I've just recently come to realize that the rhythms of my poems follow the rhythm of the physical work I'm doing and life I'm leading at any given time—which makes the music in my head which creates the line. Conditioned by the poetic tradition of the English language & whatever feeling I have for the sound of poems I dig in other languages. *Riprap* is really a class of poems I wrote under the influence of the geology of the Sierra Nevada and the daily trial-crew work of picking up and placing granite stones in tight cobble patterns on hard slab. 'What are you doing?' I asked old Roy Marchbanks.—'Riprapping' he said. His selection of natural rocks was perfect— . . . I tried writing poems of tough, simple, short words, with the complexity far beneath the surface texture. In part the line was influenced by the five- and seven-character line Chinese poems I'd been reading, which work like sharp blows on the mind."

There could be no more lucid introduction to Mr. Snyder's poems, which have so far appeared in two volumes: *Riprap* (Ashland, Mass.: Origin, 1959) and *Myths & Texts* (New York: Totem/Corinth, 1960). None of his poems included in the Grove anthology is short enough to quote here. However, since I am primarily interested in the good poets and only secondarily in the anthology itself, I feel free to quote the following short poem from *Myths & Texts*, in order to illustrate Mr. Snyder's work at its most characteristic:

> Out the Greywolf valley
> in late afternoon
> after eight days in the high meadows
> hungry, and out of food,
> the trail broke into a choked
> clearing, apples grew gone wild
> hung on one low bough by a hornet's nest.
> caught the drone in tall clover
> lowland smell in the shadows
> then picked a hard green one:
> watched them swarm.
> smell of the mountains still on me.
> none stung.

What strikes me most deeply about this modest little poem is its precision and the purpose which the precision is made to serve. In a few spare lines, the poet makes me feel the presence of a living man in a living place, many of whose vivid details I am now familiar with. He has made the language record his own human presence, and he has been able to say something about his own deep, fundamentally human experience in that place. He has made me feel a little more at home in the world.

This short poem by no means fully represents Snyder's work. It is a poem of solitude. In his other poems, he explores the landscape of the western United States—its physical look and feel, its laborers, its unassuming and humorous animals, its perpetual freshness—with a powerful delicacy all his own. He is perhaps the only living American poet who can use swear-words and make them sound as if they were spoken by a human being instead of by an IBM. Finally, his very patience and modesty enable him to see ghosts—the real ghosts of men who once lived and worked in real places that have names; and these ghosts embody Snyder's power of revealing a historical dimension to the imagination of the reader, a power which Robert Lowell and Louis Simpson have been almost alone in possessing among recent American poets. Snyder's ghosts are well illustrated by the following passage, which I find profoundly moving:

> A ghost logger wanders a shadow
> In the early evening, boots squeak
> With the cicada, the fleas
> Nest warm in his blanket-roll
> Berrybrambles catch at the stagged pants
> He stumbles up the rotten puncheon road
> There is a logging camp
> Somewhere in there among the alders
> Berries and high rotting stumps
> Bindlestiff with a wooden bowl
> (The poor bastards at Nemi in the same boat)
> What old Seattle skidroad did he walk from
> Fifty years too late, and all his
>   money spent?

Gary Snyder's poems are attractive in their ability to contain both tenderness and a certain rough honesty at the same moment and to express these manly qualities in the same breath. It should be unnecessary to say that gentleness and courage in dealing with a subject matter very close to life as the creatures live it are primarily matters of personal character; and that, where the character is lacking, no amount of literary skill can substitute for it. And yet, when the character is there to be expressed, how seemly is the effect of a sensitive craft! I find Snyder's work invariably humane and intelligent, and it makes me feel the dignity of being human. There has been a good deal of noise about bringing poetry back to the subject matter of real life. I'm sure that few people would admit outright that they want poetry to be dead. Everybody is against sin. But the real issue is to determine what is meant by "life." It is a question that can be answered, as Mr. Snyder has answered it, only by recording the actual physical details of living things, and allowing those things to speak—or simply exist—in and for themselves. Snyder's patient simplicity holds a lesson for all poets of any "school" whatever.

Of course, a man may struggle in his own solitude to make sense out of the creatures of the natural world; and the struggle may be expressed through the style of the language itself, so that entire poems may be dramatic stages where the interest lies not only in the poet's subject but also in his very effort to grasp it. Such is the case with Brother Antoninus, the last of the poets with whom I am here concerned. Although the Grove anthology contains only three of his poems, they are well chosen. We see him struggling to subdue himself in order to pay attention to the objective and miraculous existence of natural things and creatures. The dramatic impact of his poems derives largely from his struggle to see and feel the creatures come alive and endure on their own terms—which turn out to be God's terms, and miraculous. Yet the miracle of living things in Brother Antoninus' poems is anything but sweetish or merely consoling. Time and again we are forced to recognize that the full responsibility of a human being involves his willingness to recognize the frequent division between comfort and magnificence, life and sloth. There is drama in his own struggle to come alive so as to allow his subjects to come alive on their own terms. Brother Antoninus has finally achieved a language in which a natural melodiousness is often suddenly wrenched into cacophony. It is as though the poet refused to allow the language itself to subside into slick rhetoric. Consequently, the moral passion, always alert, saves the poem for the imagination. I am delighted to find the beautiful poem, "A Canticle to the Waterbirds" included in this anthology. Brother Antoninus' deliberate rejection of easy tunefulness, his constant effort to subordinate the language to the vision—an effort which recalls the similar drama in the language of Hardy's poems—may be illustrated by the following quotation, in which the poet is addressing the birds:

You leave a silence. And this for you suffices, who are not of
    the ceremonies of man,
And hence are not made sad to now forgo them.
Yours is of another order of being, and wholly it compels.
But may you, birds, utterly seized in God's supremacy,
Austerely living under His austere eye—
Yet may you teach a man a necessary thing to know,
Which has to do of the strict conformity that creaturehood
    entails,
And constitutes the prime commitment all things share.
For God has given you the imponderable grace to *be* His
    verification,
Outside the mulled incertitude of our forsenic choices;
That you, our lessers in the rich hegemony of Being,
May serve as a testament to what a creature is,
And what creation owes.

I would like to conclude with a few comments on a matter which troubles me. Some of the good poets in the Grove anthology have spoken respectfully, and even gratefully, of the teachings of Mr. Charles Olson; and, as one perceptive reviewer noted, Mr. Olson "looms" over the anthology. I myself do not feel that his work "looms" because of the excellence of his poems. They seem to me very much inferior to the work of any of the poets whom I have discussed in this essay. Neither can Mr. Olson be said to "loom" over the book because of the clarity of his prose. I have read his famous essay "Projective Verse" several times now, and I confess that I still am not quite sure I understand it. Now, it is obvious that I might be refusing to understand—out of stupidity or the cheap desire to be clever. Stupidity is beyond my control; but I am certainly not trying to be cute. I am simply admitting my failure to grasp the plain sense of such passages as the following:

"Now (3) the *process* of the thing, how the principle can be made so to shape the energies that the form is accomplished. And I think it can be boiled down to one statement (first pounded into my head by Edward Dahlberg): ONE PERCEPTION MUST IMMEDIATELY AND DIRECTLY LEAD TO A FURTHER PERCEPTION. It means exactly what it says, is a matter of, at *all* points (even, I should say, of our management of daily reality as of daily work) get on with it, keep moving, keep in, speed, the nerves, their speed, the perceptions, theirs, the acts, the split second acts, the whole business, keep it moving as fast as you can, citizen. And if you also set up as a poet, USE USE USE the process of all points, in any given poem always, always one perception must must must MOVE, INSTANTER, ON ANOTHER!"

I think I understand Mr. Olson down as far as the phrase "is a matter of" in the third sentence of the passage. After "of," I lose him completely, so help me. "Of" what? I had similar trouble following the meaning of the sentences throughout the essay.

Gravity and Incantation

Gangs of versifiers in America have oft made night hideous with a miraculous variety of blats, gunks, and skreeks. Among them were the professionally "female" poets once wickedly labeled the "oh God the pain girls." Today, of course, we have several poetic schools of our own, and in their way they are probably even worse. But at least the caterwaulresses are gone. They are old, unhappy, far-off things, and battles long ago.

We have our own howls to inspire mad dreams of having an eardrum perforated for reasons of health. But the howls are not those of women. On the contrary, many women are writing fine poetry. Perhaps Nature herself has sent them to rescue us from a poetry that has become so bad as to be almost hair-raising.

I wish to discuss new books by two noble women who are also two of the best living poets in America. They differ from each other; but their differences define their identities. By nature they resist absorption into any school. And, in being themselves, they touch certain beauties which are essential to poetry itself, whether written by man, woman, or child.

Miss Levertov has published several books during the past few years. Born in England, she first wrote with startling skill in

This review of *The Jacob's Ladder*, by Denise Levertov (New York: New Directions, 1961) and *The Looking Glass*, by Isabella Gardner (Chicago: University of Chicago Press, 1959) first appeared in *Minnesota Review* 2, no. 3 (Spring 1962).

a traditional iambic style. After moving to the United States, of which she is now a citizen, she began to write poems in a measure which is sometimes called (mistakenly, I believe, as does Miss Levertov herself) "free verse." I have neither the space nor the full understanding required to discuss her prosody, but it should be discussed, for it is one of the most rewarding features of her moving poetry. Perhaps Miss Levertov herself will eventually write on the subject in relation to her own work. I hope she does. I have the impression that she is often misread and misinterpreted. I once read, in a foolish review, that Miss Levertov was simply writing imitations of W. C. Williams, whose style itself, compact of originality and even eccentricity, could not be imitated. Elsewhere, I have seen Miss Levertov associated, almost identified, with the Beats. (It is as though one had described Horace as one of the hangers-on of Byron during the later, riper part of his career.) Whether or not some person has approached her at a party to ask why she isn't Yeats, I do not know; but I would not be surprised; she apparently has had to put up with every other critical inanity imaginable, and she may as well finish the course. At any rate, she cannot be understood as a British poet who came to America and tried to assimilate the American language through the expedient of appropriating Dr. Williams' language bag and baggage. She has made her own discovery of America. The character of her poetry is remarkably American precisely *because* it is genuinely international. I have read that her father was a great Jewish scholar and that she was educated at home. Her father must have been delighted; he must have felt like one of her readers; for her imagination is always religiously open, and it always responds to what touches it awake. It is a quick, luminous mind, protected by wisdom against falsity till its spirit is strong enough to do its own protecting. Her poetry caresses the English landscape, as in "A Map of the Western Part of the Country of Wessex" in her new book. It naturally embraces the local details of America, as in so many of her new and earlier poems. I begin to believe that her poetry is so beautifully able to acclimate itself to different nations (to their true places, not to their latest political lies) because her imagination was given its first shape and direction by a spirit of culture that traditionally has belonged to different nations. As far as I know, Miss Levertov's work has rarely been judged from this perspective—Kenneth Rexroth seems to have pointed it out only to be ignored by subsequent reviewers. In any case, the advantages offered this poet by her international heritage are displayed inescapably in her new book *The Jacob's Ladder*.

She has poems that lovingly touch the places of America, country and city alike, each with its continuous spirit and body. There are some poems—like the really splendid "In Memory of Boris Pasternak" and the difficult, harrowing sequence about the Eichmann trial—which explicitly confront international themes. But the international spirit blossoms most fully in the new poem entitled "A Solitude." Here the poet helps a blind man find his way through and out of a subway in New York city; and she allows the international inspiration to find its own fulfillment. For it touches the great theme: the particularly human. Her considerable talent blooms in this poem, which is, in Johnson's phrase, "a just representation of general nature." "A Solitude" is a special joy to those who have always felt the deep gravity which underlies Miss Levertov's work. "A Solitude" can stand up in the presence of Rilke's poems on the blind. Yes, I know what I am saying. And if it is justified, then it is easier to see why Miss Levertov's poems have been so maddeningly categorized by fools among fools. If Rilke, completely unknown in the United States, were to publish *Neue Gedichte* right now, it would probably be brushed off in an omnibus review. (Let's see, now . . . where did I leave that box of prefabricated phrases for omnibus reviews? . . . Ah, here it is: "Mr. Rilke should realize that, after all, Dr. Williams' notorious 'new territory' is really inseparable from his methods of arriving there, and it cannot be explored by the young. It is a pity that such a promising young writer should waste his energy by following roads already travelled by others. Besides, why isn't he Yeats?") Well, I am not called, much less chosen, to console Miss Levertov for the frustration of being misread by dead asses. Anyway, it just doesn't matter. "A Solitude" will outlive misreaders, and categorizers, and her, and me, and perhaps that isn't enough. The poet must judge for herself. I will merely record my gratitude for the appearance of a noble poem— indeed, for a noble book.

Miss Gardner's new book gives me a pleasure equally strong but of a different kind. It is a pleasure appropriate to the different kind of poetry which she has written. This poetry is more lyrical in the great ancient sense. Except for an infrequent occasional poem like "Little Rock Arkansas," Miss Gardner, here in her new book as in her earlier book, the distinguished *Birthdays from the Ocean*, writes of personal and urgent themes. In doing so, she frequently displays a sudden, dreadfully strong gift which I will call the power of incantation. It is the rhythmic and musical form of the authentic poetic madness, the madness of the ancient poets and rhapsodists.

The character of Miss Gardner's poetry is, first of all, sensitive and civilized. But you are not advised to hold a lighted match near it. The atmosphere of cultivation becomes the occasion for those poems in which her lyrical powers most truly fulfill themselves. Two conditions seem present in her best poems: the civilized setting and the dark musical force; the Apollonian and the Dionysian; the feeling for order joined with the understanding of disorder; possession and abandon. It is this drama of self-definition which makes Miss Gardner a lyric poet of authentic power. She belongs to the tradition of Sappho. As everybody knows, Sappho instructed other poets in the secrets of craftsmanship which would both release and shape the poetic demon. We can infer one of these secrets from Sappho's own practice, if we are willing to take Miss Mary Barnard's word for it; and I am so willing. I quote the following translation in its entirety:

> Pain penetrates
> Me drop
> by drop

In her note, Miss Barnard says that "Sappho used the word stalagmon, a constant dripping, of pain." I do not have Greek, but a scholarly friend tells me that the word *stalagmon* is the root of "stalagmite." One word. I have never seen a more powerful conception in a poem about pain, and, frankly, I would prefer not to. Too much is quite enough, thank you. The conception is not charming; it is appalling; there is something demonic about it. Its precision releases huge recognition and anguish. Simplicity is the highest of lyrical achievements. It presents us, not with the stages of a struggle, but only with the outcome of that struggle; it is the victory after the bodies have been cleared away. Nietzsche remarks in *Twilight of the Idols (#6)* that "the first preliminary schooling for spirituality is "not to react at once to a stimulus, but to gain control of all the inhibiting, excluding instincts. . . . All unspirituality, all vulgar commonness, depend on the inability to resist a stimulus." Control of a stimulus of whose power one is fully aware is the true lyrical grace. So I called Miss Gardner a lyrical poet in the great manner. We have few of them among us; but so did the age of Sappho. Consider a poem of Miss Gardner's which illustrates a combination of forces which can produce the genuine incantatory lyric: "In Memory of Lemuel Ayers, Scene Designer." The feeling is a severe personal grief. The occasion is public and formal. The poet is not concerned with vanity, with self-display. She embodies the violence of grief in a poem whose very movement and diction are themselves significant meanings: the restraint which is the true strength.

Coleridge once compared the standard bad performance of his time with the works of some poets who happened to live in the seventeenth century but whose virtues, as Coleridge implied, are the essential virtues of all poetry. He observed that great poets could deal with complex themes in a simple style; whereas the poetasters wrote of simple-minded matters in a style top-heavy, inappropriately complex. So men have faced our own literary disasters before, and some have survived. Keats, Landor, Clare, and Coleridge himself managed a few victories in the solitary struggles of lyrical poetry. So has Miss Gardner. Moreover, the power in her best poems is a fertile one, and promises to renew itself again and again.

A Plain Brave Music

The poetry of David Ignatow has so far appeared in three books: *Poems* (Prairie City, Ill.: The Decker Press, 1948), *The Gentle Weight Lifter* (New York: Morris Gallery, 1955), and *Say Pardon* (Middletown, Conn.: Wesleyan University Press, 1961). A number of periodicals have also printed his work; but it was not until quite recently, I believe, that his work began to receive the critical attention that it deserves. I suppose the first of his volumes is out of print by now. But by good luck I have found a copy, and I have been reading it with delight.

The book contains a remarkable introduction by Milton Hindus. He points out the strength of Mr. Ignatow's imagination and the courage which nourishes that strength; the "organic" form of the poems that "have emerged in shapes a little more natural and crude than those of artificial, hothouse growths"; and the poet's kinship with Whitman. It is fascinating to observe that the relation to Whitman is not merely a matter of artificial influence or the mentioning of a name. Mr. Hindus says that "real poems such as these should need no introduction—they are their own best introduction." It is true. Whitman once said the same of himself and his own poems: "We convince by our presence."

Nevertheless, Mr. Hindus noted, in 1948, that the poems *did* need an introduction, for the good reason that "the novelty of their style may stand between the reader and them." Well, in 1962 we have our own troubles; but at least we can say, with whatever relief it may afford us, that we are able to feel the joy of reading Mr. Ignatow's poems. The fact is heartening, because the poems themselves are distinguished in the later volumes by the same original power which Mr. Hindus noted in the first. I cannot improve on his words: "This novelty consists in a rock-bottom, uncompromising truth which allows for no ornamentation or embellishment." A recognition of the power which emerges from Mr. Ignatow's deliberate discarding of rhetoric is necessary to an understanding of his poetry in all three volumes.

Current academic rhetoric does not illuminate the poet's vision, but insulates it from the shock of the reader's imagination. The effect is a kind of death. When I was a child I was told that the beards and fingernails of cadavers continue to grow in the grave. But even were some scavenging critic to steal abroad by night, shave the jowls of his favorite rhetorician, lay wolf-bane on his coffin, and stride forth at dawn proclaiming the dreary equation of poetry with deodorants, it would make little difference to the corpse whether he is a bearded Beat or a member of the faculty club: a rhetorician is a rhetorician. Blessed be the name of the Lord. It would be pleasant to pretend that the word "rhetoric" retains its ancient meaning: a way of arranging words to convey a vision and evoke a true response in the feelings of readers. But today the word signifies the manipulation of words with the purpose of drawing unqualified attention to themselves and to the dubious charms of their manipulator. We endure a bloated body of verse which drops a shroud between the true feelings of the reader and the true character of the poet.

But the true character of a poet is just what Mr. Ignatow exposes to us through his work. No doubt his poems have their autobiographical origins; and no reader can intelligently deny their direct, personal force. But it is important to distinguish between such personal poetry and that mechanical listing of data untouched by imagination which clutters the verse of selfish men who possess no talent except vicious self-praise.

The true person who is born in David Ignatow's poetry is

remarkable for his self-knowledge. His struggle against rhetoric is the labor of his birth.

This character—a suffering, unselfish, honest man—is a poetic counterpart of another creation of spiritual autobiography, Dostoevsky's man from the underground. Of course, Ignatow's underground man is not literally identical with Dostoevsky's. The latter defiantly refuses to be happy, whereas Ignatow's man insists on his own happiness—and any wretched man in our America who dares to be happy is more than defiant—he is practically subversive.

Tough happiness is part of Mr. Ignatow's poetic identity. I think he has conveyed images of private happiness more convincingly than any other American poet I have ever read except Dr. Williams. He has a love poem in *Say Pardon* which describes the beloved woman sitting in an apple tree and concludes with these lines:

> She smiles the whole crop in
> and the one she throws me
> as the best I believe
> even if it will not chew
> because I too am smiled in,
> just like you,
> old battered skin.

It is only after the most devoted labor that a poet can strip his language of everything except what he sees and feels. Purification of one's language is purification of the heart. It demands courage. It requires the character which must exist and stand forth once the rhetoric is taken away. Much current critical hullaballoo can be clarified by a plain horrible statement: many American versifiers are lacking in courage; David Ignatow is a very brave man.

He is true to himself. The novelty which Mr. Hindus discovered in his first book is sustained through all three collections: the "rock bottom, uncompromising truth which allows for no ornamentation or embellishment." I cherish this novelty. But it is not the only virtue of this poet's work. For example, there is his music. I read one reviewer (I forget where, and I don't especially care to remember) who claimed that the poems in *Say Pardon* were without lyricism. That reviewer must have a built-in iambic metronome, or perhaps a cauliflower ear. For if anything is immediately lovely in these poems, it is their music. It is based on the colloquial syntax and the rhythms of our American language as we speak it. Dr. W. C. Williams is one of the persons to whom Mr. Ignatow dedicates his third book. I presume the dedication is offered in personal friendship. In any case, it is an appropriate dedication to the older poet, who has sounded the depths of the music in our own language so lovingly and long, and whose generous teachings now, in the fullness of his noble life, are finding such beautiful listeners and learners as Robert Creeley, Denise Levertov, and David Ignatow. A whole poem from *Say Pardon* will give a sound of Ignatow's music. It is called "Brief Elegy":

> In every beautiful song is a promise of sleep.
> I will sleep if you will sing to me,
> but sing to me of sleep
> when the bells have hushed in the towers
> and the towers have hushed from their sounds.
> Sing to me, strolling through silent streets.

I have spoken of this poet's power of creating a spiritual characterization in his poems, and of singing a beautiful, true music. But my description of his work is still incomplete. The decency in the man's character carries him even beyond personal lyricism. We are dealing here with a healing imagination, which comes to a man after he has scaled his dark mountain. The power is terrible; it is love; nothing else could have created the following little masterpiece, called "Mother and Child":

> She feared the baby would fall,
> Upside down she held it.
> She loved her child.
> As a born baby, it was a practical thing,
> handled by doctors. As a drowned baby,
> it still would exist.

By accident it died inside its tub.
She carried it carefully to its crib
and there rocked it, as she called for help.
Help, help, she called.
Help, help, she whispered,
hands resting upon her.

After I read this poem aloud to myself, I can hear Thomas Hardy muttering under the earth, "Shut up and drink the whiskey."

But this is no time for a critic to quibble about the incompleteness of his own descriptions. What is completely clear is that we have before us a poet of magnificent powers which are still growing. Let us be quiet, and listen to his new poems.

James Wright on Roger Hecht

Roger Hecht has been working silently and devotedly at his poems for more than a decade. Last year he published his first book. These *Twenty-Seven Poems*, however, cannot be described simply as a selection made at large from the substantial body of work which he has so far produced. The selection was rather guided by this poet's preoccupation, through an unpopular style, with a painful and necessary set of themes, the latter largely having to do with the rupture of American national idealism, a rupture long ominously prefigured by the sentimentality of American private life and the hysteria of our public life. The most ambitious of these poems, and the one probably most splendid in its achievement, deals with the confrontation between President Wilson and what one must call something like the cracked old Adam of human reality in this world. Roger Hecht's style, which I call unpopular, is the great plain style in English, deriving its wide range of rhythms from three main sources: the author's familiarity with the English and American masters of prose; his mastery of lyrical verse; and his wonderfully fresh pleasure in the spoken rhythms of the American language. There is always something forbidding in the tone and measure of these poems, and this quality is the surest value of the style. The author's integrity is such that he devotes all of his stylistic bril-

This review of *Twenty-Seven Poems*, by Roger Hecht (New York: AMS Press, 1966) first appeared in *Voyages* 1, no. 1 (Fall 1967).

liance, all of his passionate intellect to his insistence on the irreducible difficulty of his subject matter. The poems are disturbingly beautiful, like the poems of Melville; beautiful because they are disturbing. Moreover, by their very existence they provide a relief to the mind of any reader who cares about a literary culture, for they are the basis of such culture: a steadfast devotion to language itself, and an abiding moral seriousness.

"I Come to Speak for Your Dead Mouths"

By this time it is clear to everybody who has ever heard of him that Neruda is a very great poet.

It is the folly of Americans to assume that to say as much is to say that a man is a great man, worthy of worship, a relief to us in our frantic and temporary deaths.

But a great poet is a disturbance. If poetry means anything, it means heart, liver, and soul. If great poetry means anything, anything at all, it means disturbance, secret disturbance, that can be disposed of in public, as the pharmacist's delivery of prescription disposes of lonely midnight daydreams. But that cannot be so easily disposed of privately, as the insomniac discovers that the soporific provides him with sleep only to follow the hand of sleep into a land of secret wakening, nightmare, or illumination, that he wished to escape in the first place. It is bad enough to be miserable; but to be happy, how far beyond shock it is. To be alive, with all one's unexpected senses, and yet to face the fact of unhappiness.

There is a critic in the English language whose nobility and spaciousness allowed him to make the statement about poetry that can in turn allow us to cherish what is great. It is a statement about Shakespeare, and it applies to Neruda's poem "The Heights of Macchu Picchu." In his preface to the works

This review of *The Heights of Macchu Picchu,* by Pablo Neruda, translated by Nathaniel Tarn (New York: Farrar, Straus and Giroux, 1967) first appeared in *Poetry* 112 (June 1968).

of Shakespeare, Dr. Johnson wonders why we should care about a poet after he has been dead for more than a hundred years. After all the envious reviewers are dead, something lives. How do we know it lives? We love it. It is alive. It is all we have. But why? Why do we love it? What is alive?

It combines a flowering in language with a cold pruning of form. Great poetry folds personal death and general love into one dark blossom.

I don't know why you read it, but I read it because I like it. I want poetry to make me happy, but the poetry I want should deal with the hell of our lives or else it leaves me cold. Why should I care? Why should I let it touch me?

Here is Johnson's remark on great poetry, which on this particular occasion happens to be Shakespeare:

> Nothing can please many or please long but just representations of general nature. Particular manners can be known to few, and few only can judge how nearly they are copied. The irregular combinations of fanciful invention may delight awhile, by that novelty of which the common satiety of life sends us all in quest. But the pleasures of sudden wonder are soon exhausted, and the mind can only repose on the stability of truth.

Neruda's abundance is clear in every country whose citizens care about poetry. He is too huge to handle in an essay, but I think we should try to identify his genius in a single poem.

Neruda wrote *The Heights of Macchu Picchu* in the fall of 1945. In 1943 he had returned to Chile, and it is very odd to reflect that on that return from his travels as Chilean consul general in Mexico, a "triumphal journey, on which he found himself acclaimed in capital after capital by huge crowds" (in the words of Professor Robert Pring-Mill, whose introduction is one of the most valuable features in this volume), he should have written this great poem. He had achieved fame, all right. And we know what fame is. Milton has told us. It is an infirmity. But Neruda responded as follows.

In a sequence of twelve poems, the poet tells how he had spent his early life wandering in the cities of his country, sick to death of his loneliness, longing for love. The love he longed for was partly sexual, and this love had already been achieved and celebrated in the *Twenty Poems* that made his poetic reputation (by the way, the best English version of these love poems can be found in the neglected masterpiece, Kenneth Rexroth's *Thirty Spanish Poems of Love and Exile,* published by City Lights Books). But Neruda's love is human, and human love is a hell. Coming home, acclaimed, he responded by grieving over his failure to achieve a fulfillment of love with the living. And yet they were cheering him! Imagine. He is a very great poet. Instead of writing an Ode to His Readers, he composed the "Macchu Picchu."

But how can that be? Macchu Picchu, the big city of the Incas, was dead. And the people who built it were dead.

No, they were living in the modern cities of Chile. They were also living in Cleveland, as we know. (If we are sane.)

Neruda couldn't find them in Cleveland, or in Santiago.

So he ascended.

I would paraphrase Neruda's argument as follows: Appalled by loneliness I sought my human brothers among the living; I do not really object to their death, as long as I can share with them the human death; but everywhere I go among the living I find them dying each by each a small petty death in the midst of their precious brief lives. So I ascended to the ancient ruins of the city of Macchu Picchu in the Andes; and there I found that, however the lives of my human brothers may have suffered, at least they are all now dead together. Look at the gorgeous things they have made. But wait a moment. Weren't their lives just as petty and grotesquely fragmented as the very people who die early and pointlessly in the modern cities where I have just been celebrated? Yes, they were. And therefore I love the poor broken dead. They belong to me. I will not celebrate the past for its perfect power over the imperfect living. "I come to speak for your dead mouths." The silent and nameless persons who built Macchu Picchu are alive in Santiago de Chile. The living are the living, and dead the dead must stay.

In conveying this idea, Neruda writes twelve poems that

move from his despair in the living cities to his ascent to the city of the dead, and thence to his invocation of the dead who, in his poetry, are the living. As Professor Pring-Mill remarks, the poet's ascent through space is also an ascent backwards through time. In fact, that is the form of the poem; to discover the living in the past is to discover the living in the present. The image which fulfills this grieving discovery is enclosed in a passage which, in the words of Mr. Tarn, seems to me tragic and beautiful.

> Let me have back the slave you buried here;
> Wrench from these lands the stale bread
> of the poor, prove me the tatters
> on the serf, point out his window.
> Tell me how he slept when alive,
> whether he snored,
> his mouth agape like a dark scar
> worn by fatigue into the wall.

The translation of Neruda into English is a problem which has engaged several poets. One of the most effective of these is Mr. H. R. Hays, whose version of "Walking Around" remains, to me, one of the greatest poems in the modern American language. Mr. Clayton Eshleman has also done a Neruda notable for its daring and force. Now we have Mr. Nathaniel Tarn, the gifted English poet. He has tried to solve the most difficult poem by Neruda which involves not only the stylistic and imaginative brilliance of the great poet's language but also his formal mastery of these elements which enables Neruda to illuminate for us some of the meanings of life. Although personally I would hem and haw over this and that detail of Mr. Tarn's translation, I have to confess that I think it is a beautiful poem in the English language, worthy of the noble and spacious poem which identifies Neruda as one of the precious few great masters of our time and of any time.

Secrets of the Inner Landscape

It is good to have the selection of new poems by Richard Hugo in the *American Poetry Review,* particularly the "Letters to Friends." These are beautiful and vital in themselves, as poems, and they show Hugo rediscovering and giving new life to a form of poetry that is as valid as any other. Richard Howard has touched the form, in this wide-open and personal way, in his vibrant and surprising "Letter from Europe." As far as I know, in the last few years no other poet except Robert Duncan has been rummaging and singing and reflecting into the personal letter as a poem.

But for my present purpose Hugo's "Letters" are mainly important for the light they shed on his work as a whole, and, in a curious and retrospective way, on the form and focus of his new book *The Lady in Kicking Horse Reservoir.*

The new book contains many of the best of Hugo's poems, and before I am done I will quote one of these. In the meantime I intend here to gather a context for the splendid new poems, because Hugo, like Thomas Hardy, is a writer whose work is all of a piece. Some of Hugo's best poems appear in his first book, *A Run of Jacks.* And some of his best poems appear in *The Lady in Kicking Horse Reservoir.* So we are not dealing with a poet who presents us with a sudden dramatic change from one language to another. We are dealing with one of the precious

---

First published in *American Poetry Review* 2, no. 3 (May/June 1973).

few best poets of our age (how he would hate that phrase! but I can't help it) who has, and sustains, an abiding vision.

To make full sense out of Hugo, it is necessary to recognize that, in spite of his "Letters to Friends," he is not a "confessional poet." He has great powers of affection, but he does not write lightly about them, and, God help us and thank him, he does not tell us endlessly about how it feels to menstruate at forty, pick your scabs at suburban coffee klatches, and get even with your mate after you've committed suicide. Every poem is a confession in the sense that it is impossible to write a word on the page without revealing some personal feeling. As Orwell, another honest person, took great pains to point out, all art is propaganda, and every book above the level of a telephone directory reveals, if only we knew how to read it, a feeling about persons and reveals a reflection, if only we knew how to see it, of what human life is and how it might be lived. The *Iliad* is a good adventure that suggests to me sometimes that I can meet my enemy and hold hands with him in the shadow of death. Petya Rostov runs down the hill with a wooden sword and shouts Hurrah! into the fantasies of my childhood, only to turn down another hill on another day shouting Hurrah! only to get killed by somebody who doesn't know him but who— here we return to Hugo—might have cared about him if only they both had known.

Known what?

The special and secret details of places. The secret faces of friends. And the wild secrets of the inner landscape, the inner face, the face we are all dying to share in a century when in our terror we have all been running to hide, only to discover our places in the other place, our secrets in the other secret. In Richard Hugo's great poem, "Mission to Linz," a poem about a bombing raid which is a secret account of the spiritual life, the poet sings of a place away from the sky where the air is always summer. What did he mean by that? We cannot understand it without realizing that he had been in a bombing plane, and that having once more survived the real threat of death, he had returned to the summer, to the earth. Earth to him, in that shockingly graceful poem, was.

Was what?

It was Italy. But wait. Hugo the bombardier fell down with great relief out of heaven and what he did when he got on the earth again was to "study friends' faces." There is no escape from the earth, as Emily Bronte knew, but she didn't want to escape from it any more than Hugo does.

It would be too easy, and so to my mind silly, to think that Hugo visited Italy again, many years after his war, merely out of guilt. Many poems have no doubt been written out of guilt, but I find it hard to remember a good one. Hugo's poems about Italy, some of them included in *Good Luck in Cracked Italian*, are not guilty poems. They are poems of discovery.

How do you discover Italy if you are born and grow, grasping into despair, in the American Pacific Northwest? I don't know about you, and I suppose you don't know about me, but in Hugo's poems he tells us that the first thing he does is to go fishing, and I guess his purpose is love, but in his poems we find that we have discovered, and studied, the secret faces of the fish. There is a trout that has a certain smoky shadow on its sides under the gills, and that shadow looks like "apples in a fog." I like those trout, because I ate four of them one afternoon, but that is not the only reason I like them. I like them because I know now what they look like, and I would not have known if Hugo had not told me in his poem. Fish have secret faces, but they have a good deal more than faces. I am not about to paraphrase Hugo's descriptions—is fulfillment the word?—of a gar gliding through the water. I am about to confess that I too have secret apples in me and on me somewhere behind my gills, and if anybody is going to eat me alive I wish I could recommend to him my own choice lakes and stones, where I swim day and night. If you are going to kill me in this century, friend, first try to know me.

Know what?

The side of a trout that looks like apples in a fog. A beach near Kalalock where the waves come in with the tide like the eyes of all the cats in the world stampeding. An airfield near Naples, where the poet was as lost as the people in Linz. A fish flying away from the earth, where the air is always summer.

Hugo's poetry is rich with images like these. I believe that his "Mission to Linz" was also his "Introduction to the Ho," a place in the Pacific Northwest most of us are not likely to know about until we read Hugo's poems, because the fish are secret there, and it takes a good man to discover them. I didn't say a skilled man, although Hugo is wonderfully skilled. I said a good man.

A short while ago, delighting in Hugo's poetry again, I happened to be reading in George Orwell's most beautiful novel, *Coming Up for Air*. His narrator, George Bowering, most appealing, honest and true, has got through World War I, which was as bad as any war, and has somehow managed to get near a childhood place where it might be possible to go fishing. Here are the passages that remind me most of the spirit of Hugo:

> I stayed there for a bit, leaning over the gate. I was alone, quite alone. I was looking at the field, and the field was looking at me. I felt—I wonder whether you'll understand. . . . What I felt was something that's so unusual nowadays that to say it sounds like foolishness. I felt *happy*. I felt that though I shan't live forever, I'd be quite ready to. . . . Farther down the hedge the pool was covered with duckweed, so like a carpet that if you didn't know what duckweed was you might think it was solid and step on it. I wondered why it is that we're all such bloody fools. Why don't people, instead of the idiocies they do spend their time on, just walk round looking at things? That pool, for instance—all the stuff that's in it. Newts, water-snails, water-beetles, caddis-flies, leeches, and God knows how many other things that you can only see with a microscope. The mystery of their lives, down there under water. You could spend a lifetime watching them, ten lifetimes, and still you wouldn't have got to the end even of that one pool. And all the while the sort of feeling of wonder, the peculiar flame inside you. It's the only thing worth having, and we don't want it. But I do want it. . . .

Like Orwell, a man with whom he has deeper and truer spiritual affinity than any man I know, Hugo has labored to cluster the best labors of his art around his best theme. It is "the peculiar flame inside you." In one of his "Letters to Friends," Hugo catches himself using the phrase "breaks my heart" to suggest his feeling about the inarticulate drunks in one of those

God-forsaken taverns in the Northwest, and then he adds that he hates the phrase. But it is what I would have said, if I had Hugo's courage, and so would you, unless, reader, we are both liars. And we are *not* liars. I don't give a damn how stupid we have made our lives, our lives matter whether we like it or not.

That is a huge thing to say, especially if a poet can say it without sentimentality and with what has become an almost perfect precision. The music of the new poems is a masterful shift from a perfect control of traditional English; the diction constantly reveals itself, the offhand slang becoming a stony music. I believe that Richard Hugo has become one of the best poets alive, in any language I know. The best way to conclude a review of his work is to quote one of his new poems. It is about a place that most of us did not know, but we will know it now. It is dedicated to Hugo's friend Stanley Kaufmann, but it is also dedicated to every person who owns the death of every bird he names. The poem is called "Montgomery Hollow."

Birds here should have names so hard to say
you name them over. They finally found
the farmer hanging near the stream.
Only insect hum today and the purple odor
of thyme. You'd bet your throat against
the way a mind goes bad. You conquer loss
by going to the place it happened
and replaying it, saying the name
of the face in the open casket right.

People die in cities. Unless it's war
you never see the bodies. They die in print,
over phones in paramouric flats.
Here, you find them staring down the sun,
flies crawling them like bacon. Wives
scream two days running and the pain is gone.
Here, you find them living.

To know a road you own it, every bend
and pebble and the weeds along it,
dust that itches when the August hayrake
rambles home. You own the home.
You own the death of every bird you name.

To live good, keep your life and the scene.
Cow, brook, hay: these are names of coins.

As Orwell says elsewhere, "fishing is the opposite of war." I think that Richard Hugo is a great poet, true to our difficult life.

IV

Memoirs

On the Occasion of a Poem
Richard Hugo

New York
June 7, 1974

Several years ago I went fishing with Richard F. Hugo, an employee of the Boeing Aircraft Company and a softball player of some distinction. We spent a pleasant afternoon drifting in a skiff all around the lake—I believe it was Lake Kapowsin, the destruction of whose congenial tavern has since been described by Hugo in one of his many beautiful books. His many friends will agree that Hugo is a fisherman of long experience and great skill. During the afternoon, he also presented an attractive appearance in his fishing togs. Standing in easy balance at the bow of our skiff, he would have served as an excellent illustration for a cover of *Field and Stream* magazine. He even carried, slung casually at his side, one of those old-fashioned wicker baskets in which serious fishermen used to carry their tackle. I myself was, of course, no fisherman at all. I enjoyed the lake, the peace, the laziness. With the understanding of a good friend who knows that he doesn't have to explain, Hugo would occasionally reach into his wicker basket and, with a certain professional flair, hand me an uncapped stubby of excellent beer.

Getting on toward dusk, we had drifted toward one end of the lake. Fifty yards or so up in the woods we saw a shack, to all

From *American Poets in 1976,* ed. William Heyen (Indianapolis: Bobbs-Merrill, 1976).

appearances abandoned—unpainted, with only a few shingles left, generally ramshackle. Since the fishing for the day was more or less finished, Hugo suggested that we might walk up and explore the shack, just for the fun of it. I begged off. It's not that I was afraid of anything or anybody there. I happen to be one of those people who enjoy snakes. Since I spent a happy visit to the Sonora Desert near Tucson with my friend the poet Richard Shelton and his wife and son, I have even grown fond of tarantulas. I would far rather stroke a tarantula than attend a concert by Rod McKuen or spend an evening at dinner on the *Sequoia*. No, I just didn't want to explore the shack at the end of the lake.

It is interesting to learn, from a moving interview by Richard Hugo, recently published in *The New Salt Creek Reader*, that, even at the time of which I am writing, he was very fond of exploring abandoned houses. So it turns out that I deprived him of an innocent pleasure without knowing it. He didn't object to my reticence, though. We just returned to the shore. I think he understood that I didn't want to get out of the boat because I was too lazy or too drunk. Probably both.

Here is the poem I wrote afterwards:

> Ignorant two, we glide
> On ripples near the shore.
> The rainbows leap no more,
> And men in boats alight
> To see the day subside.
>
> All evening fins have drowned
> Back in the summer dark.
> Above us, up the bank,
> Obscure on lonely ground,
> A shack receives the night.
>
> I hold the lefthand oar
> Out of the wash, and guide
> The skiff away so wide
> We wander out of sight
> As soundless as before.
>
> We will not land to bear
> Our will upon that house,

Nor force on any place
Our dull offensive weight.

Somebody may be there,
Peering at us outside
Across the even lake,
Wondering why we take
Our time and stay so late.

Long may the lovers hide
In viny shacks from those
Who thrash among the trees,
Who curse, who have no peace,
Who pitch and moan all night
For fear of someone's joys
Deploring the human face.

From prudes and muddying fools,
Kind Aphrodite, spare
All hunted criminals,
Hoboes, and whip-poor-wills,
And girls with rumpled hair,
All, all of whom might hide
Within that darkening shack.
Lovers may live, and abide.

Wherefore, I turn my back,
And trawl our boat away,
Lest someone fear to call
A girl's name till we go
Over the lake so slow
We hear the darkness fall.

Having given a brief account of a poem, I must now come to the real point of this brief essay. On another afternoon, Hugo and I went fishing again. To the best of my recollection, the Bumping River flowed near an indescribably beautiful meadow called Goose Prairie. It was surrounded by mountains whose roads were difficult to drive on even in the daylight. We and our wives rented a perfectly comfortable cabin for a reasonable price, so that we could spend the night.

Now, for some reason, serious fishermen who stay overnight always run out of beer. It's no use asking me why. I do not know. I have done it myself at least a hundred times, and many trustworthy persons have told me about their own suffering from this same curious lack of what would seem, to any reasonable person, a normal and necessary foresight. A fisherman who neglects to bring an adequate supply of beer is as unaccountably silly as a man who travels from the very northernmost tip of the Bronx to spend three days with close relatives in Far Rockaway, only to remember, as he changes trains at Times Square, that he has forgotten to bring his *petit-mal.*

Nevertheless, such things happen, and they always seem to happen to overnight fishermen.

Goose Prairie—oh, that lovely place, where we even saw some elk browse slowly across the meadow in the evening—featured only one tavern. Its proprietor and manager was a man named Ed Bedford. His wife tended bar. I do not wish to denigrate Mr. Bedford. He was not what you would call particularly intelligent or charming, in the ordinary meanings of those words. He was not handsome, but presentable. He shaved. I suspect that, as we used to remark in Ohio when I was a boy, he took a bath every March, whether he needed it or not. Generally speaking, I think it is fair to describe him as an ordinary chap, doing his best, trying to make a living, just like most other people.

But Ed Bedford possessed another quality for which I have often tried to find the appropriate word, and I am afraid that I must use the word that even approaches accuracy: Ed Bedford was a genius. In his combination of simplicity, mediocrity, and sudden, astonishing grasp of solutions which ought to be obvious to everyone else but which almost never do become obvious until it is too late to do anything but weep, I can think of only three persons in my lifetime who resemble him: Bobby Fischer, Richard M. Nixon, and the late Baldur von Schirach.

Mr. Bedford's genius consisted, first of all, in his instinctive grasp of human nature. He simply remembered what all fishermen consistently forget. Consequently, he never ran out of beer.

The second feature of Bedford's genius was geographical. He knew the severe difficulty of driving on those mountain roads even by daylight. He knew that not even Steve McQueen or Gene Hackman would have attempted to drive those roads after dark. Not even their stuntmen would have tried it. (Evil Knievel might have tried it, but I don't think he was born yet, and in any case I doubt if Ed Bedford would have hired him. He would probably have got sidetracked and tried to leap on his motorcycle from Mt. Rainier to Mt. Whitney. Worse, he might have succeeded.)

With the unapologetic aplomb of Napoleon at the battle of Austerlitz, Ed Bedford disregarded conventional tactics and disposed of the enemy (that is, the frustrated fishermen) by two classically simple strokes. He kept his beer available in unlimited supply; and he doubled the price. (Perhaps he tripled it. But the reader must remember that these events took place many years ago, and, admitting my own usual tendency to exaggerate, I am studiously attempting to write moderately.)

In spite of these difficulties, we all recognized the futility of our position. It never occurred to any of us that Bedford's practices might have been illegal. For all I know, they may have been. For that matter, for all I know, Ed Bedford may have been the game warden.

We bought his beer at his price. And we drank it.

It was obvious that I cannot hope to be a prose stylist like, say, Harold Robbins, Jacquelin Susann, Faith Baldwin, or even John Updike. But I do sincerely attempt to avoid triteness as well as I can. So I cannot, in good faith, say that Ed Bedford's beer tasted like shit. As a matter of fact, I have eaten shit, and more than once. I don't mean just bad inedible food. I mean shit. To tell the truth, it wasn't as distasteful as the prejudiced reader might assume. Nevertheless, I must make some kind of effort to suggest the quality of Bedford's beer. A direct, literal description is beyond my powers. Still, as a Professor of Literature, I do from time to time have certain belletristic aspirations. And so, as the master Henry Fielding likes to say to his friendly readers: since we are in no special hurry, I believe I shall essay a simile: The flavor of Ed Bedford's beer suggested a somewhat watery puree of White Castle hamburgers, half-green with decay; and this in turn offered a pungent bouquet of blend of at least two distinct underarm perspirations: one from Ms. Hermione just as she was acknowledging perhaps her tenth curtain call after the evening performance of *A Little Night Music;* and one from the late Rocky Marciano at the very moment when the referee was raising his arm in a gesture of victory after his eighth-round knockout of the gallant Archie Moore.

Recently Richard Hugo claimed that Ed Bedford is dead. Having more than once recorded in print my admiration for Hugo's splendid poetry, I think it pertinent to add here my equal admiration for his personal honesty. He is as straightforward and trustworthy a person as I have ever had the honor to know. I am not implying that he is a liar in his report of Bedford's death. What Hugo does not seem to realize is that his claim has created problems in my mind which I am not able to cope with. These problems are both physical and metaphysical. They are so abstruse, that I had better sketch them one at a time.

First, the physical. What exactly could they do with Bedford's stiff? If they tried to bury him at sea, he would poison the fishes and even the nuclear submarines. If they buried him conventionally in the ground, then, given the realities of geological time, he would eventually seep into the workings of the Anaconda Copper Mines and thereby—perhaps by interfering with the alloying process, threaten the company's profits; and I doubt if anybody, even Ed Bedford, could get away with that sort of thing. After all, even Christ was crucified. If Bedford were cremated, he would likely outlast the operators of the furnace, the way Fearless Fosdick, having scientifically determined the exact temperature which would melt his archenemy Anyface, courageously trapped Anyface and himself into a fiery furnace and waited as the temperature rose; when it reached the appropriate degrees, of course, it was Fosdick who melted, while Anyface escaped. I once considered the possibility, not at all unlikely, that Bedford's wife might have been persuaded to eat him. But this solution quickly turned into another problem. Bedford would certainly have been indigestible, and, in the event of his wife's death, what in God's name would the embalmers have done with her tripas?

The metaphysical problem is even worse. I thought of consulting the illustrious Dr. Abram von Elsing, who drove the silver stake through Dracula's heart in the daytime. But Bedford had no heart, and, besides, he stayed awake night and day. As for the afterlife, I don't wish the poor man in Hell. And how can he be in Heaven? I always thought that beer, like everything else in Heaven, tasted good and was free of charge.

The problem is too much for me. As far as I can figure it out, Ed Bedford is a white elephant on the hands of the Deity.

If Dick Hugo had known about the consequences of his perfectly reasonable report of news about an old acquaintance of ours, I think he would just have told me that Ed Bedford had retired, and let it go at that.

But I can conclude on a cheerful note. I have stopped drinking, and one sure sign of my improved health is the fact that I seldom think about Bedford's beer and other outlandish things.

On the Occasion of a Poem
Bill Knott

Lake Minnewaska
New Palz, New York
June 14, 1974

Although I will directly quote some verses of my own, the most important part of these reflections will deal with the poet Bill Knott, partly because of his rarity but mainly because of his value. Such persons are bound to be rare on the earth at any time, for reasons that are probably biological, although it is obvious to the reader that both my training and my knowledge in this science are more than ordinarily limited. When I speak of his value, I refer to his friendship, which I cherish, in spite of our too infrequent meetings, and most of all to his poetry, which I consider to be very fine and likely to endure long after most of our contemporary smoke has done me the unintended but nevertheless genuine personal favor of just simply drying up and blowing away.

I first read a few of Bill Knott's poems on a pleasant afternoon in Robert and Carol Bly's chicken house, which had long since been converted into a comfortable study and which also contained a perfectly lovely antique bed where, in those earlier times, so dear to me, I spent many a comfortable sleep and had many pleasant dreams. I also slept there with a girl whom I

From *American Poets in 1976*, ed. William Heyen (Indianapolis: Bobbs-Merrill, 1976).

loved. The previous sentence is beside the point to you, I am sure, but not to me.

There are authors in this world who work with great facility. May I offer them my respectful envy. I myself am one of those people who, granted the choice between writing the opening sentence and being hanged by the neck until I am dead, would cheerfully prefer the latter. I think I would even volunteer to slap the horse's buttocks, if my arms were as long as those of Rose Mary Woods. Since this physical condition does not obtain in my case, I have been forced to develop other devices for avoiding work, and I must confess that I pride myself in having developed over the years a good deal of adroitness in this art.

I had not reckoned with the natural and experienced intelligence of Carol Bly, however. On the afternoon in question, when I was supposed to be finishing an essay to be published in the magazine *The Sixties,* she made sure that I would finish the essay, or at least work on it, by employing the simple and effective expedient of a Napoleon at the height of his career. She locked me into the chicken house, including the door and the windows. My delicious lunch was delivered to me promptly by my incomparable goddaughter Mary Bly, who prevented my escape by simply standing at the door and watching me eat it. When I was finished, she proceeded to relock the door and leave me to my work. To this day, I remember those afternoons in the chicken house as a curious combination of a pleasant study, Yaddo, and Devil's Island. The only thing that was missing to make the comparison perfect was the butterfly tattooed for some reason that still escapes me, on Steve McQueen's chest. In those days, by the way, I was a drunk; and, no doubt with the intention of inspiring me to responsible literary labors, my realistic friends made sure that the chicken house contained no booze whatever.

During my frantic and resourceful efforts to evade the typewriter, I happened to come upon a sheaf of poems. They were unsigned. I read them.

They were short poems. I must have read them twenty times. Robert later told me they had been sent to him by a young poet named Bill Knott. They were then, and they are now, among the most beautiful poems I have ever read in any language. They were brief, gentle, totally clear in their meaning on the most casual first reading, and shocking only in the sense that they were so original: in short, they were the true thing, finally unaccountable, as even Longinus had to admit, and yet unmistakable. I remember thinking then, as I am thinking now, something that Louis Simpson said to me when he had made a similar discovery: in that sinister moment when it is so frighteningly difficult to tell the difference between the feeling of pain and feeling of gratitude, Louis observed that "sometimes, even in the weariness of literature, poetry can happen."

I did not know Bill Knott personally. We had never corresponded. We had absolutely no way of knowing that each other even existed, except for the possible fact that Yale had published a single book of mine; and, in case the reader has to be reminded of what is banally obvious, I tend to doubt that either John Updike or Jacqueline Susann need ever fear being driven into panic at the threat that my books will force one or even both of them (since, for all I can tell, they are the same person writing under two different names) into position number eleven on some bestseller list, whether it be that of the Sunday *New York Times* or the Pickwa, Ohio, *Herald-Tribune and Livestock Report.*

Some months later, I received a note from Bill Knott which I believe I can quote word-for-word. The note was quite brief. I recall that it did not even address me by name:

"I'm so lonely I can't stand it. Solitude is all right. It's not the same thing. Loneliness rots the soul." He signed the postcard and included his home address.

In case the reader hasn't noticed, we live in a strange world. The poet's desperately unhappy message arrived at a time which turned it into a happy coincidence. I received his postcard about a week before Thanksgiving. I myself had just recently recovered from an illness and been released from a hospital. My friends Alva and Edna Miriam, parents of one of my nicest students, had invited me to Thanksgiving dinner at their home in Ogden, Iowa. Moreover, they had made plans to travel to Chicago the succeeding weekend, and they kindly invited me to accompany them. I accepted their invitation, and instantly wrote to Bill Knott that, come Hell or high water, I would arrive at his room in Chicago some time during the afternoon of the Saturday immediately following Thanskgiving. I also informed him that I would arrive in the company of two pretty, hilarious girls and a bunch of fresh bananas. And by God I did it. By this time the reader will be thinking that I am making up this whole story, but I don't care what the reader thinks. It is the truth. I wish I could add that the bunch of bananas was my own idea, but the fact is that one of the girls thought of it. I haven't the faintest notion how or why the thought ever occurred to her. She had never read any of Bill Knott's poetry. She had never even heard of Bill Knott. All she knew was that I had asked her if she would like to join me in a brief visit to a friend who lived in Chicago, and I had no sooner finished asking the question than she instantly suggested that we take him a bunch of bananas as a house gift. I love women.

At the time, Bill Knott was working all night at some charity hospital or other. By the time we arrived and persuaded the superintendent of the building that we were neither narcotics agents nor gangsters in disguise, Knott had had time for a morning nap. He was refreshed when he warmly greeted us. I doubt if anybody can be said to know Bill Knott really well. But he has some devoted friends—William Hunt, John Logan, Thomas Lux, and others—and I believe they would agree that Knott is nearly always reticent in manner, sometimes painfully so. But on the afternoon of the visit which I am trying to describe, he was as happily friendly and sociable as one could wish. Perhaps he was simply surprised that I had actually succeeded in fulfilling so quickly a literally nutty promise. Perhaps it was the presence of the girls, both so pretty and natural and charming. Perhaps it was the bananas. I don't really know. I do know the four of us spent a delightful half-hour or so, before the girls, having appointments with their respective families, unfortunately had to leave.

Bill Knott's room, like his clothing, was shabby and worn. He had to share a single toilet down the far end of the hall with other tenants, of whom there were many. His room contained few things: a sink, which gave only cold water; a single swaybacked bed; a shelf stuffed with books, neatly but un-alphabetically arranged. Whether Bill Knott ever finished high school I do not know. I do know that he never attended college. His collection of books was what more formally and professionally academic persons like myself would call erratic. I remember in particular one volume which will serve as a typical example. It was a worn copy—thoroughly read and reread with obvious devotion and intensity—of the collected works of the great Greek contemporary master Odysseus Elytis. But my most striking memory of Bill Knott's skimpy room was an object placed right in the center of his single bare wooden table. It was a full unopened quart of the finest Jack Daniels whiskey, clearly placed there as a token of welcome in the poet's anticipation of our arrival. Now, my friends, my enemies, and any number of strangers who have had the dubious experience of hearing me speak in public need hardly be reminded that I used to be what, in gentler and more civilized times, would have been known as a heavy drinker of spiritous liquors (or, for those who prefer the more euphemistic phrase, a two-bit drunk). On the afternoon of my first meeting with Bill Knott, however, the girls drank nothing at all. Knott and I drank no more than a single shot each. (Lest the reader assume, as he naturally might, that my memory on this particular is flattering me with my own virtue, I must add that I did indeed get stone-blind drunk late that evening. I awoke next morning in a room in a theological seminary. How I got there I don't remember, and, in any case, it doesn't matter. I could probably lie about it, but space is limited.)

What made Bill Knott's bottle of Jack Daniels so moving an experience to me was the fact that he could not afford to buy it. His salary at the hospital where he was working at night could not possibly have provided him with very much more than what he needed for bare subsistence. Consequently, he had clearly been saving every extra penny he could possibly spare in order to buy that bottle of whiskey as a token of greeting to his visitors. To quote a remark by Oscar Wilde which has always been dear to me: I do believe in my heart that men have gone to heaven for less.

Bill Knott was poor. I record with horror the fact that I have sometimes heard some persons, personally acquainted with Knott, describe his poverty as affectation. My personal meetings with this singular man—meetings all too infrequent—give me the authority to assert that he is poor. He is not one of those persons who, dressed in tie-dyed trousers and puce buckskin blouses, frequently suck around Lincoln Center fountain in the patient hope of procuring Alice Cooper's snake's autograph (and then, of course, selling it).

Bill Knott was poor.

Part of the vitality and difficulty of the American language is its capacity for rapid change. It may therefore be useful—to those too young to have experienced the Great Depression of the thirties—to digress briefly on the meaning of the words "poverty" and "poor."

Of course, the Depression struck the entire country. But my native place was southeastern Ohio and the West Virginia Panhandle, and I will confine my remarks to those parts of the United States which I knew best during my childhood.

The fathers of the great majority of my childhood friends were ordinary working men. For example, my father was officially employed for fifty years in Wheeling, W. Va., by the Hazel-Atlas Glass Factory, now absorbed by the Continental Can Company. Other friends' fathers worked at such places as Wheeling Steel, the Laughlin Steel Mill, Blaw-Knox, and the usual coal mines, which were nearly as interesting and newsworthy during the Great Depression as they are today.

Some of these working men were fired from their jobs outright. Some of them managed to support their families in unaccustomed ways. Some made a few cents a day by emptying people's garbage cans and hauling the garbage by pushcart to the town dump. (How I remember that old town dump. It was as thrillingly unpredictable as the planet Jupiter. It contained everything from mysteriously unopened boxes of sanitary napkins to young and frolicking blacksnakes to unaccountably unemployed condoms somewhat past their prime to out-of-tune player-pianos to decaying paper flowers [sometimes even poor people love their wives and do their best to remind them of it]). Others, like my uncles Sherman and Emerson, of blessed memory, ordered boxes of something called Dr.

Dade's soap (which by the way, was totally incapable of raising lather, though I personally experimented with it scores of times), drove their senile Model-T Ford into the surrounding mining towns, and occasionally succeeded in bartering their dubious product with the unsuspecting housewives of the unemployed miners in exchange for such items as undernourished live chickens. I have myself often dined on these. I would not go so far as to compare these fowl with *coq au vin* as served at Maxim's or La Belle Epoque. But our skinny hens had their points. Besides, you can manage to eat quite a few improbable things when you get hungry enough. Believe you me.

Other working men, like my father, were more fortunate—theoretically, at least. They were not given the kindly choice of either getting their asses the hell off the company property instantly and voluntarily or else getting those very selfsame asses kicked off, even more instantly, by the company's trained and courteous personnel (i.e., the muscular company finks of the old days, who were for some reason constantly employed and decently paid for their services, which they were always willing and even eager, to perform with competence and dispatch). No, men like my father were never fired outright. Instead, they were frequently "laid off." This term means simply that they were told by the management to just go home and stay there, often for weeks at a time, without being paid. I have often wondered why such men's names were retained officially on the company's payroll. Perhaps the management thought of it as an "honor" of some kind. I don't know. If you should ever by chance figure out just what goes on inside the skull of a factory manager, please don't waste your time by trying to explain it to me. I just don't get it, and it is unlikely that I ever will.

These men were poor. In spite of their remarkable courage and resourcefulness in their determination to support their families in the face of sometimes appalling difficulties beyond ability to describe, which in fact only a great novelist could manage adequately—Nelson Algren and Dreiser got at least some of the truth on paper, and I trust the reader will excuse me when I point out that, in spite of my respect for his genius, we are not exactly dealing with Henry James country at this moment—my father and my friends' fathers were often understandably discouraged. They used to have a phrase that attempted to express their discouragement, and they repeated it so often that it became almost a kind of folk saying. Hundreds of times I must have heard a man returning home after a long day's futile search for work, any work at all, and dispiritedly whispering to his anxious wife, or mumbling absent mindedly to himself in his baffled loneliness: "I ain't got a pot to piss in or a window to throw it out of."

That is the kind of thing I meant when I said that Bill Knott was poor. For all I know, he still is, though God knows I hope that, wherever he may be at this moment, he is getting enough to eat. Let me conclude this digression by asking a favor of the reader: if you should see me and approach me with the intention of informing me that Knott's poverty is an affectation, please be kind enough to forget me and just go talk to somebody else. In my youth I used to be able to listen patiently enough to liars, cowards, and other ignorant, mentally retarded sons of bitches. But Nature catches up with all at last, and I am unfortunately getting too old to listen. I would probably go to sleep right in your face. Or *on* your face, if I had the strength left.

Now let me return to that first meeting with Bill Knott. After the girls hurried off to keep their appointments, Knott and I chatted for a few minutes and were pleased to discover our mutual devotion to the art of shooting pool. Almost immediately we started to stroll in the direction of a local parlor.

This is where my old poem comes in.

A clear account of this odd little episode will require a few words of preliminary explanation.

Several months before I met Bill Knott, or had even heard of him, my brother Jack informed me in a letter that our uncle, William Lyons, had died. An adequate description of Uncle Willie's life and personality is hopeless. But I will do my best to offer a few suggestive details about him, because they might help the reader make a little more sense out of the poem that I will soon quote.

Willie's usual personal appearance was somewhat misleading. Though by no means a dandy, he preferred to dress in a conventional black suit, black tie, white shirt, well-polished black shoes, and, when he was outside, a conventional black hat. Seeing him standing idly on a street corner in Martins Ferry, you might naturally have taken him for one of our local morticians out for a few minutes of fresh air; or, given his somewhat puritanical dress and stance, one of our local ministers half-lost in his secret romantic fantasy of suddenly, without preliminary announcement, dropping the entire fiasco, getting decently drunk, and devoting his meager life savings to the hope of giving Mae West a proper jump in a rumble seat; he might even have seemed a dentist. In short, to the casual passerby, he could have appeared to be any one of a thousand of our typical, conventional, respectable citizens. In his formal dress, he looked slight of build, perhaps even frail.

In reality, Willie was a highly skilled carpenter by trade. I have watched him for hours at work. I never once saw him fail to drive a long thin nail all the way into a two-by-four at a single flawlessly accurate stroke. Consequently, I never heard him curse. (I speak of his working occasions, of course.) With his denim sleeves rolled up, his forearms resembled those of the late Rocky Marciano. Willie's skill was such that he could have made good money at his trade, even during the Great Depression. He could have taken a job any time he chose. There was a lot of money around even then, though only a small minority of people owned it. And yet, Willie preferred to work only as long each year as he needed to achieve two goals: to earn enough to live on; and to pay the government as little income tax as was necessary to keep himself out of jail. In a word, Uncle Willie was a patriot. I am aware that the old-fashioned word "patriot" will be as unintelligible to most occupants of the United States as the punchline of an in-joke among the slaves of the Hittites. But in Uncle Willie's prime, the word had a perfectly clear and common meaning. Willie considered himself a free man. I remember his sentiments on this subject so vividly that I believe I can quote some of them with middling accuracy:

"The gummint? I don't work for the gummint. They work for me. I work good and I work hard when I choose to work. I pay them what they force me to pay them. If they don't like it, they can go hump a castrated snake."

Uncle Willie had a dour face. I can't remember ever hearing him laugh out loud. But he smiled once in a while. And when he smiled, his eyes gleamed with a wickedness of almost supernatural beauty. He wore an upper denture, which he sometimes could wiggle with his tongue into positions so improbably ugly and grotesque that these performances made my younger brother Jack nearly collapse into an epileptic faint out of sheer unqualified delight.

Willie has been dead for years. Nearly everybody alive, except a few remaining relatives like Jack and me, has forgotten him. After the few short years that remain to us, nobody will know or care that my Uncle Willie ever existed on earth. I loved him very much. I still do, even as I write these few words about him.

The afternoon Jack informed me of Willie's death, I was very busy in my office at the University of Minnesota. But the hell with busy, I thought. A few things matter in this world. I just dropped everything I was doing, whatever it was, and took a half-hour's walk all alone, to mourn Willie by myself, in my own way. While I strolled along University Avenue, deaf even to the diesel trucks that seem to roar along there one after another all day and all night, I thought about Willie. I knew he would never be an immortal historical figure, Julius Caesar, Christ, Alice Cooper, or President Nixon. So I thought it might be nice to write a poem in his memory. I had to get back to work at once, so I made a mental note to try the poem whenever I managed to get a free hour or so. Then out of sheer economic necessity I forgot about the whole thing: death, Willie, poem, and all.

Bill Knott and I continued our slow walk toward the pool parlor. In his usual reticence, he didn't say a word. I didn't mind. Usually if a friend feels like talking, I'm willing to converse. If he feels like staying quiet, I'm willing to be quiet, too. (Since I've quit drinking, the reader can trust this statement.)

Abruptly Bill asked, "Do you want to hear a poem?"

I thought he meant a poem of his own, so naturally I was pleased. I answered, "I sure would."

Here is the poem, which he recited to me with flawless accuracy:

Willy Lyons

My uncle, a craftsman of hammers and wood,
Is dead in Ohio.
And my mother cries she is angry.
Willy was buried with nothing except a jacket
Stitched on his shoulder bones.
It is nothing to mourn for.
It is the other world.
She does not know how the roan horses, there,
Dead for a century,
Plod slowly.
Maybe they believe Willy's brown coffin, tangled
        heavily in moss,
Is a horse trough drifted to shore
Along that river under the willows and grass.
Let my mother weep on, she needs to, she knows of cold
        winds.
The long box is empty
The horses turn back toward the river.
Willy planes limber trees by the waters,
Fitting his boat together.
We may as well let him go.
Nothing is left of Willy on this side
But one cracked ball-peen hammer and one suit,
Including pants, his son inherited,
For a small fee, from Hesslop's funeral home;
And my mother,
Weeping with anger, afraid of winter
For her brothers' sake:
Willy, and John, whose life and art, if any,
I never knew.

I stopped stone-still on the sidewalk and glared at him, angry.

"Who the hell do you think you are?"

He looked hurt and puzzled, and mumbled, "I don't know what you mean." Not that he would have minded much, but he must have really done it this time: got himself mixed up with an authentic psychotic. Such persons are not sentimentally amusing, in spite of Jerry Lewis' feeble attempts to make them seem so by imitating their hilarious pain.

I answered, "You know what I mean. I never got around to writing those verses, but they were my idea. It was my own uncle, for Christ's sake."

Knott just looked at me for a long moment. Then he asked if I would please come back to his room with him for a minute. Still furious, I went along. I had no idea what he had in mind—maybe he was going to offer me some more Jack Daniels, to calm me down.

When we got back to his place he said nothing. He just took a magazine from a shelf and opened it to a certain place. I said then, and I say still, "Well, I'll be a son of a bitch." There it was: the poem he had just recited to me, with my own name printed right under the title.

The matter explains itself.

Evidently, some time after I had spent my lonely afternoon mourning for my Uncle Willie, I actually did get a chance to write the poem. Almost immediately after I wrote it, my friend Dick Foster, then editor of *The Minnesota Review*, was caught in an uncharacteristic panic. He had a new issue all ready for the printer, and to his horror he discovered at the last minute that the number of pages hadn't come out even. He was in danger of printing an issue that contained a blank page. Usually a man of good cheer, he saw me and asked, in a hangdog way, if I happened to have something I could give him to fill in the magazine. He was a good friend; I knew how he felt; I had just finished the poem about Uncle Willie; he printed it. This sequence of events happened so fast that I had forgotten I had written the poem and even that it had been printed.

But Bill Knott found it and liked it.

In order to write this memoir, or whatever you want to call it, I had to reread the Uncle Willie poem. It doesn't seem like much to me now. Reader, if you and I felt like puking all over each other with boredom before we both sank into terminal catatonia, I could easily name you a list of at least five hundred other persons who could have written it or something very like it. It's not a bad poem. It's not a good poem. What is it, actually? It's a conventional exercise in modish free verse or whatever the hell this week's cant word may be, which I neither know nor care to know. The real value the poem has for me is that it still reminds me of Uncle Willie. I love him, he is in the ground, he is mostly forgotten, soon I'll be forgotten, and that's the end of that. He's my precious secret.

> Ist auf deinem Psalter,
> Vater der Liebe,
> Ein Ton seinem Ohre vernehmlich,
> So erquicke sein Herz!

But when Bill Knott quoted my own commonplace poem to me, it sounded magnificent. No, he wasn't trying to imitate the great voice of Dylan Thomas. He wasn't even trying to imitate Vincent Price. He just read in his own ordinary voice: the plain midwestern twang (I have heard that he was born in Michigan, but I don't know for sure); the softness, part of his reticence no doubt, that sometimes made it hard to hear him clearly, so that you have to ask him to repeat a word or even a whole phrase. It was just Bill Knott, quoting to me my ordinary poem, and making it sound glorious. I have often wondered what the experience meant. The nearest I've ever managed to come to an explanation is that, in some way I don't hope to understand, the poem struck a live nerve somewhere in Knott and somehow became important to him. In a way, it seems to have become part of his living spirit. When that sort of thing happens to a person of great natural gifts, God alone knows what incredible beautiful thing it might move him to create. The odd thing is that the original occasion, or material, that sets a great and original artist in motion doesn't in itself have to be anything out of the ordinary. Take, as just one example of many possible examples, Beethoven's "Diabelli Variations."

Diabelli, a man of good will, had had a little extra money to spare, offered it to any good composer who would write a set of variations on a theme of his own invention. Did you ever happen to hear that theme itself, played in its naked original version on the piano? I don't know about you, but the original theme invented by Diabelli sounds to me neither good nor bad. But that's not quite accurate. It sounds better than a duet by Rod McKuen and Florence Foster Jenkins; but then, what in the universe doesn't? But once Beethoven got hold of it, he transformed it into one of the immortal glories of human life on earth.

This short piece began as an attempt to describe my first meeting with Bill Knott, for the purpose of further describing just how a certain set of verses came to be written and first published. It ended mainly as a discussion of Knott himself. But that's all right with me. If it's not all right with you, I can't help it.

I once heard Knott read a poem of his own. At one point, he was describing the appearance of a wretched skid-road drunk, half-starved and yet probably unable to keep any food down, literally dying for a mere sip of rotgut, leaning on a corner of an old building that must have looked as though it had been saturation-bombed and then half-reconstructed by an architect from McDonald's. The man stood there, in Knott's phrase, "crucified in his clothes." I'm not even jealous of that phrase. What's the use? Even a hack can feel gratitude when he hears true poetry, of which we have very little in the world at any time.

I don't know where Bill Knott is at the moment. The last I heard, he had a job and enough to eat. The thought makes me happy, because we are friends, and because it means that he will be able to give us more of his indispensable poems, poems that nobody else could write.

The Infidel

Garrison, N.Y.
June 9, 1974

The strange man stepped slowly out from the sumac trees. He didn't look afraid, but I think he looked suspicious—certainly cautious. I reckon he must have been hiding for a long time back in the brush. Probably he had been waiting till we got the fire good and going and had given it enough time to burn down to nice red coals. It's also possible that the stranger had enough sense to make sure we weren't likely to be receiving a cordial social visit from a railroad dick (we had built our fire only a few yards from the B & O railroad track) who was acquainted with us and with most of our fathers. Our visitor, on the other hand, was a stranger, and a stranger is, shall we say, well advised to be discreet in his relations with a railroad dick. My friends and I, all of us between eight and ten years old, had little experience of the real world, but we did have some, and some of it was useful, and remains so even to this day.

Take the procedure of dealing with a railroad dick. If you met one walking along the railroad track, or anywhere within sight of it, you smile, say, "hello, sir," and immediately go away from there as quickly as possible. Don't run. Do not ever run.

From *American Poets in 1976*, ed. William Heyen (Indianapolis: Bobbs-Merrill, 1976).

Railroad dicks during the Depression were not easily employed merely for their rugged good looks and their irresistible personal charm. They were talented men. In spite of their age, and in spite of their advanced paunches, they shared yet another quality of the elderly Jim Thorpe. They would run quite rapidly and adroitly for surprisingly long distances.

Then, if you happened to meet a railroad dick while you were actually aboard a B & O freight car, even if the car were rusted and isolated on a side track, as so many of them seemed to be in those days, you faced two possible consequences, either of which was certain. If you were lucky and the railroad dick was in a genial mood (drunk), he might just chuckle avuncularly and say, "Kid, you know you ain't allowed on these cars. Now, you git on out of this or I'll tell your old man on you." If he happened to be in a bad mood, he might do anything to you.

For the benefit of readers unfamiliar with the idiom of southeastern Ohio and the West Virginia Panhandle, I should point out that the word "anything," as commonly used, is neither an abstraction nor a vague generalization. The term has a specific meaning. I am not going to define it here. I don't like to think about it. I knew a boy who got caught by two railroad dicks and they did something to him. He didn't die. I am old enough to realize that the process of human dying is sometimes very long and painful. But it is easy to be dead.

The stranger seated with us at the fire had two black eyes. Even an eight-year-old can distinguish between bruises and dirt. The man needed a bath. He plainly hadn't washed for some time. The fact seemed odd to me. Though I myself had no passion for daily cleanliness, there were times when I felt the need. At the moment, we couldn't have been more than two hundred yards from the western channel of the Ohio. It wasn't dangerous there. There could have been no fear of drowning. On our August evening, the channel ran shallow. You could touch bottom all the way from the Ohio bank to the north tip of Wheeling Island. Of course, even in those days the river water was not quite as sanitary as a bottle of sealed Perrier. An open sewer from Martins Ferry poured into the river about a mile upstream; and, a little further up, such factories as

Wheeling Steel, Laughlin Steel and the Blaw-Knox Company were constantly presenting their modest contributions on which the health of our American economy continue to depend. Still, the water in the river was flowing, at any rate, and the stranger could have refreshed himself briefly and got the scum off, at least. I guess he was just too tired to bother.

"You boys happen to have any mickies in that fire?"

"Sure," said Junior Pugh, and speared him a nice one with a sharp little willow stick.

It was then that we understood how hungry the stranger was. To be properly roasted, a mickey has to be buried under the hot coals for a long time. The mickey Junior offered the stranger had roasted so long that its entire crust must have been charred half an inch thick. You can imagine how hot it must have been. I wouldn't have even touched that mickey till it had lain on the ground for at least five minutes, maybe even ten. But the stranger plucked it right off the end of the willow stick, broke it in half, and ate it in four or five bites.

"Thank you, son. Appreciate it."

"You happen to have any more?"

"Oh, we got plenty more. Crum's old man worked a couple days last week, unloading potatoes up at the A & P." This was a lie, of course. We had stolen that sack of potatoes. I forget where.

The stranger ate the second mickey just as he'd eaten the first.

He sat silent a while. Just to make conversation Jack asked, "Where you just come from? Hop a freight?"

"No, matter of fact I hitched a ride with a truck driver down in Bridgeport. Nice fellow. Came right out and admitted he was a company fink. I didn't mind. Everybody's got to make a living. He let me out right down by this bridge you got at Aetnaville."

"Where you headed now?"

"Well, I got to meet a guy in Pittsburgh tomorrow, so I figured I'd catch that B & O freight they run by here at five in the morning."

"You better watch out for the railroad dick. They got a mean one here on the night shift."

"Oh, don't worry. If I see him see me, I'll jump off the train. I know how to do it." He looked drowsy to me, but something told me he would make it through the night. I didn't really believe he had a friend in Pittsburgh; but, for that matter, I don't believe anybody else does either.

He sat quiet again, for a longer time than before. He was thinking. Then he said, "Boys, I'm an infidel. You know? An unbeliever?"

I didn't have the faintest idea what an infidel was, and I was pretty sure that the others didn't know either. But several of us said, "Oh, yeah, sure, we know."

He scared me a little. For all I knew, Infidel might have been one of those strange diseases like that one they used to call infantile paralysis, in the days when people were forever warning you to keep away from swimming pools and pool rooms and cheap crowded movie theaters and other places where any rational person would be likely to spend the summer vacation, except maybe church, which somehow never seemed to cause any hygienic anxiety to the Board of Health.

But we left the stranger alone. We sat there with him while he slept for about an hour. Then we went home. We never saw him again. I kind of liked him, and if he died, I hope he had a good easy death, as I hope I will some day have one, too.

I look back over the sometimes confusing years, and I remember with affection several people who were believers. I am not myself what I would call a man of much particular faith, religious or otherwise. But it always quickens my joy in the value of life to think about my friend Father George Garrelts, S. J., with whom I spent so many happy hours in Minneapolis years ago. Most of all I remember how one evening in Saint Paul my precious beloved friend, almost my brother I might call him, Ghazi Ismail Gailini, the poet from Iraq, read in Arabic and then translated into English for some students and me a little poem from his country. I forget the name of its author. But what strikes me most sharply in my recollection of Ghazi's incomparably beautiful recitation is the almost total difference between the students' response to the poem and my own response. The students were without exception highly intelligent and attentive. And yet to them the poem seemed totally obscure, impenetrable, a poem written in a tradition so exotically oriental and foreign to them that they found it hopeless. They said that they could never understand the poem in a million years.

To me, the poem was instantly perfectly accessible. Even as I write down these memories, the poem seems to me one of the clearest and most comprehensible poems I have ever heard or read anywhere. It is possible that Ghazi's poem reached out and touched, as with a kindly and understanding hand, my half-buried memory of that strange infidel, the hobo with the unwashed eyes, who stepped out of the sumac trees near the railroad track just above the Ohio River so long ago and shared with my friends and me a little of his time, a little of our time, some serious conversation we only partly understood, a few of our lies, a couple of our mickies, and the social comfort of our August fire.

Here is the poem that Ghazi translated:

> As I drifted near shore
> In the first light of morning,
> I saw my country
> Hunched over in a blackened boat,
> A fire between her knees.

Home, New York
Feb. 25, 1974

This afternoon, after I had lectured for an hour or so, a girl came up to me and exclaimed, "I feel so shaken! How can you go on and on so passionately about the poems of Robert Herrick? I think he's too—too pretty. I don't think I like him."

Ears small and delicate as the inside of a monarch butterfly's wing; her nostrils seemed strong and careful enough to catch something beyond the fragrance of the sea beside Eype, Fowey, Mousehole, the whole of ancient Cornwall. I would have liked to ask her to take her shoes off and walk across the floor of that dismal classroom. I don't know how I know, but I know that her toes would have been as sure and strong as the horns of a snail.

Anthea, Julia, Electra, why do I love Herrick?

I don't know. Lucky, I guess.

Childhood Sketch

I was born on December 13, 1927 on Union Street. I don't
know why I should cling to that particular useless detail. It may
have something to do with the frequency of my family's mov-
ing. By the time I was ten years old we had lived in at least half a
dozen houses, which were scattered apart from one another
about as widely as possible in a small town of 16,000 inhabi-
tants. All this restless moving around didn't bother me es-
pecially at the time. On the contrary. I love the variety of
neighborhoods in Martins Ferry, a skinny place stretched out
along the river between the railroad and the abrupt hills. By
the time I was in the fifth grade, I had attended three different
grade schools. It was mildly disconcerting to make new friends,
whole worlds of friends, so often. But, in a small town as in any
town or city, a single grade school is an entire human society,
with its own heroes, beauties, snotty sons of bitches, cruelties,
lonelinesses, and basketball teams. By the time I entered high
school, where all the local nations gathered together like all the
bewildered Buddhists, Taoists, Mongolians, and Hindus wan-
dering puzzled along the Streets of Ch'ang-an during the high
days of the T'ang Dynasty, I sometimes rejoiced in the gifts of
my wandering and my restless dwellings for I cherished the
friends I had made in distant places all the way from Kuckkuck

From William Saunders, *James Wright: An Introduction* (Columbus:
Ohio Authors Series, 1978). Also published in *Antaeus* 45/46 (Spring/
Summer 1982).

Lane in the north of town, just above Wheeling Steel and the Blaw-Knox factories, all the way down south along the river, always the river, below the La Belle Lumber Company and its yards of sawdust, fragrant as rancid pollen, down to the old empty mill fields, the cherry lanes and hobo jungles lost in the wilderness of Aetnaville, the junction where the traveling carnivals camped during the summer and besieged the citizenry of Martins Ferry and Bridgeport. I had lived in all of the neighborhoods except the wealthy ones up on the hills away from the factories and the river, and I knew most of the languages, and carry with me today the affections of those words.

My father worked as a die-setter at the Hazel-Atlas Glass Company in Wheeling, West Virginia. He was a handsome man of great physical strength and the greatest human strength of all, an enduring gentleness in the presence of the hardship that the Great Depression brought to everyone.

My mother's family came from West Virginia, and they were honest-to-God hillbillies to fare-thee-well. All her life my mother was moved by a longing to return to the kind of farming life she had had as a child, and by the time I had finished high school and gone to the army, my parents did succeed in buying a small farm in the tiny community of Warnock, Ohio, a bleak little crossroads about twenty-five miles back in the hills from the Ohio River. The hills I have in mind were cornfields, some of them, but many others were smoldering slag heaps, crazily shaped piles of bluish-gray waste from the mines. After the army I was away from the Warnock farm at college except for parts of the summers, so I never became as well acquainted with the local inhabitants as my younger brother Jack did. There was something darkly West Virginian about the country store in its perpetual fog, and Jack has told me of a place nearby called Blood Hollow, whose citizens frequently provided business for my father in his capacity as Justice of the Peace.

During the last couple of years before his retirement from the factory my father rose at four o'clock in the morning and rode a rickety bus down through the dank hills to Bellaire, Ohio, where he would take another bus across the river to

Wheeling, where he worked. The difficulty of this arrangement finally persuaded him to rent a small furnished room near the factory. Until my parents were married around the time of World War I, my mother, too, had worked in the towns. She had slaved—it is the true word—in a laundry. I have visited such places more than once, and I can still understand my mother's dream of green quiet places and her struggle to reach them.

And there were green places. As I think now of my own childhood, I can still feel an abrupt pang that rises not only from the shape of my parent's lives but also from the very disruption of the earth in southeastern Ohio. Take the river. In form and body it remains itself one of the magnificent rivers of the world. It could gather into itself the Seine, the Arno, and the Adige, and still have room for a whole mile of drifting lost lives.

Many lives were lost to the river, and a few were saved. My friend Harry Schultz, who was in the first-grade class with me at the old Central School, got caught in a suck-hole one afternoon just above the Terminal Bridge (long since condemned), and maybe he would have drowned; but a strong and courageous boy named Joe Bumbio saved him. At the same time and place, little Patsy di Franco was lost. Even Joe Bumbio couldn't find him, and turned the search over to the hands of a man named John Shunk, a professional diver skilled in the use of those awesome hooks that James Dickey has described toward the end of his novel *Deliverance*. I still do not know what Mr. Shunk did for a living during those days and nights when the river ran on quietly minding its own strange business. But whenever somebody drowned, sure enough Mr. Shunk would appear from somewhere and, sooner or later, perform his ghastly labor. For many years he seemed to me to carry a kind of solitary holiness about him in my mind. His very name in the local newspaper hinted at the abiding presence of some hopeless and everlasting grief that waited for us all as we looked at one another and wondered about ourselves. This summer, after all these years, as August approached me far away from the Ohio River, I thought about Mr. Shunk again, and I mourned for him, for he carried the visible terror of good and frightened people in his arms, and he was brave as even the river never knew how to be brave. I wrote something in his memory.

For all its dangers, the river still had the power to make the banks green, and some of us children of the blast furnaces and factories and mines kept faith with the river. Even after the workers of the WPA had built a modern swimming pool next to the Martins Ferry City Park, where the citizenry repaired on weekend afternoons, my father would take my older brother Ted and me to swim in the river. Later I often joined my friends from Aetnaville and southern Martins Ferry to swim naked from the bare-ass beach to the northern tip of Wheeling Island. The water there was beautiful in its rawness and wildness, though something was forever drifting past to remind us of the factories that lined the banks to the north. They were always there, just as the Martins Ferry Cemetery overlooked the entire town seemed, wherever one stood, to hang in the sky above the Laughlin Steel Mill.

I am afraid that I must have seemed often solitary and morose in my childhood, and it is true that I did a good deal of wandering around all by myself, daydreaming along the river bank or plundering certain apple trees in the hills behind home. But I think also of the vividness in the lives of my brothers and my most beloved cousin. My brother Ted is only two years older than I, and two years seems little enough to me now. But he still seems to me an admirable man, and his authority rises from his character, not his age. He is a photographer in Zanesville, Ohio. My younger brother Jack has long since left Ohio for southern California. I suppose I spent more time in the close company of my cousin David Lyons than anyone else. His parents were divorced when he was a small boy, and he was raised by my Aunt Grace, and by our grandmother, Elizabeth Lyons. I will leave my grandmother as she is, for she blessed my childhood with such a glory of intelligence and anarchic humor that I have had to find other ways of writing about her. She appears in every one of my books in one form or another.

It seems to me that José Ortega y Gasset was speaking the plain bone truth when he said that, at the start, life is a chaos in which one is lost, and I have certainly spent most of my own life in confusion. But some people when I was young brought me the sense, the vista, the realization of a deep world in the Ohio Valley itself and the huge world of time and space beyond the place. I am thinking of my teachers, and now that I am middle-aged, I look back and marvel at the vitality and devotion of all those young men and women in the public schools of my home. I think of them all with affection and there are two I want to name. Miss Elizabeth Willerton (now Mrs. Henry Esterly of Cupertino, California) introduced her high school students to literature with a clarity and intelligence, a kind of summons to enter whatever nobility there is in the human race, with something very like genius. As for Miss Helen McNeely Sheriff, an authentic aristocrat of mind and character, her teaching of Latin embodied a vision of uncompromising excellence. She is now in her nineties, in Cadiz, Ohio; and, no matter what life has flung down on me during the past thirty years, I have never lost touch with her, thank God. Her hair is white now and she needs a cane. But she has the same classic and exalted face, the same eyes, so witty and so deep, the most beautiful intelligent eyes. It will come as no revelation to many critics that my own writings are not always distinguished by clarity and grace; but I have never written anything without wondering sooner or later, whether or not Miss Sheriff would find it worthy.

I want to return sometime. If I do, I imagine I will feel what George Orwell felt when he thought of returning to the place of a particularly vivid childhood: How small everything has grown, and how terrible is the deterioration in myself.

The friend I loved best, as radiant a spirit as any I have ever known, was Harley Lannum. Dear Pete, where are you? Once, among the shadows of the years, I heard that you were working on a newspaper in Sandusky, or some such place? I wonder if you have ever read anything I have written. I wonder if you will read these words. Salvatore Quasimode said that every man stands alone at the heart of the earth, transfixed by a ray of sunlight, and suddenly it is evening. Pete, why don't we go home? Why don't we find each other, and go home, while we are still alive?

UNDER DISCUSSION
Donald Hall, General Editor

Volumes in the Under Discussion series collect reviews and essays about individual poets. The series is concerned with contemporary American and English poets about whom the consensus has not yet been formed and the final vote has not been taken. Among those to be considered are:

Elizabeth Bishop and Her Art
by Lloyd Schwartz and Sybil P. Estess

Adrienne Rich *by Jane Roberta Cooper*

Richard Wilbur *by Wendy Salinger*

Robert Bly *by Joyce Peseroff*

Allen Ginsberg *by Lewis Hyde*

Please write for further information on available editions and current prices.

Ann Arbor   **The University of Michigan Press**